TRAMPS LIKE US

TRAMPS LIKE US

A NEW JERSEY TALE

Kristen Buckley

CYAN

First published in 2007 by

Cyan Communications Limited
119 Wardour Street
London W1F 0UW
United Kingdom
T: +44 (0)20 7565 6120
E: sales@cyanbooks.com
www.cyanbooks.com

A CIP record for this book is available from the British Library

ISBN-13 978-1-905736-23-2
ISBN-10 1-905736-23-1

Printed and bound in Great Britain by
TJ International Ltd, Padstow, Cornwall

CONTENTS

LOVE AND THANKS TO

Stephanie Staal
Richard Pine
Brian Regan
Howard Altman
Kate Probst
Lester Probst
Jennifer Harrington
Nak Ho Choe
Lee DeGross
Stacie Probst
Gabriela Johansson
Tubbs Pike

To my mom, the North Star in my dark night sky.

and Peyton and Liam ...
Big and Little Dippers, respectively.

A LITTLE FORWARD

THERE IS JUST SOMETHING about New Jersey that breeds a certain type of life and by extension, a certain type of person. It's as if all those murky swamps, water gaps and rivers formed a natural economy that led to the confluence of jug handles, diners and highway stink. This in turn, begat an enormous amount of interstate travel options, which caused a lot of lost travelers to just settle in New Jersey rather than spend another hour on the Turnpike or its better looking sister The Parkway. This would at least explain how New Jersey came to be the most densely populated state (with a whopping twenty percent of the population foreign born). Of course, crowded areas make for strange bedfellows, which is how it is that soccer moms and gangsters can shop at the same stores and how such disparate entities as the World's Oldest Nudist Camp, the Medieval Times Theme Park/Dinner Theater and the International Castor Oil Association can all co-exist in perfect harmony.

But I would argue that there is a larger factor shaping the people of New Jersey, and that is, with the exception of Mall Rats and nail salon owners, just about everyone from the Garden State wants to escape. And because New Jersey is such a difficult state to escape from (mostly because wherever you turn there are tolls and tunnels all requiring cash payment), there is little room for error. You have to be strong, fierce, determined, tenacious and good with maps. In its essence, New Jersey is one giant chrysalis, inside which all us desperate caterpillars spin and rotate until we can become butterflies and fly away.

And much like the way that a butterfly flapping its wings in Brazil can cause a tornado in Texas, the escaped people of New Jersey exert tremendous influence over the world as we know it.

Take Bruce Willis as an example.

Walter Bruce Willis grew up in Penns Grove, New Jersey, and later went on to become the über, box-office success that he is today. But let's suppose for just a moment that Walter Bruce Willis didn't grow up in the armpit of the nation. Let's say for argument's sake, he grew up in Akron, Ohio. What would have happened?

For starters, he would've most definitely stuck with his first name, Walter, and Walter would have grown up content with his surroundings, comfortable in his own skin and state. He would have vacationed at Cedar Point, made out with girls to the strains of The Michael Stanley Band and eventually found work in the tire business. After that he would probably have married a local girl, with a name like Elizabeth or Mandy. They would have had two children and passed their leisure hours watching college football or visiting the Rock and Roll Hall of Fame. And life for Walter and his family would have been just dandy, until 1995 when Russian nuclear missiles would have attacked the Eastern seaboard, killing millions instantly and causing others, including Walter, to die a slow and debilitating death from radiation poisoning.

But, Walter Bruce Willis grew up in New Jersey and due to that intrinsic desire to escape, he pushed himself to the limits and ended up becoming one of the world's greatest movie stars. Of course, this wasn't all he did. Let's pause for a moment and ponder a few of his minor accomplishments:

He coined the phrase, *"Yippie Ki Yay, Motherfucker"* thus enabling tough guys the world over to replace the outmoded and circumstantially limiting "I'll be back!"

He named his daughter Scout, which in turn boosted readership of *To Kill A Mockingbird.*

He divorced his wife Demi, whose name I might add is actually a preposition. The resulting coverage of the divorce and Demi's subsequent relationship boosted *People* magazine to record profits. The result was a rise of Time Warner Inc. stock prices, which in turn fueled the bull market.

But all of these pale in comparison to his most major accomplishment which occurred in 1994, when he agreed to star in the *Color of Night.* The film was instantly green-lit and ultimately made. And though it was panned by critics and is considered to be one of his lesser box office successes, the film was in fact responsible for saving the lives of millions, thus proving the Butterfly Effect once and for all.

Color of Night starred Bruce Willis opposite the very toothy Jane March and was an intricate story involving sex, psychiatry, art and murder. But what most people don't know is that *Color of Night* is the favored viewing of the sea-based leg of the United States Strategic Deterrent Forces (a.k.a. the SSBN), who prowl the oceans in sleek, stealthy submarines for one-hundred day stints. Their primary mission: Nuclear deterrence. Their mission profile: To avert war while remaining undetected. There isn't a crew member on the force who won't testify to the positive masturbatorial effect that *Color of Night* has on the entire SSBN fleet. Something about that Jane March keeps them lucid, clear headed and alert, which is a good thing because on the morning of January 25, 1995, Norwegian scientists launched the largest sounding rocket ever from Andoya Island off the coast of Norway. Designed to study the northern lights, the rocket followed a trajectory to nearly nine hundred thirty miles altitude. To Russian radar technicians, who were no doubt foggy from the plethora of substandard Eastern European porn, the rocket appeared to mimic the flight of a U.S. Trident missile. From their perspective it seemed obvious that the U.S. was trying to blind Russian radar by detonating a nuclear warhead high in the atmosphere, so it could then launch an attack of some sort on Mother Russia. The response time was nearly instantaneous and Russia was suddenly poised to launch a full-scale, pre-emptive nuclear attack on the United States. President Boris Yeltsin put down his vodka, activated his "nuclear football" and lo and behold, WWIII was *on*. The United States scrambled to find an answer and thankfully it arrived from a SSBN crewman, who after a recent viewing of *Color of Night*, was so clear headed, lucid and mentally sharp that he determined that the rocket was no rogue, Neo-Conguided Trident, but rather an annoying Norwegian rocket. Yeltsin got the message just in time and put away the nuclear football. The Eastern seaboard was saved and millions were spared a debilitating death by radiation poisoning. To this very day, whenever statesmen discuss the Norwegian Rocket Incident, they secretly thank Bruce Willis for getting *Color of Night* made, because even the most inexperienced spy can tell you, Jane March could never have gotten that movie green-lit alone.

All this, from one tiny escaped butterfly from New Jersey's polluted chrysalis.

What follows is a list of other people from New Jersey.

Buzz Aldrin, Bud Abbot, Jason Alexander, Charles Addams, Count Basie, Yogi Berra, Robert Blake, Judy Blume, Jon Bon Jovi, Zach Braff, Grover Cleveland, Tom Cruise, James Fenimore Cooper, Lou Costello, Steven Crane, Danny DeVito, Helen Gahagan Douglas, Michael Douglas, Thomas Edison, Connie Francis, Jon Forsythe, Daisy Fuentes, Derek Jeter, Allen Ginsberg, Leslie Gore, William Frederick Halsey Jr., Lauryn Hill, Whitney Houston, Ice T, Alfred C. Kinsey, Ernie Kovacs, Dorothea Lange, Huey Lewis, Jerry Lewis, Norman Mailer, Thomas Mitchell, Jay

Mohr, Ricky Nelson, Jack Nicholson, Shaquille O'Neill, Joe Pesci, Zebulon Mongomery Pike, Joe Piscopo, Paul Robeson, Philip Roth, Antonin Scalia, Norman Schwarzkopf, Brooke Shields, Elizabeth and Andrew Shue, Paul Simon, Frank Sinatra, Tony Soprano, Kevin Spacey, Steven Spielberg, Bruce Springsteen, Alfred Stieglitz, Meryl Streep, Dave Thomas, John Travolta, Frankie Vallie, Sarah Vaughan, Dionne Warwick, Denzel Washington, William Carlos William.

Consider the Butterfly Effect that each one of them has had on the world, then see if you have something lousy to say about New Jersey after that. Better yet, the next time you meet someone who is originally from New Jersey, thank them, because the odds are, their very existence has no doubt helped maintain the delicate balance that ultimately allows for all life on earth to exist.

1. FIVE AND A HALF STAGES OF GRIEF

SHORTLY AFTER MY SIXTH BIRTHDAY, my dad and I got up early and drove from our home in New Jersey to nearby Rye, New York, for a day of sailing on the Long Island Sound. We had been on the water for only a few minutes when he told me he was leaving. "I've been wanting to do this for a long time," he explained, "but you were sort of young, so I waited. Now that you're six, you don't need a dad anymore."

This was what he said.

I considered his words, trying to figure out where they had come from. I suppose for him, they had been formulating for some time, but for me, they had just appeared out of some unfathomable depth that I didn't even know existed.

"What?" was about the only response I could manage, hoping that maybe I'd just heard wrong.

But I hadn't. He repeated himself word for word. My life had suddenly run dead downwind. It had happened in a blink, and just like that I was emotionally overboard. A tiny speck in the deep blue sea; struggling to catch my breath, desperate to keep my head above water. But it was a hopeless fight and I soon found myself being pulled under. Eventually, I surrendered to it. My life as I knew it was ending. The water was cold, but the visibility was good. And in the distance

I could see images of my family and me sinking into the abyss.

All of us ...

Playing by the red swing in the backyard.

Eating sukiyaki at the white Formica table in the kitchen.

Dancing in the living room to *Sweet Caroline.*

Vacationing on Martha's Vineyard

Laughing at *The Carol Burnett Show.*

I stared at the images as they sank into the murky waters, and then I felt my body surge upward. When I popped back to the surface, the sun was shining and my father was still on the boat. I saw the faint outline of my shadow sitting next to him. He was saying something about visitation and alternating Christmas holidays, when the sea suddenly shifted. It became choppy and dangerous. I tried to get back to the boat, but I wasn't strong enough. Soon enough, a massive wave crashed down on me, and the next thing I knew I was back at home. My dad carried me inside to my mother, who was lying on her bed with my newly adopted brother and sister, Lee and Jenny, who had come from Korea two months earlier. Though they were only four and two respectively, they seemed to sense that something was wrong, but I guessed that the dissolution of our family meant less to them than it did to me. After all, they had just lost their Korean mother and father, so this was really just small potatoes. Just another case of bad luck in a string of catastrophic events that had ultimately brought them to New Jersey of all places. And now here I was, half an orphan, and my parents hadn't even died. I was just being abandoned. Somehow it seemed worse.

I crawled onto the bed, which seemed like a giant raft, and promptly clung to my surviving parent for dear life. My dad muttered, "Goodbye, Kate," and then left us there. The house felt empty and still. It was as if we were the only people on earth and the quiet was unnerving. After a few minutes, my mother pulled me in close and said, "Everything is going to be alright," but I didn't believe her. I'm not so sure she even believed it herself. After all, she was 32 years old and she had already buried her mother, her father and a daughter who had been born before me. And now here she was with three kids, no husband, and no work. Somehow I didn't think "alright" was going to be part of our foreseeable future. I so wanted concrete answers from my mother, I wanted to know exactly how things would turn out and what would become of us, but for that moment there were none. I looked into her eyes, but all I saw was uncertainty. In a different life, with her long, lean body and her icy blue eyes, my mom might have been Maud Gonne, averting famines and winning the hearts of poets. Or maybe Grainne Ni Maille, captaining her ships from her pirate stronghold in Clew Bay. But in this life she had toed the line, just like all the other women in her family. She became a teacher, got married, and supported her husband through medical school. This was what women like my mom were expected to do. And with it, came the rewards of "being good." She eventually moved to the suburbs, pursued her master's degree at NYU and tried to feed her adventurous spirit by reading and learning, as if a life of the mind would be enough. It was a schizophrenic existence. The intellectuals in the city were unable to comprehend why my mother had bogged herself down with all the trappings of a traditional suburban life. And the Jersey housewives couldn't understand why my mom didn't spend more time at the Country Club, or more importantly, why she would clutter her living room with enormous, teetering piles of books. She was like a nomad moving between two worlds, searching for her place inside each. And she may have found it, but that was before my father left and we found ourselves lost in a strange land called "'70s Divorce Hell."

It was 1974 to be exact, and this new, vast landscape

bore a striking similarity to the Wild West in that anything went, including all the furniture. I began to think that maybe I was just a chance protagonist in someone else's story, because this was certainly not *my* life. Without realizing it, I'd entered the first stage of grief: A state of complete and total denial. After all, there had been no warning signs. My parents went out to dinner every Saturday night. We had two cars, a boat, and a nice house. My father was a doctor; my mother had a master's degree. We had just adopted two kids from Korea. Our life was perfect. Too perfect for this to be happening.

But days turned into weeks, and there seemed to be no end to my waking dream. I felt myself floating in and out of reality. I was unable to fathom any of it, until one night my father came to take the stereo system. There was something so incredibly final about it. All those wires and cords. As if we'd been on life support and he'd just pulled the plug.

And all I wanted to know was why. *Why had this happened?*

But all I could do was stand there, with my mouth open, as my father removed the speakers from the wall, gave me a quick kiss on the forehead, and headed off toward his new life.

I looked up at the white squares where the speakers had been. Then down at the dusty imprint where the sofa once sat. I tried to remember what it had looked like before, but I was having trouble remembering. It seemed like my life was being erased, one object at a time.

I was mired in "Why?", this being the second stage of grief, commonly referred to as anger. And while I couldn't ask my father anything, I was more than happy to inundate my mother with questions.

"Why the hell are we driving down Route 17 in the middle of the night to trade in the VW for some shit Gremlin?" I asked one evening.

“It’s not the middle of the night, Kristen. It’s daylight savings,” answered my mom.

Ever since my dad left, I had been allowed to openly curse in front of my mother. “Why the Gremlin? I don’t want a Gremlin. Joe Riela says a Gremlin is the biggest piece of shit car there is,” I continued.

“It’s not the biggest piece of shit, there are bigger ones. And we’re doing this because your father won’t pay for the lease on the VW, and I can’t afford it myself,” said my mom.

I could only stare out the window. My mom always gave me answers, but they weren’t the ones I wanted to hear. We entered the dealership, and scanned the assortment of cheerful Gremlin ads that graced the walls:

Haulin’ Half Pint!

The car with the heart of a Javelin!

America’s first subcompact car!

There was no sign of the dealer and so we looked around at the yellow floor model, which came with AM radio and black plastic seats.

“See, it’s a good car,” said my mother, trying to remain upbeat.

“The thing’s a shit box, Mom. We all know it,” I replied.

I turned to Jenny and Lee, who had barely been in the country for three months. From the look of disappointment on their faces I knew I wasn’t wrong. But before I could go further, Jerry the Dealer emerged from the back. Jerry was very tan and wearing a short-sleeved plaid shirt. He was one of those guys who loved his job. Nothing made him happier than selling cars. Jerry never dared to dream big, and as a result, he was not burdened with the stinging disappointment that usually went along with being a car salesman. He took one look at us, clapped his hands together and called out playfully, “What looks like a sports car, loads like a wagon, and drives like fun?!”

I was about to say, "My mom's Volkswagen," but she cut me off at the pass.

"Watch your brother and sister, I'll try to make this fast," she told me.

Jerry handed us day glow Gremlin stickers and said it would be okay for us to sit in the Jeep CJ5 while he went over the paperwork with my mother. The CJ5 was my dream car, and the one my father had promised to buy me when I turned seventeen. As I was brooding about this, Lee and Jenny began papering the inside of the jeep with the Gremlin stickers. I was about to tell them to stop, but it occurred to me that the little Gremlin on the sticker was mocking me, as if he found this all very humorous. In fact, I couldn't help but think that I was being punished. And if I was being punished, then perhaps all this was somehow my fault. I racked my brain for trespasses, but none stood out. However, it was pretty clear, given all that had happened of late, that I had sinned. Why else would this be happening? Like any self-respecting sinner, I turned to my lapsed Catholic faith and asked St. Rita, the patron Saint of Desperate Situations, to intervene on my behalf. In return, I promised to be a better person. Without realizing it, I had entered the third stage of grief (bargaining), but it was too little too late. We left in the Gremlin, and all there was to do was wave goodbye to our VW as we pulled onto the highway. Clearly, the promise to be a better person had fallen on deaf ears. Still, I clung to the hope that the message would get through. If I cleaned my room, and helped my mom; if I thought good thoughts for people careening past in ambulances; if I helped everyone I possibly could, then perhaps St. Rita could turn fortune's tide for us. Until then, I floated in the penumbra, trying to pretend that driving a green Gremlin didn't have any larger metaphorical meaning in our posh Northern New Jersey neighborhood, where dads worked, moms played tennis, and kids rode shiny new bikes. But of course there was no getting around facts. Everything about our town was new; new money, new houses, new cars, new roads. It was essentially paradise and no one wanted to see it sullied by a family that had been forsaken. The Gremlin was our scarlet letter. Of course we could have done the sensible thing and gotten the hell out of town. Moved to a working class neighborhood, filled with single moms who wouldn't have judged us or whispered as we passed them in the grocery store. But my mother would not have it. We were staying in Upper Saddle River. She wasn't going to let a cheaply-made American car drum her out of town. "Hell no, we won't go!" became the unspoken rally cry around our house. We were sticking it out, and even though I continued to secretly pray to St. Rita each night, I moved into the next stage of grief and deluded myself into quasi-believing that I did not care what everyone else thought. And I may have pulled it off, if it were not for one issue unforeseen by the divorce experts. I'm not talking about depression. I'm not talking about sudden changes in socio-economic status.

I'm talking about lawn care.

My mother always liked to point out that the lawn was an American invention dating back to the mid-nineteenth century.

"It's nothing more than a social contrivance designed to delineate between common space and private space," she'd yell to the old guy across the street as he pruned his roses. "Lawns distance the house from the road, and the owner from the world of labor," she'd say as the lady next store spread fertilizer.

"It's a cultural and economic symbol, an *idea* and nothing more," she'd say to my dad as he paid the boy who mowed the lawn.

The neighbors humored my mother pre-divorce. She

was the smart wife of a doctor who was going to be getting her PhD any day now, and hopefully find work at a university, and leave them to enjoy the guilt-free pursuit of a cushy bourgeois existence. But after the divorce, things changed.

We lived on a full acre, which differed from a builder's acre, though I wasn't enough of a yard enthusiast to know how. What I know is that we had a big-ass front yard. Sprawling might be a good way to describe it. And the trouble with big-ass, sprawling front yards is that they had to be mowed every now and then. And with each passing week, my prayers to St. Rita went from, "I promise to be a better person if you would just get us out of this mess," to, "I promise to be a better person if the kid who mows our lawn up the street just shows up."

But it was clear that my father got the kid who mowed the lawn in the divorce. My mother – overwhelmed with small children, no work, legal bills, and a newly healed broken back from a car accident the year before – was in no position to be pushing a mower around. And so the lawn sat, or rather it spawned, in some sort of natural frenzy that our neighbors came to see as a blight on property values.

Still my mom clung to history in her defense. "They had no lawns a hundred years ago," she would say. "It's a useless decoration bespeaking a certain culture and a wistfulness for class."

But it was so out of control that even my mom couldn't keep up the front, and in a moment of weakness (following the discovery of a nasty anonymous note taped to our door that read: *What the hell is the story with your lawn?!*), she admitted, much to my chagrin, that lawns also told stories.

"If a lawn tells a story, what the hell does our lawn say about us?" I cried.

"It says that we're having a tough time of it," was her answer.

And not the answer I had wanted to hear, mostly because I felt deeply ashamed by the recent turn of events in my life. Of course I blamed myself, because the truth is, it usually is the kids' fault when parents split up. Kids are time consuming, exhausting, and demanding. They require you to change the entire way you live your life, and the burden of the responsibility can be overwhelming for even the best of parents. So, I think it's safe to say that I was at least partially responsible for the divorce. After all, my dad had said he didn't want to be a dad anymore, and I was his kid, so do the math. But the last thing I wanted was this horrible secret to be revealed to the entire neighborhood and every car taking the short cut past our house on their way up to Route 17. I didn't need my dirty laundry out there for all to see. I did not need every kid on the block to know that I was a home-wrecker and the ultimate cause of our out of control lawn. Still, my mom wanted me to let go of it.

"What do you care what people think?" she asked. "We've got bigger fish to fry."

And she was right. We did have bigger fish to fry. It turned out that my brother Lee had severe hearing loss. The strange thing was he didn't sound deaf at all, but the doctor explained that this was because he could hear high frequencies rather than low. This was also why he lacked that typical guttural inflection associated with the deaf. I had just thought he was rude, my mom had thought he might have a learning disability, but it turned out to be severe hearing loss, and he desperately needed hearing aids, for which there was no money. Then we learned that my sister Jenny had smallpox. Apparently, she had been ill in Korea and when she got to Alaska (en route to New Jersey) they inoculated her with smallpox. Given her weakened immune system, this was not a smart thing to do. The result was that she came down with smallpox, and was losing her hearing as well. Yes, we were mired in misfortune. But I couldn't wrap my head around low frequency hearing loss, or smallpox; so instead, I fixated on the damn lawn.

My mom turned to the Romantics to try and rouse me from my funk. She tried to instill in me the notion of Romantic individualism over the representative ideals of a civilized society. She would read Coleridge and Byron to me and then explain, "Look, basically they're saying sometimes you need to give 'the man' the finger." And I would nod my head half-heartedly. Out of desperation, she moved on to John Locke's treatise *Of Property*, after which she would ask me questions like, "What would John Locke say about a well-manicured lawn?" And I would mumble, "He'd say it's a load of shit." My mom would pat my head and say, "That's my girl." But I still didn't feel any better. Finally, my mom got tough with me. "Look at your sister Jenny," she said. "She got smallpox, but she's not giving in. She's fighting it, she's standing up to that virus and telling it to piss off. You need to do the same thing."

And she was right. Jenny was fighting hard, and so was Lee for that matter. In the space of a year he had lost both his parents. Then he had been adopted by a new family, only to lose another father. I looked around and saw that my mom was right. It was time to rise to the occasion. I would talk the talk and walk the walk. I would believe the lie, and accept that our lawn was a deliberate throwback to the days of yore. I was a modern day Aurora Leigh, living my life free from the constraints of modern society, informed by the tenants of the Romantics. Our lawn was the equivalent of a '70s fro. It was beautiful and natural. If we had Black Panther neighbors, we would have been considered righteous. I didn't care what anyone thought.

"Man in a State of Nature did not have a mowed front lawn!" I would shout at the rubberneckers in their passing cars. Yet, through it all, I continued to pray to St. Rita, asking for her intercession. But my prayers seemed to be falling on deaf ears, as our continued streak of bad luck seemed to have no end. First the plumbing in the upstairs bathrooms went, then the water heater broke, and then the washing machine broke. And as if that weren't enough, our septic tank overflowed. I fell hard into the fourth stage of grief, better known by its more common name, "depression."

Our house was located at the bottom of a large hill, and everyone in the neighborhood was sporting their own septic tank, so between entropy and gravity, and a very bad rainy week, we woke to find that our overgrown lawn had become a fetid, bubbling, living, breathing, mass of fecal waste and soap suds. If we had been a little more enterprising, perhaps we could have billed it as some sort of natural geyser, but alas, we were tired and broke, and did nothing of the sort. With the grasses so tall and the ground so wet, the lawn became imbued with a sense of foreboding. My mother likened it to the bogs of Ireland or the moors of England. It told a story indeed. Beware it said, tread upon this land and you may never return again. In fact, many a UPS man, thinking he'd skip the driveway for a quick cut across the lawn, had fallen in the septic hole, only to pry his foot out and find it covered in excrement. Of course with no money, pumping it out or repairing it was out of the question. After a few weeks, the back-up flow began to stink, and this stink was so virulent and so offensive, that our neighbors began to hate us. Of course no one looked up the hill, no one eyeballed the neighbors up the street, whose waste was contributing to our flooded septic tank. No, we bore the brunt of the proverbial load. It was all on us. Our lawn was an epic disaster, the outward manifestation of our inward disarray. It was the symbol of my parents' failed marriage, and the crumbling of everything that we had known, into the warping of what now was. We were a wasteland. We were the Asbury Park of divorce. If Bruce Springsteen had lived nearby, or even passed our house on his way to The Stone Pony, he would have written a song about it. The only thing missing from our disaster of a lawn was a car propped up on cinder blocks, and for that we were grateful.

I entered the hazy grief netherland known among a select few as stage four and a half. I am of course referring to the "I'm ready to blow my brains out because this is so friggin' horrific" stage.

And there was nothing I could do about it. This was the maddening part. I had no control over the situation. I was too small to start the mower. I didn't own a scythe. The one large shovel we had was broken. And the neighbors were openly hostile. Of course, I felt that it was entirely my fault and yet, I could not manage to find a way out of the mess. In a sense, we were still sinking, which was amazing because every time I thought we had finally hit the bottom, it turned out there was still another fathom below us.

In a quest to feel a sense of control, I took to moving furniture. I didn't just move small tables and desks. I moved bookcases, breakfronts, sofas, and bunk beds. Nothing was beyond my reach. It is amazing how much you can move when you put your mind to it, and it makes you see that child labor really does work. I would put Lee and Jenny on the far end of a dresser and have them hold the legs. Then I would bend down, lean my back against the other side, and with all my might, I would push back on the piece as I yelled, "PULL!" I believe this was how the Egyptians had moved the boulders used to make the Pyramids; only unlike the Egyptians, I did not have the luxury of pulleys. Every time my mom would go for a walk to clear her head, I took the opportunity to move furniture. Rearranging rooms at the drop of a dime, shouting at Jenny and Lee as we inched entire bedroom sets across the hallway in my effort to exert control over a losing battle with the elements and my father's affections. My mother stayed her course with the Romantics, and indulged me by giving me the entire top floor of the house. Lee and Jenny were right by my side, and we took over the Master Bedroom, which became an orgy of bunk beds. The other rooms became playrooms, and painting rooms, and dirty laundry rooms. We put tables in broken showers and bookcases in closets. We turned sofas upside down and pretended they were ships. We put books in dressers and clothes in bookcases. We were doing things our way. Meanwhile, my mother escaped into the dank confines of the basement, drowning her despair in Virginia Woolf novels, and semimonthly dances at Parents Without Partners. In between we ate, slept, and bought food. Once, in a great while, we even went "clothes shopping," though this involved rummaging through Good Will bins at the local Protestant Church on Saddle River Road. Of course, my mom would dupe us into thinking she was throwing away clothes, when in fact, she was there to look for us. This was an offense that none of us could tolerate. Lee barely knew English, Jenny could barely speak and was still weak from the pox, but they both knew enough to know that having your mother knee deep in the local Good Will container, with only the lights of the Gremlin to guide her, was unacceptable. But still, my mother was undaunted. "Do you like this?!" she'd shout as she held up various shirts and pant ensembles, while Lee, Jenny and I would cower in the back seat. Of course we never wore those clothes. It was a small town and the thought of being caught in someone else's shirt was more than my shallow heart could bear. Since we were unwilling to wear the former clothes of present schoolmates, my mother took to bargain shopping, often with a blatant disregard for gender specifications. This led to the embarrassing first-grade photo shoot, during which Joe Riela and I wore matching outfits. All the while, my father pursued his every whim. He drove fast cars and attended Friday night dinners at the Stamford Yacht Club, which included a ten gun salute before the serving of chocolate mousse and tea. His life was martinis in shiny metal shakers, European vacations, heated swimming pools, a young girlfriend, and a rather large collection of leather driving gloves. My life was septic tanks, smallpox, and the used clothing of my classmates. Visiting him every other weekend was like traveling to a foreign country. Never mind his love, or his various personas, which seemed to ping pong from Dr. Marcus Welby to Jacques Cousteau. I just wanted him to spring for a tree-trimming service.

It was with great despair that I endured the next year of my life. I was so inside my head, and so full of pain, and resentment, and quiet stoicism, that I nearly missed the one redemptive glimmer that enabled me to pass into the fifth stage of grief: the final acceptance of my new life.

It was a gloomy November morning. The leaves were all turning, and the air was filled with that damp chill that gets inside your bones and doesn't leave. I was standing at the bus stop at the end of the street, a bleak corner of my personal universe, aptly named Ware Road. There were other kids with me, but they didn't speak to me, or look at me for that matter. I was hating my life and thinking up depressing haikus, when I noticed a massive dead tree lying prostrate on the lawn right across from the bus stop. Behind the tree, was an old rickety house. I had never noticed it before, I suppose because it had the luxury of being covered by the massive tree and its surrounding hedges. But now that the tree was down and the hedges crushed beneath it, I could see it in all its dilapidated glory. The windows were filthy, the front stoop missing a bottom stair, and the roof was covered in blue tarp. And off to the left, near the gravel driveway, though not actually on it, sat a '72 white Dodge Dart, propped up on four cinder blocks. In a world filled with despair and disillusionment, that car up on blocks, caught my eye like a brilliant ray of hope. I felt the clouds part, and heard the faint murmurs of angels humming, and sensed that St. Rita was somehow behind this. Just then, a woman came from within the house, wearing a faded floral housecoat. This caught the attention of all the kids at the stop, mostly because her grey hair was cut in an aggressive mullet and she had a cigarette hanging out of her mouth. She saw that we were all staring at her, but interestingly enough, she didn't care. Taking in the fallen tree and its close proximity to the car she turned to one of the boys near me and said quite cheerfully, "Damn lucky the tree didn't get the car."

The boy was mortified and answered back, "What do I care about your car?"

While the other kids teased him about his "new hot girlfriend," I continued to stare at the house. From inside, I heard the sound of the television and a baby crying. Then a teenage girl emerged from the house, yelling, "Shut your trap!" to someone inside. She had two different colored eyes and was wearing a shirt that looked vaguely familiar. She scowled at the lady with the mullet, grabbed a wet sweater out of the back of the Dart, and headed up the street toward the highway. And while every kid on the bus stared at her, I was filled with an overwhelming sense of relief because, for the first time in a long time, they weren't staring at me. That night at dinner I told my mother about my experience.

"Stay away from that house, the Stevens are crazy," was her response.

Such shock on my part, as I realized she knew the name of the owner!

"You know who they are?" I asked.

"Of course, everybody knows who they are. They leave cars up on blocks."

"But what about John Locke, he would say that was okay, wouldn't he?"

"Don't get crazy Kristen, even John Locke wouldn't have left a car on his lawn."

"But I thought he didn't have a lawn."

"Of course he had a lawn, he just didn't think that everyone *had* to have a lawn."

I was so confused. My own mother knew of these people. She knew of the woman in the strange housecoat and the girl with the different colored eyes. Why had she been keeping this such a secret!?

"Well, what's their story then?"

It was with true fascination that I listened to her tell me the story of those people. It turned out that the mother had been the girlfriend of a rich man who owned a publishing company. The rich guy had knocked her up (which I learned meant "got pregnant") not once, not twice, but *thrice*, after which he promptly left her for another woman. Since the mother was never married to him, she was entitled to nothing, but the rich guy, wanting to get her off his back, bought them the crappy bungalow behind the giant sycamore tree on the corner of Ware Road. He made her sign some paper that essentially said that everything that had happened between them had been a play they were in, and then he went off on his merry way.

"How come you don't feel bad for the woman? She got left and all?" I asked my mom.

"You don't shack up with a man and have kids one after another. That's just moronic. She had no protection," was her answer.

"But you were married and look at us," I said.

"That's different," she said

"How?" I asked.

I could see that my mom was getting annoyed, but I sensed that there was something she wasn't telling me.

"They're White Trash," she said.

"Sort of like us?" I said.

"Don't be ridiculous. I have my master's. I know about oil painting and Japanese poetry."

"So, we're *not* White Trash?" I asked.

My mother looked at me like I was insane, "Of course not. We're Middle Class."

"Really?"

"Yes, how could you not know that?" she said.

I guess I had just forgotten.

"But we don't mow our lawn," I stammered, still in uncertain territory.

"No, but the difference is we justify it with philosophy. The Stevens think their hill of weeds is normal."

"But we *know* this isn't normal," I said.

"Exactly," was my mom's response.

All at once, I no longer saw myself as a pariah, because that slot had long since been filled by the Stevens down the street. And even though we lived in a dump, we were not riffraff. We were a Dickensian novel in reverse, a riches-to-rags story. And like Horatio Alger characters, we could rise from the depths. One day, this ship of ours would return to our homeland. We'd wash ashore and realize we were home. We'd look back on our long journey and be filled with a sense of grateful appreciation for all that we had seen and accomplished. But until that day, we'd have to be content with the knowledge that we were not "one of them" (i.e. White Trash). We were merely the victims of bad divorce laws and a lack of a handyman. We would read, and grow smart, and figure a way out of this deathtrap. And maybe *that* was the story that our lawn told, the story Bruce Springsteen would have seen as he took the short cut to Route 17 on his way to Asbury Park.

2. FORt APACHE

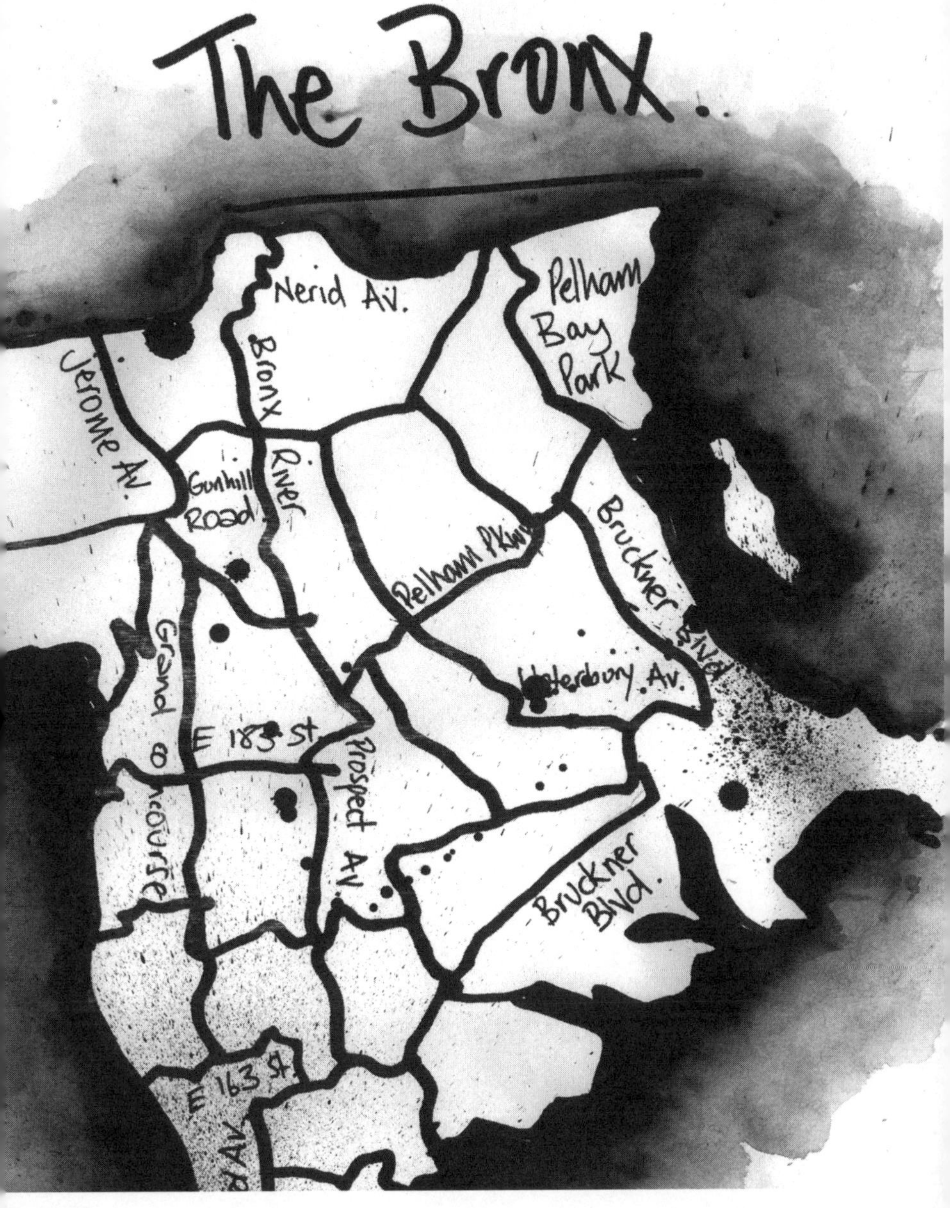

The Bronx..
Nerid Av.
Pelham Bay Park
Bronx River
Jerome Av.
Gunhill Road
Pelham Pkwy
Bruckner Blvd
Waterbury Av.
Grand Concourse
E 183 St.
Prospect Av.
Bruckner Blvd.
E 163 St.

WHEN JIMMY CARTER VISITED the South Bronx in 1977, he called it the worst slum in America. Filled with abandoned buildings and rubble-strewn lots, the place was a monumental failure in public planning. In one four-year period during the 1970s it saw over 40,000 arson fires. A study of three streets in its Hunts Point section, published by *The New York Times*, found that residents had only a one in twenty chance of dying of natural causes. Most were murdered or died of drug overdoses.

As luck would have it, this was where my mother managed to find a job teaching. She drove us in on a Sunday so that she could familiarize herself with the route, and also look for a safe place to park. I was sort of excited. My mom's father had been from the Bronx, and I remembered my mother telling me that Edgar Allan Poe and Woody Allen had both grown up in the borough as well. My mother warned me that the neighborhood was bad, but I remained upbeat. After all, if Woody Allen and Edgar Allen Poe had lived there, how bad could it be? As we headed off the Bruckner Expressway onto Charlotte Street, I gazed in wonder at what was outside the window. War zone, might have been a good description. Post-apocalyptic nightmare was close. It was like nothing I'd ever seen. Just burnt out building, after burnt out building; there were hookers, glassy-eyed junkies, and cars on the sidewalks that were literally on fire. I looked at my mother with wide eyes. "Have we left the United States?" I asked.

My mom shook her head. "No, we've just entered the South Bronx."

We drove around a few blocks and my mom explained that the buildings were burnt out due to a bad city policy. Welfare recipients who lived in decaying city-owned buildings naturally wanted to find a better alternative, but regulations forbade payment of moving expenses to anyone who had not lived in the same place for at least two years. There was one exception to this rule, and it was posted in large type in neighborhood welfare offices. Any tenant burned out of his or her building automatically became eligible for a grant, usually about $1,000 but sometimes as much as $3,500 – to cover the cost of new clothing, furniture, and moving. Also, burned-out families went to the top of the waiting list for public housing projects. As a result, arson was rampant. Clearly, this was not a safe place. I noticed that people were staring at us as we drove around the neighborhood, circling the dilapidated school (complete with barred windows) where my mother would now be working. I was suddenly nervous.

"What if you get hurt?" I asked.

"I'll be fine, Kristen," my mom said.

"How can you be sure?"

"'Cause no one screws with me," she answered.

Something about the tone in her voice was fused with certainty and I believed her. My mother was nothing if not tough. She had grown up in a working class, Irish neighborhood in Jersey City. A place known as much for its corruption, mobsters and number rackets, as it was for its stellar Manhattan views.

As we rounded the corner two men approached our car, and began washing the windshield. My mother tried to wave them off but they didn't listen. We were suddenly being held hostage by men wielding squeegees.

"Jesus and me gonna wash your window real nice ..." said one man. I swallowed hard. My door wasn't locked, even though my mom had told me to lock it. My brother and sister were in the backseat. I was terrified. But my mom barely blinked. "You and Jesus better move your asses or I'm going to run you both over, and believe me, *that* won't be 'real nice.'"

I slid down in my seat. The anger in my mom's voice was palpable. She was about to unleash a torrent of rage on Jesus and his friend and they had no idea what was about to hit them. Since my dad had left, my mom's anger had become an invisible current that moved through the house. It was impossible not to feel its presence, even on the best of days. It was this force that overshadowed every aspect of our life. And it wasn't just anger against my father. It was anger toward the 1950s mentality that dictated the course of my mother's life. It was anger at not being given the opportunity to express yourself, to be yourself, to find your true place in the world. It was anger toward the conservative thinking of immigrants who didn't want to make too much noise, or alert the powers-that-be that they were in fact here to stay. It was anger at the misguided notion that a woman was to know her place and reap the rewards of a big house, nice children and a comfortable existence. My mom had played the proverbial game. She didn't put up a fight when her family told her in no uncertain terms that she could only be a teacher or a nurse. She didn't protest when she was asked to help pay for her brother's college tuition, or when she was expected to support my father through medical school. In all instances, she humbly obliged and where had it gotten her? A run-down, shit-stain of a public school in the South Bronx.

And now the Squeegee Brothers had to add insult to injury.

"Don't give us a hard time, baby," said Jesus.

"Get the fuck away from my car or I will mow you down!" screamed my mom.

I slid further down in my seat. My mother and her anger were apparently trying to get us killed. But to my surprise, Jesus and the other guy backed up from the car and let us go. I looked at my mother, clearly impressed. She patted my leg, "I told you, no one screws with me."

And suddenly it occurred to me that everything happened for a reason. And that perhaps within the crumbling hallways of her new school lay our redemption. In that moment, I saw our future play out in my head. Yes, this was a horrible place to work, but if this was any indication of what was to come, my mother was going to turn the South Bronx around. She'd start at the crumbling school, wielding an iron hand. She would force all the kids to wear uniforms, which would in turn boost their reading skills, and after having conquered Shakespeare, they would all become Mathletes. Simultaneously, she would take all the hookers loitering outside the school and put them to work. First, she would have them remove the bars from the school windows. Then, she would have them repaint the school. At this point, it would be revealed that a few of the hookers had artistic talent. My mother would hatch a plan with the hookers, and at night they would paint by the light of the Gremlin headlights, and every morning a new mural would appear on the side of a dilapidated building, each one more spectacular than the next. The murals would inhibit arson because no one would want to harm them. The drug addicts would sober up, and as luck would have it, they would possess hidden construction skills. My mother would introduce them to the pro-housing group Banana Kelly, whose motto was "Don't move. Improve." And along with revitalization pioneer Father Louis Gigante (brother of the famed mobster Vincent "the Chin" Gigante), they would work to fix the decaying buildings.

The crippled vets who smoked on the corner by the school would begin a basketball league. Spike Lee would shoot Nike commercials at the local courts, and the money from the commercials would be used to refurbish the playgrounds. And most importantly, my mom would meet a hunky cop, who would bear a striking resemblance to Ken Wahl (pre-the facial disfiguring car accident), and he would take us to Yankee games and buy us nice birthday gifts. Eventually *60 Minutes* would come to the school and do a big piece on my mother. Film rights would be sold. Sally Field would play my mother. Quinn Cummings (of *Goodbye Girl* fame) would play me, and my brother and sister would play themselves since there were no Asian child actors at the time, and they had very good bone structure and photographed well. We would be on the cover of the *New York Times Magazine*. My mother would explain her French Romantic ideals and we (along with our giant unwieldy front lawn) would become the new rage. Then we'd take the money, having been enriched by the process, and move to a big-ass house across town. My mother would become Secretary of Education under Jimmy Carter and we'd refer to our ordeal from time to time (between tennis matches at the Country Club). My brother and sister would become famous actors, and I would sleep soundly knowing that I had a total in at the Georgetown School of Foreign Diplomacy, where I could continue in my mother's footsteps and attempt to change the world, with an eye toward stamping out illiteracy.

Unfortunately, it didn't quite work out that way. My mother endured the South Bronx and did what she could. Most kids were reading five years below grade level, so my mother focused on the basics. Since just about every night a building burned, my mom began to put words like "arson," "fire," "get out," and "tonight" on every vocabulary list. To be on the safe side, my mother reminded them to sleep in their shoes. She brought in washcloths and band aids, and vitamins for the pregnant girls. And while she worked hard to teach her students, the reality was that most of them were so far behind they were doomed.

Since my mother had a long commute and Lee and Jenny were not yet in school, my mom hired a woman named Deanna to work as a live-in housekeeper. Deanna was from Paterson, New Jersey, by way of the Dominican Republic, thus dashing my hopes of a British Nanny who could drive a flying car. To add insult to injury, Deanna didn't drink tea or break into song. In fact, I don't think she really liked kids much at all. She tolerated us at best. Sometimes she'd let us come into her bedroom, but always with the implicit understanding that we weren't allowed to touch anything, which made for a boring stay since we were nosey and liked to poke around. She called my mother Miss or Ma'am, which unnerved her. My mom would say things like, "You're part of the family now, so please just call me Kate." Deanna would just look at her with those dead fish eyes. Clearly, the last thing she wanted was to be a part of *our* family. But the one saving grace was that Deanna could cook. The Dominican delicacies were flowing. Black bean soup, corn pudding, red beans and bacon. My two personal favorites were fried chicken in a mayo sauce and *mangu*, which was the Dominican answer to mashed potatoes, only it was made with plantains, bacon, cheese, and half a stick of butter. The only problem with this food was that it contributed to the "Nanny 10" and my mother promptly put an end to it. She had no problem with eating, in fact my mom was a bottomless pit, but fat children were a big no-no in her world. We had enough issues to contend with without bringing morbid obesity into our already growing pantheon. This infuriated Deanna, who took to sulking and giving us the silent treatment.

"You better do something, because she's going to make a mojo bag and curse you," I told my mother.

"What's a mojo bag?" she asked.

"It's her voodoo stuff," I explained.

"Voodoo? Don't talk crazy."

"Why do you think she saves the chicken feet, Mom?"

"She likes to eat them."

"She doesn't eat them, she reads them," I said.

"You've lost your mind," was my mother's response. However, I had not lost my mind, because I had snuck into Deanna's room and unearthed her stash of Dominican voodoo paraphernalia. She had dolls, and strange astrological looking charts, as well as a smattering of statues of loas, which were the voodoo equivalent of saints. She also had mojo bags, which were filled with charms, like hair and teeth and sticks and smelly herbs that I presumed were used to either curse or help, depending on the situation. I admired Deanna's commitment but I feared that dark forces would be used against my mother because of her fat-rationing edict.

Ever the peacemaker, I convinced my mom to let Deanna take us on field trips. My thinking was that we would get out of the house and Deanna wouldn't have time to fester over the fact that she had to make boiled potatoes and broccoli for dinner. Deanna seemed to like the idea as well, and soon enough, we were on our way behind the wheel of Deanna's beat-up station wagon. I figured we would hit a few museums, maybe take in a park or two, if we were feeling really crazy we could even go to the beach. But Deanna's field trips were always a mystery to us, as she would make a point of dropping us at her mother's house in Paterson before heading off on her own.

Located on the banks of the Passaic River, Paterson had once been a great mill city. But hard times had fallen, the mills closed and now it was just the ugly stepsister to neighboring Newark. Deanna's mom had a spacious pre-war apartment and we'd spend hours there watching Jackson Five on the television while Deanna went out. I remember she had a retarded brother, or rather, mentally challenged brother (back then we said retarded without fear of reprisal), and he was pleasant. I began to suspect that my mother didn't know that Deanna was leaving us at her mother's house, but Jenny and Lee really liked her mom, who was super friendly, and I enjoyed the endless bingo with the retarded brother, mostly because I always won. So, who was I to complain?

Given an inch, Deanna decided to take a mile. Soon she was hustling us out on weekends. And one night, after an argument with her mother, she left us in a car and went out dancing with her friends. It was dark, and it was Paterson, and we were three kids alone in a car, which even in the late '70s seemed downright terrifying. I remember huddling with Lee and Jenny in the wheel-well of the car, thinking we were a moment away from being stolen and then sold into some sort of slave-labor ring. When we got home that night and my mother returned from her Parents Without Partners dance, I sang like a canary. Deanna gave me the evil eye, grabbed her mojo bags and left, thus ending The Live-in Situation and ushering in The Daycare Solution.

In my mom's quest for acceptable daycare, there were two main issues. First, it had to be affordable, and second, the staff had to know what the hell they were doing. She was looking for master's degrees in early education, teachers in training, or anyone who had a sense of phonics and early childhood development. Of course, the solution presented itself in the unlikeliest of places. The Salvation Army Daycare Center in Mahwah, New Jersey.

Like many towns in Northern New Jersey, Mahwah was named after an Indian word that meant *mouth of the river*. Before New Jersey became the capital of shopping malls and bad hair, it was the dumping ground for Lenape Indians who had been booted off their land in New York and Connecticut. The Lenape were a huge community, but due to chronic infighting, they had become divided into many different groups, none of whom spoke to each other. When the French settlers came, they figured there were too many different tribes to bargain with and just started kicking the Lenape off the land. Many of the displaced natives fled to New Jersey, probably thinking, who the hell would want to live there? But sadly, the white man thought New Jersey would work just fine and headed over. The twice displaced Indians were then pushed into the Ramapo Mountains of Mahwah where they were renamed the Jackson Whites. There they lived like social pariahs, watching the white man down below in the valley as he built car dealerships, mini malls, and my personal favorite, Consumers Warehouse (where you could buy everything from calculators to bicycles with the aid of a code number and a small pencil). The big rumor swirling around the Jackson Whites was that they were inbred. This stemmed from the fact that they all had the same last names (DeGroat, Mann and DeVries being the three most popular). They didn't look at all like Indians in the stereotypical sense. They had very light skin (thanks to the French) and very dark features (thanks to the runaway slaves) and in a confusing twist, preferred to be called Ramapo Mountain Indians though everyone called them Jackson Whites. They had lived in the hills of the Ramapo Mountains for hundreds of years and over time they began to get that glossy, angry, glazed-over look of people who are at their core, pissed off. Of course, the Salvation Army Daycare Center was perched at the top of Stag Hill, which was their central hub. Word in the area was that if you drove up Stag Hill Road you could be shot. But my mother had been working in the South Bronx for nearly six months and was undaunted. The price was right and there was a young teacher who had a master's degree in Early Childhood Education. We'd risk it.

The drive up Stag Hill seemed treacherous enough without the fear of imminent gunfire. The road was narrow and winding, and the Gremlin barely had enough horsepower to make it up the steep hill. While I obsessed about how we would make it up the hill during the winter, when the roads were frozen, my mother focused on the positives.

"This is an adventure," she'd say. Or, "We're seeing a part of New Jersey that most people don't know about!"

While the mountain had the feel of *Deliverance*, it wasn't as bad as I had expected. It was just a poor community full of shanty houses and chicken coops, and lots of cars parked on what I assumed were supposed to be front lawns. My mom would always point out interesting facts as we chugged up the hill. "The residents of Stag Hill are like a lot of other groups, such as the Downland People of Iowa and the Melungeons of Tennessee," she'd say. "All these groups were of mixed-race descent, all were regarded as social outcasts, all had mysterious pasts. The Melungeons, for instance, are believed to be the descendants of the Roanoke colonists."

"They're like us too because they all have messy front lawns," I pointed out.

"This is true. And like them we also have a unique and isolated history," my mother added.

But unlike them, we did not have the luxury of commonality. They were surrounded by people living the same story. They were bitter, tired and poor, but they had each other. No one in this 'hood looked down on anybody else. There were no whispers at the supermarket, no eyeballs at the pharmacy. My mom always liked to say, "Like seeks out like." And I began to wonder, where were the people like us? I looked for them on that mountain, but I never saw my own face staring back at me. I looked for them down below, in the valley and in strip malls and in towns with Indian names. But there was no one like us anywhere. In fact, it seemed to me that everyone else had a place where they belonged, and the sad truth was that we were still terribly adrift.

3. tAKING tHE BAtH

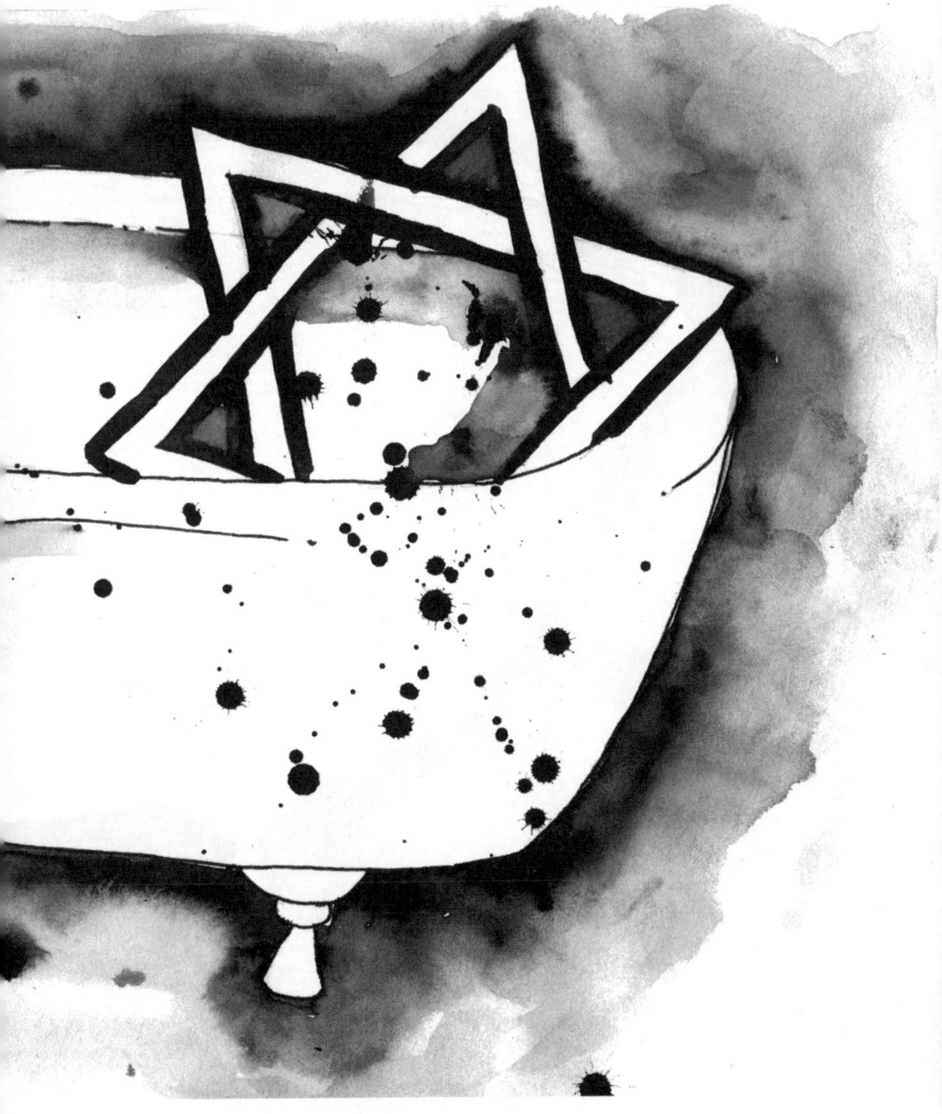

AFTER TWO YEARS of trolling the stellar singles at Parents Without Partners, my mother managed to find a suitable gentleman friend to date. His name was Lester and according to my mother, he immediately caught her fancy because in addition to paying for her drinks, he didn't pass out at the mention of her three children. While my mother might have been taken with this blatant display of generosity, it took a lot more than a few free drinks to impress me.

I wanted to run a background check on him, but my mom felt that would be intrusive. But there were so many questions to answer. How much money did he make? How many kids did he have? Where did he stand politically? Could he mow a lawn? I wanted answers and my mother didn't really have any. The best she could do was to let me loose in his apartment, which was a clean one bedroom, with fairly acceptable rented furniture. He had framed photos of his three kids on the mantel and a stack of mysteries on the side of the bed. The bathroom had matching towels, which was more than I could say for our bathroom, and the medicine cabinet seemed organized. From what I could tell, he wasn't a serial killer. Then there was the stack of *Playboy* magazines under his fish tank. This was an intriguing development. As I leafed through the glossy pages filled with tasteful shots of '70s-booshe, I assessed the situation. On the plus side, Lester had a job. He also drove a Buick, which wasn't a Benz, but after the Gremlin, I'd take it. In addition he seemed to have an interest in gardening and he also owned a toolbox. On the downside, he parted his hair on the side, in a sort of swept-up comb-over, which troubled me slightly. My mother reminded me that he was eight years older than her, which explained the hair, or rather loss of hair that demanded the comb-over. Hair issues aside, the idea of having a man around the house was appealing and I began to warm to the idea of Lester being around. After a few months of dating, the sleepovers began. Without even so much as a prod, Lester mowed the lawn, fixed the shower and even bought a waffle iron. Shortly thereafter, we began attending his kids' softball games, until finally one night, we ended up at McDonald's for a casual first joint family dinner. There we were, sitting across from each other like two nations at a summit, wondering if we had what it took to become the next Brady Bunch. Jenny and Lee were too excited about the French fries to be considering larger issues, but I had their backs, and was sending messages to Lester's kids with my eyes. They may have been older than me, but I was top dog of this outfit. I was only eight, but I had been living on the mean streets of Bergen County, and unlike them, my dad didn't shell the shill for McDonald's dinners, nor did he attend softball games. If they thought they were going to move into my territory and exert any influence or control, they were sorely mistaken. If I had been a dog I would have peed all over my siblings, our crappy car, and our home for that matter. Moreover, I could sense that Lester wanted his kids to come live with us, and I could see them sussing out the situation to see if it would indeed be in their best interests to do so.

After the meal, I let my mother know exactly where I stood on the issue.

"You said I'm the Majordomo around here," I reminded her.

"Everything will be fine," she assured me. "You're in charge and nothing's going to change that."

"How can you be certain?" I asked.

"Because Lester's Jewish, and Jewish men like being bossed around by women."

I was almost too stunned to speak.

"Lester is Jewish?"

"You seem surprised," she added.

"I just don't think I know anybody who's Jewish," I said.

"Well, now you do."

"But, what's the deal with being Jewish?" I asked.

My mom looked at me like I was insane.

"There's no deal. You are what you are."

"But we're not Jewish."

"Correct."

"And don't you always say that 'like seeks out like'?" I asked.

"Yes, but he's nice, so what's the difference?"

"I don't know."

Truth was, I didn't know. I was just trying to get my religious bearings. I knew what it meant to be a Protestant because our town was loaded with them. Protestants were what my mom called "old money," which meant that their grandparents had not been laborers. They often had lawn ornaments such as flamingos gracing their front lawns. They ate casseroles on a regular basis and did a lot with thank-you notes. Then there were Catholics, and their lesser cousins, lapsed, half-practicing Catholics like ourselves who thought Jesus was a great guy, but couldn't be bothered to attend mass regularly mostly because we didn't like those bossy priests who insisted on calling us sinners all the time. Regardless of status, all the Catholics were "new money" as our grandparents had all been poor laborers. We celebrated the same holidays as the Protestants but we had names like Mancini, Murphy and Makowski, and instead of eating casseroles we ate roasted meat and/or ziti. In addition we prayed to saints and our grandmothers had elaborate nativity scenes, which often included toy soldier figurines and Hummels. Christians I understood, but the Jewish thing was still a mystery.

"Jewish...," I muttered to myself.

"I don't know why you're so shocked, he was discussing his son's upcoming Bar Mitzvah," said my mom.

"I thought that was a medical procedure or something," I answered.

"Why are you acting so dumb? Your friend Alyssa is Jewish," my mom said in her annoyed voice.

Mother of God, she was right. Alyssa was a Jew. And what did this mean?

Alyssa sang Christmas songs with us and even had a tree, albeit one decorated with silver and blue ornaments.

"I will not have blue and silver ornaments!" I blurted out.

What else was there? I was in a froth trying to think. At Alyssa's house there was pasta night and the sauce was made from ketchup.

"You better not start making tomato sauce with ketchup," I warned her.

"What are you talking about?" my mother asked.

But I was too inside myself to answer. Alyssa had an extra freezer in her garage.

"Will we be getting another freezer in the garage?" I asked.

"No, the outlet's broken."

"Do we have to have Carvel cakes at every birthday?"

"No, of course not," she answered.

What else did I know of Alyssa and her Jewishness? All at once it hit me like a ton of bricks. Alyssa and her siblings were shipped off to camp for the entire summer; her belongings packed in these intense, heavy-duty cases with metal buckles.

After that, I eyeballed my future stepfather wearily. I wanted to be sure he didn't have some hidden camp agenda up his sleeve. I'd drop subtle hints like, "If you think you're shipping my ass off to camp, you're living in a dream world pal."

As a precautionary measure, I put pictures of Jesus up around the house. I also watched for signs of yarmulkes, and blue Christmas ornaments, and glared at my mother every time she uttered the word *bubula*.

And though my mom had taken to invoking Yiddish terms, it was pretty clear that we weren't going to have to take some group mikva bath and become Jewish ourselves.

Scared off by the cornucopia of Crucifixion scenes, Lester's kids decided they didn't want to live with us and instead moved down to Boca Raton with their mother. The status quo seemed to be holding, I wasn't going to be out of a bedroom, and so I approved the union.

The wedding was at home. It rained in the morning before the ceremony, but then thankfully it cleared up, although the humidity made my mom's already frizzy hair so big people kept mistaking her for Patti LaBelle. We lost a few cousins to the septic tank, and a few more to West Nile, given the fact that the mosquito population was running on full tilt. But despite those minor glitches, it was a fine day, and a welcome improvement from my father's second nuptials when I rode the elevator at the Hilton Hotel up and down for a few hours, and then threw up, mostly because nobody (and by nobody, I mean my dad) realized I was missing from the wedding.

After the wedding, my stepdad fell into a routine. He'd go to work early and come home late, and just like the Sphinx, he would greet us with a question.

"Why is this here?" he'd shout out from the foyer.

My mom would then yell out from the kitchen, "Why don't you try sticking a noun in there hon? We're not psychic!"

But after a long day tackling transportation concepts and services (which was his business niche), Lester was often at a complete loss for words. He'd merely sigh and then head up the stairs of our crumbling split-level. He'd give my mom a kiss hello and launch into his triangulated litany of complaints that covered the Holy Trinity of Lester's world: The electric bill, the front lawn and the thermostat.

"There are too many lights on in this house. Money doesn't grow on trees you know," he'd intone while pouring himself a giant glass of diet root beer. "I'll go to the store tomorrow and pick up some torches," was my mom's typical answer.

"The kids need to stop leaving their baseball equipment all over the lawn. The grass is starting to spot," he'd complain as my mom popped his frozen Weight Watcher entrée into the microwave. Incidentally, we learned post-nuptials that Lester was a serial dieter whose ultimate goal was to find the perfect balance between the weekend Jewish deli gorge and staying under two hundred pounds. During the first few years of the marriage, it was all about diet root beer and Weight Watchers frozen entrées. So, while his Barbeque Glazed Chicken with Mixed Vegetables cooked, Lester would continue to rant about the yard and how our playing on it translated into some sort of lack of respect. And by the time he moved off that and reached his finale, "Who turned up the thermostat?!" the Weight Watchers dinner would be done, and Lester would be sent upstairs to eat in his bedroom and watch TV.

Oh, how we envied his freedom.

During the week he was sort of like a boarder but on the weekend, he'd come alive. Making breakfast for everyone, gardening like a pro, and organizing field trips to sporting events. It was all going great, until one day, after several months of this marital bliss, he went old world on us and busted out the smelly, morning fish foods associated with fine Jewish cuisine. Creamed herring, pickled herring, gefilte fish, or, as I liked to call it, diarrhea in a jar. Then there were bagels and their more delicate cousin the bialy. Of course I'd heard of bagels because I watched the kid's show *Wonderama*, which always featured Lender's bagelettes as gift giveaways. However, I was under the impression that they were ornamental objects to be worn around the neck, rather than food. My first true lesson as Lester's stepchild was that Jews ate bagels. My second lesson was that there were entire towns in New Jersey, towns like River Vale and Cherry Hill, which were teeming with Jews. Suddenly we were being whisked to kosher joints for Saturday lunch. Places populated with people named Saul and Murray and Ida. I found myself in yet another unfamiliar landscape, filled with people who were clearly outsiders.

"Are the Jews similar to the Melungeons of Tennessee?" I asked Lester as I chomped on my corned beef sandwich.

Even if he knew who the Melungeons were, Lester was too busy eating to answer me. "They're not like the Jackson Whites," I pointed out, "'cause they have nicer houses and they're much more talkative." My mom nodded her head, content to let me play the role of anthropologist as she choked down her whitefish sandwich. I was sort of fascinated by this new "tribe" of people known as New Jersey Jews. I wouldn't say that they were friendly, because friendly would imply a sense of congeniality. The Jews seemed to dislike one another, and yet at the same time, they seemed to revel in the contention. There were always a lot of arguments. Backhanded compliments and snide greetings were the norm, and just about every statement was followed by a rhetorical question, like "Who am I?", "What do I look like?" or "What do I know?"

I kept waiting for my stepfather to get into it with

someone, but he was only in it for the food and kept to himself. Still, I looked forward to our kosher outings. I was fascinated by these Jews and I wanted more than just deli. How did they come to be in New Jersey? Were the Jews who wore their yarmulkes off to the side part of an elite group or were they just trendy? And what was with that strange double-inverted triangle that they wore around their necks? There was an element of mystery that I yearned to unlock.

All this was Before Fort Lauderdale. BFL was a period of blissful ignorance, when the world of Judaism was revealed to us in tiny incremental packages wrapped in challah and noodle-dishes involving fruit. Things were bound to change, and they did once Lester decided that we needed to go down to Florida to meet his folks. We were going deep into the heartland. I grabbed my yarmulke and packed my trunk.

They played *April in Paris* on the plane, which really annoyed me. I had been hoping for a Chevy Chase movie and I felt that it was a cheap move on the part of the airline to go with some old musical, even if it was a classic. I was way too young to appreciate a hoofer like Gene Kelly and I sure as shit wasn't going to sit through an entire Technicolor musical. My mother likes to point out that it was one of the last peaceful flights with me, because a few years later I projected the failure of my parents' marriage onto the image of a plane crash. After that, I harbored a quasi-hysterical fear of flying, which made traveling with me, now as well as then, an arduous task.

Nonetheless, we arrived in Fort Lauderdale to oppressive humidity and an unbelievably flat landscape, filled with old Jews and girls in bikinis. My hair fell victim to the humidity, and I made a mental note to never marry anyone who lived in Florida. This of course negated a large assortment of professional baseball players, and considering all the anti-frizz products on the market these days, may have been a bit hasty on my part.

We rented a car at the airport, which frankly impressed me. Even my sister Jenny, who hated everything, thought the rental car was pretty swank. Jenny even managed to find an old piece of gum in the ashtray, which she promptly began chewing. Yes, this was class.

We were going to meet our new grandmother, Nana Ruth, and her husband Jessie, who was Lester's stepfather. Jessie had married Ruth after the death of Lester's real dad, who was described as "a man who knew great meat." Jessie had been the owner of a very popular clothing store that bore his name in Fair Lawn, which was one of those secret Jewish towns in New Jersey. He and Ruth had moved to Florida after he retired to bask in the heat and humidity, and lived in a Jews Only Retirement Community.

We arrived at the gate and were buzzed in by the security guard.

"How can it be Jewish only?" I asked.

"It just is," said my mom.

"But what if a nice Buddhist couple wanted to live here?" I reasoned.

My stepfather laughed on that one, "I don't really think it's an issue."

But I was troubled. "Does the ACLU know about this?"

"Kristen, *please*," said my mother.

"What about Rosa Parks?"

"She doesn't want to live here," sighed my mom.

"Jews only is discriminatory!" I yelled, working myself up into a tizzy.

"No one is bent out of shape about the Jews Only rule," said my mom.

"How can you be sure?" I asked.

"Because no one wants to live with the Jews, except for other Jews," adding, "No offense hon," to my stepdad.

"None taken," he muttered.

My mother then turned around, and mouthed "shut up"

to me, which I took as an indication that perhaps I was on the right track. Still, I inferred from her steely glare that equal protection under the law had to be put on the back burner because it was time to meet the step-in-laws.

As we drove into the complex, I looked around at all the deliriously happy octogenarians.

Unlike my grandmother's neighborhood in Weehawken, where no one looked each other in the eye and longstanding grudges were met with silence and indifference as people muddled along leading lonely lives and ignoring each other from their kitchen windows, this place was hopping. They had tennis courts and pools. There were shuffleboard tournaments, movie nights, date nights, mahjong, yoga, even early-bird-special nights. These people were not sitting in their kitchens waiting to die; they were living it up Jewish style.

Lester's mom Ruth was a handsome woman, who looked a bit like Anne Bancroft, only with red hair. She was well-read and had a wry sense of humor. Reserved was a good way to describe her, which was probably a good thing since she balanced out Jessie, who was like Groucho Marx without the moustache or the assortment of talented siblings. He'd give us dollar bills, clap his hands, and yank us all in for group hugs. We loved the bug shield on the front of his car and we loved that he had to have cake everyday at three. "What's life without good cake?!" he'd shout before digging in. Jessie was also the president of the retirement community, and we were his new step-step-grand children. As such, he paraded us proudly around the pools and canasta games, showing off his assortment of pan-ethnic, semi-disabled, step-grandchildren. The Jews love a cause, and as such, we were initially embraced, even though everyone in the complex knew that our mom was Catholic, which was a serious *shanda*, but one that they were willing to overlook considering she had taken in orphans.

Still, there were a lot of rules governing pool use, so we

ended up spending a great deal of time inside, enjoying the never-ending stream of air conditioning. I began having tea in the afternoon with Nana Ruth, who would pepper me with questions about school. Of course, I loved school and was more than happy to prattle on endlessly about social studies and geography. It was during this time that I became particularly taken by the raised oil painting of a geisha girl walking among cherry trees on her wall. Strangely enough, the girl bore a striking resemblance to Jenny, and the more I looked at it, the more disturbed I became, until finally I had to ask the big question.

"When was that painted?"

"Why do you ask?" she said, in typical Jewish fashion. Answering a question with another question.

"Well, I'm just wondering how long it's been up on the wall," I said.

"Why would you wonder about something like that?" she asked.

I was getting antsy. The geisha was suddenly troubling me.

"Well...," I started, unable to finish.

"Well, what?" she said

Mother of god, would the questions ever end!

"Did you paint this recently?" I tried again.

"Who asks a question like that?" she responded.

There was no choice but to get to the heart of the matter.

"Did you have this painted as some sort of homage to your new Korean step-grandchildren?"

Nana Ruth had her poker face on. "And what if I did?" she asked.

"Well, did you know that the Koreans were subjugated by the Japanese for centuries, and that for many Koreans, being referred to as Japanese is like the biggest insult in the world?"

Rather than being insulted by the mouthy ten-year-old before her, Nana Ruth seemed to admire my candor.

"It was painted about ten years ago," she explained.

A wave of relief washed over me, and we sat there admiring it for a few moments, then she added, "I think it's pretty classy." I wasn't sure about classy, after all, there really wasn't anything classy about Japanese hookers, but still I liked her out-of-the-box thinking. I guessed that she was the only woman in this place with a geisha on her wall, and I dug it.

But there was a darker side to this joyful enclave of Jewish retirees. They harbored an obsession with dietary laws and dish-washing practices that didn't seem to make the food taste better, and frankly, smacked of a little discrimination. They ate on the plates with the flowers, and we got the crappy Oneida set. I wondered if they would have liked it had the tables been turned. I told my mother that we should have a separate set of sheets for them when they came to our house to visit, just to make the point. Or perhaps we could take a bus ride and make them sit on the back of the bus. But my mother felt that new sheets would always be interpreted as a positive. And while Nana Ruth privately copped to the fact that she didn't give a crap about the kosher of it all, she was still playing the game, and I have to say, I lost a little respect for her because of it. After all, we were new to this; we hadn't even been versed in the ways of this unleavened-bread eating people. And there was my poor sister Jenny, trying so hard to be helpful. And all she got in return was grief, as various old women took turns berating her just because she kept putting utensils in the wrong sink. Then my brother Lee made the mistake of asking for cheese on his burger, which literally prompted an emergency meeting of the retirement community. Harsh words were exchanged. *How could Jessie let these gentiles invade? Enough with the cute orphan routine, we want them out!*

I sensed conspiracy everywhere. Every phlegm-rattling cough was a signal, every *oye gevalt* a code word. They were up to something. My spidey senses were tingling, and my suspicions were confirmed when Irv and Dana Liebowitz invited us to their apartment for a "nice meal," and then proceeded to serve us tongue. They had thrown down the gauntlet and we responded in the only way we knew how. Choking back our tears, we staged our first walkout. Like the Romantics, we fled to the tennis courts to declare our independence. But my mother had taken on smallpox, Jackson Whites and an angry Dominican housekeeper bearing mojo bags. A few testy Semites weren't going to scare her out of Dodge. We huddled next to her, trying to avoid the avalanche of tennis balls being hit in all directions. It was a clear night and the air felt like pea soup, without the ham of course.

"Who was this Moses?" I cried to our mother. "And what did he have against Jesus and shellfish?"

"Remember the Ten Commandments?" my mother asked.

"Thou shalt not kill…," I began.

"No, the movie! With Charlton Heston."

"And Yul Brynner!" I shouted.

"Remember how good Charlton Heston was as Moses?"

We all nodded our heads, because he really did seem convincing, although the big beard and giant red cloak helped lend an air of authenticity.

"Well, I'm gonna let you in on a big secret," she said; "Charlton Heston was convincing as a Jew, despite the fact that he *wasn't* a Jew."

"What is he then?" I asked.

"A casserole-eating, saint-hating Protestant!" my mom declared.

"So we can pretend to be Jews?" Lee asked.

"No, we just need to respect the customs of the people whose land we are visiting," she said.

"When in Fort Lauderdale?" said my sister Jenny.

"Yes! When in Fort Lauderdale!" laughed my mom.

Finally, my brother pointed out how cream cheese was not just for bagels, but also for cheesecake, which was something we all liked. We agreed that Fort Lauderdale was yet another strange and foreign landscape, and once again we were visitors in this land, just passing through until we could find our way back home. We could do this, mom stressed. We could make this work. So what if we couldn't eat off their dishes? The Oneida was actually a nicer set. My sister agreed to not help with the dishes anymore, and my brother promised to remember not to mix dairy with meat, and I promised not to gag on matzo balls, but rather to politely push them off to the side and just sip the broth. We practiced sighing heavily, then saying *kinahora* ten times fast for luck. After that, we headed back inside feeling determined and fortified. As we stepped onto the crowded lobby elevator, filled with tired Jews heading home from yet another early bird extravaganza, my sister Jenny began to sing a little song (to the tune of *Frère Jacques)*. Quietly at first, but then stronger with more conviction. *"If you're Jewish, and you don't know it, ask your mom, ask your mom. She will then tell you, she will really tell you, you're a Jew, you're a Jew."*

It was a bridging of worlds, a reaching across the proverbial matzo, and all the crabby Jews with heartburn began to hum along with her. And for that moment, that one beautiful moment, we were all Jewish.

IN PURSUIt OF LEISURE

MY MOTHER WAS NEVER KEEN on the notion of family vacations. She always maintained that it was in essence a pursuit of leisure, and for my mother, leisure was nothing but a big waste of time. Of course, I knew that there was more to it than this. After all, this was a woman who could sleep twelve hours straight and then lounge all day in her bathrobe reading the *Sunday New York Times*. Clearly, leisure wasn't really the issue for my mom. Though we never discussed it, over the years I came to see that her aversion to vacations was tied to the vacations of her youth, where as a girl she and her entire extended family spent summers on Long Beach Island. LBI was a quaint beachside town in New Jersey, that was commonly referred to as the Irish Riviera (along with nearby Spring Lake). It was filled with massive Victorian houses, an expansive boardwalk, and sandy white beaches. Every summer, my grandmother Mardy and all her sisters would sit on the beach drinking highballs all day, while their respective children, including my mom, were forced to swim in the rough ocean surf. Each day brought a new near death experience, but my grandmother and her sisters were too plastered to notice. Various cousins would be waving furiously for help, but my grandmother and her sisters would misinterpret the cries and just smile and wave back. In addition, my mother had very fair skin and would burn to a crisp if left in the sun for even a minimal amount of time. So, added to the threat of drowning was the daily pain of sunburn. Years later, vacations also became about death when my grandmother Mardy took ill, was hospitalized back up in Jersey City and then died suddenly. The irony was my mom hated the beach and would have much rather been with her mother, but her family was Irish, and rather than giving my mom the option, they kept her in the dark and pretended that nothing was happening, so that my mom never really had time to prepare or even say goodbye to her mom.

The confluence of all these things caused my mother to hate vacations. But rather than explaining all this to us and rehashing painful memories, it was just easier to blame it on the Minoans of Crete, who were basically a community of accountants that built a singular civilization in antiquity; one that was oriented around trade and bureaucracy with little or no evidence of a military state. The immense concentration of wealth in such a small population led to an explosion of visual arts that seemed to have been solely oriented around visual pleasure, rather than visual utility – political, religious, or otherwise. When they weren't painting nice pictures, the Minoans would attend boxing matches and bull jumping tournaments, cheering wildly like a bunch of rabid sports addicts. Without realizing it, they had invented the entire notion of leisure time. They made their cash and they wanted to enjoy life. And while we don't think of this as anything all that new, it was. In the history of mankind, there had never been a culture like this before. But the good times only lasted a few centuries. The military city-states on the mainland of Greece started eyeballing the leisurely Minoans and decided to invade. Had the Minoans spent a little more time building up an army and a little less time painting sunsets on their many idyllic beaches, perhaps they wouldn't have had their asses kicked by the Greeks. My mother's message was clear:

It was a tough world and you couldn't afford to go soft. But how this translated into a blanket refusal for a lousy once a year vacation to Long Beach Island remained a mystery. Clearly, we were not going to be attacked by Greeks as we played miniature golf on the boardwalk. There was an issue with logic. It was a weakness in my mother's vast intellectual fortress. And though it was barely perceptible, I knew it was there and continued to push. In fact, I begged, pleaded, whined and cajoled for the better part of six months, until finally, I wore her down. And ultimately my mother agreed to a vacation! Though in order to make the whole thing more palatable, she justified it in the name of home improvement. Her decision cannot be fully understood until one appreciates what was going on during those six months in our home.

Since Lester was a man, it was, of course, his job to fix up our house. He had conquered the lawn and was now turning his sights onto the interiors. At the same time, Lester's eldest daughter Allison, who was eighteen, had come to live with us. After her mom had moved to Florida she decided that she didn't want to leave her bevy of friends. One of these friends was a twenty-year-old guy named Lenny, who had super long brown hair and looked like he could be the missing Allman Brother. Lenny was not a painter by trade, but he very much wanted to paint our house. He lobbied fairly hard, but my parents weren't so sure. However, Lenny had one thing going for him, his price was right. And after getting bids from professional painters, it was decided that Lenny should get the job. The only trouble was that Lenny's shared love of pot and TV overshadowed his ability to work, especially between the hours of nine and three. Most days we'd come home from school and find him sleeping on various sofas. To his credit, he was very handy in the kitchen. He'd always get up and make us a snack. By the time my mom got home from her hellish Bronx commute, she was too tired to notice that there had been no painting accomplished. She just wanted a nap.

And Lenny, sensing her deepest needs, would often forsake late afternoon painting to make dinner instead. My mother would relish every bite of her grilled cheese as if it were coq au vin. Lenny was so good in so many ways. He straightened up in the morning, made us snacks, and in between his shows he'd run to the store for milk and other necessities. The only trouble was the house wasn't getting painted.

Finally Lenny, the paradigm of out-of-the-box thinking, had a brilliant idea: He'd move in with us. During the day he'd sleep, watch TV and get stoned, and at night while the family slept, he'd paint. He even drew up a timetable, estimating the job at a mere two weeks. It seemed like a perfect solution. While we slept, dreaming of the *Architectural Digest* home of the month, Lenny would be hard at work, making that very dream a reality. But Lenny often smoked too much pot and would then sleep through the night, vowing that he'd do double the work the next night, only to pass out in front of the TV once again. This went on for the better part of two months, until finally my stepfather pulled the plug when one night Lenny mysteriously "sleep-walked" into Allison's bedroom. And while my stepfather could tolerate a lazy, free-loading, non-painting pothead under his roof, he could not tolerate canoodling with his daughter.

There was a brief commotion and Lenny was never seen again. Sadly, the house never did get painted, but my mother decided to move off the walls and focus on the floors.

Our house was a split-level. The top floor contained the bedrooms and was carpeted in a pink shag, but the living room, kitchen, and dining room had wood floors, which were buckling, scuffed, and hideous. We were never going to make it into the hallowed pages of *Architectural Digest* with those babies. It was decided that we were going to pay a *professional* to refinish the wood floors. It was a new beginning to our new life. We were getting *new floors* and everyone knew that from there it was just a slippery slope to new cabinets, new carpets, and new sofas. The greatest news was we *had* to go on vacation for two weeks. During that time, the floors would be refinished and have time to dry.

It was to be a true family vacation in that all my step-siblings would be joining us for the seminal event. Of course, we weren't going to a beach. That would have been more than my mother could have handled. Instead, we were driving (in a three car convoy!) to upstate New York, where we would rent a Winnebago and then drive to Canada. From there we would tour Montreal, Quebec City, and Toronto. In retrospect it actually sounds hellish. My mother had copious notes, all under the heading "Points of Interest". Clearly there would be no "leisure" in this vacation. But I had negotiated a personal bag of Dipsy Doodles for the trip and the idea of having my own bag of Doodles coupled with the excitement of sleeping in a moving vehicle filled my ten-year-old heart with joy.

We hit the road, with only our maps and our CB radios to guide us. And after a few hours spent annoying every trucker in the vicinity with our fake southern accents and our faux trucker lingo (culled from *Smoky and The Bandit* and its various sequels) we turned our attentions to AM radio. By some miracle, as we headed up I-287, we got *Match Game* on the radio. It was thrilling! And not only was it thrilling, it was a watershed moment between my middle stepsister Stacie and myself, in that we finally managed to find common ground. I was new to *Match Game* (having only been recently turned onto it by Lenny), which was a popular game show, hosted by Gene Rayburn. There was a panel of six celebrities that were given a fill-in-the-blank sentence and their job was to try to match what the contestants put in the blank. It was a very simple concept and sounds a bit boring, but nearly all the questions had possible suggestive answers and alcohol was served to the celebrities during taping, so boredom rarely came into play. The frank sexual jokes, the constant flirting, the obvious drunkenness of the panelists, the way they smoked right on camera, the innuendos of host Gene Rayburn made *Match Game* completely brilliant. I would rush home from school every day just to watch it. But on this day, the show was on the radio, which somehow made it even better. As luck would have it, our favorite panel was on. Charles Nelson Reilly, Richard Dawson, Brett Summers, Bert Convy, Betty White and Fannie Flagg. My mother was in a different car, thankfully and didn't know about my illicit addiction to *Match Game* (television watching being a big "no-no" on par with heroin addiction). During the commercial breaks we debated what Fannie Flagg was wearing. I voted for Champagne Bubbles, my sister felt she was going with the Confederate Flag, even my stepfather chimed in, saying he thought she was wearing the Post Office uniform that she sometimes favored. It was a seminal bonding moment for us, as we headed North on I-287 with Gene Rayburn's smoky voice saying, "Lex Luthor is so evil," and the three of us shouting, "How evil is he?!"

If this was any harbinger of things to come, things were definitely looking up. I was bonding with my suddenly cool fifteen-year-old stepsister. We had even plowed through the Dipsy Doodles, but I didn't care, I was having fun. And soon I was going to be cruising in a 31-foot Winnebago! I ran through the bullet facts that I'd memorized from the brochure, impressing my stepsister with my ability to memorize pointless facts at will. "25-inch stereo TV, three 8-track players, a big, comfortable interior, Benchmark Full Comfort Dinette, 'Super Slide' Slide Out Couch, Queen-Size Bed with Deluxe Mattress, Ducted Air Conditioner & Heater, Super Quiet Generator, Awning, Sleeps Eight … "

My stepfather said if all else failed, I could get a job as the dealership spokesman.

"Is there really a niche market for youth Winnebago sales?" I wondered aloud. "Maybe I could make some extra money doing it?" I mused, which cracked up Stacie and my stepdad.

"I like the way you think," said my stepdad as we pulled into a rest stop about twenty minutes outside the Rochester Winnebago dealership. Seating arrangements were shifted and somehow my stepbrother Phil ended up in the car with Stacie and me, completely disturbing the balance. I was irritated and made a mental note to tell my mother as much. As we pulled into the dealership parking lot, Phil blurted out, "Wouldn't it be funny if our Winnebago wasn't here?"

My mouth went dry, the blood drained from my face and I sensed the onslaught of imminent diarrhea. *Wouldn't it be funny*?! No, Phil. What the hell was he thinking even uttering such a thing?! Did he not know that bad luck had followed us around like the plague and to even utter such nonsense was asking for trouble? As we headed into the dealership, I noticed a dark cloud forming in the sky above us and moments later we learned that the people who currently had our 31-foot Winnie had not returned it because a relative of theirs had died and they had driven the Winnebago to the funeral. I glared at Phil. This was all his fault. He had uttered the words that had somehow set this backward plan in motion. I wanted to strangle him, but instead, I focused on problem solving and pointed out that there were Winnebagos everywhere in this place.

"We could take the Conquest or the Coachman Freedom Classic, which incidentally has a really stellar glass shower-enclosure," I said to the dealer who glared at me and replied, "Floor models cannot be removed."

My mother, who was never one to shy away from public displays of anger, proceeded to lose her mind and shouted, "My mother died and I never inconvenienced anyone!"

This was my cue to hustle my younger siblings into a floor model and start trashing it. Being an idealist at heart, I clung to the hope that our Winnebago would somehow return, but alas, my hopes were dashed when a compromise was reached. The Winnebago people agreed to put us up in a hotel on beautiful, nearby Lake Seneca, one of the famed New York Finger Lakes. I eyeballed the brochure for the Seneca Inn and noted that it had a massive pool. Suddenly, things didn't seem so bad.

We got to the hotel and in the time it took for me to admire the walk-in closets and the pool, my stepsisters had managed to find eligible boys. They were off by the pool faster than you could say "hussy" while Jenny, Lee, and I were politely told to beat it.

My dreams of lounging poolside were once again dashed as we were given the lake. But due to my recent report on bull sharks I would not swim in it. Seneca Lake was not a glacier lake and therefore it was entirely within the realm of possibility that a bull shark could get into these waters. I forbade Jenny from going in. My mother assured her that it was safe, but Jenny knew who buttered her bread and listened to me. We huddled by the side, ever alert for signs of sharks, because after the attack, who'd be the dummy then?

In the evenings, I turned to television. My stepbrother, who was thirteen, was known for his ability to watch copious amounts of television. My mother was horrified by this, but didn't feel it was within her realm of authority to shut it off. And so I took advantage of her new-step-parent-lack-of-boundary issue and watched with him. As luck would have it, they were running a *Six Million Dollar Man* Marathon. It was Steve Austin vs. the Aliens, Steve vs. Loch Ness Monster, and the most terrifying double episode, Steve vs. Big Foot. I noted that the wilds of California bore a striking resemblance to the woody wilds of Lake Seneca and promptly spiraled into a vortex of irrational fear and frenzy. Panic gripped me. I would huddle by the window, wondering when Big Foot would strike. I told my sister Jenny to hunker down. I was going to keep her safe, but she had to listen to me. We needed to stay inside, with the blinds drawn. Sharks be damned, we now had hirsute primates to contend with.

Annoyed by my increasing hysteria, my mother decided that day trips were in order. My stepsiblings knew I was behind her change of heart and they hated me for it. Jenny sided with them, only because they bribed her by carrying her all the time. I was odd man out. A pariah. But they were all just ignorant to the world around them. Bad things happened to good people and I was the only one who had their backs.

And so it was that we visited the homes of: Harriet Tubman, which was swanker than one might expect; Susan B. Anthony, pre-coin, and as such no one knew who the hell she was; and Gideon Granger, whose big claim to fame, other than being a crony of Thomas Jefferson, was that he had a comprehensive collection of carriages. Then we visited some wine vineyards, which incidentally, are really wasted on the young, and Underground Railroad hideouts, as well as a few assorted English gardens. We also visited the Watkins Glen Park, which boasted a massive gorge and nineteen falls. At the end of that sweaty excursion, I felt that there should have been a sign that read:

Watkins Glen Park: You've seen one fall,
you've seen 'em all.

We were even subjugated to a trip to the Corning Museum of Glass, where the sign read:

CELEBRATING 3,500 YEARS OF GLASS

This would have been exciting had we cared about glass, but sadly, we didn't. My mom of course, was thrilled, drawing comparisons between the methods of Egyptian glassmakers and those of the Renaissance, and engaging the docent in hours and hours of pointless conversation. We however, were sullen and bored and that was how we remained for the duration of the trip.

Eventually, it was time for us to return home. The car ride back lacked the joyful insouciance of the ride up. We were cramped and tired. No one wanted to listen to *Match Game* and the CB radios were quiet. On the plus side, perhaps this made us a family. I was more than comfortable calling my stepbrother Phil an idiot and he was happy to return to favor.

When we finally got home, the house sat looking very quiet and suddenly I remembered the whole point of our vacation.

The new floors!

Joy returned to me, the last two weeks had not been for naught. There was still some light at the end of this tunnel. I couldn't wait to lay my eyes on the perfect *Architectural Digest* flooring, awaiting us inside. But we entered the house, only to find that it reeked of polyurethane. Oh, how foolish and naïve we had been to believe that the contractor was going to come when he promised he would. The floors were soaking wet and we were trapped in the hallway, with no way to get up to the bedrooms.

While everyone bitched and moaned about the smell and the inconvenience, I saw the wet floors within the context of a larger metaphorical picture. Upon the advice of Phil (the resident genius) my stepfather decided the best bet was to scale the flimsy aluminum banister that ran from the entrance hallway, all the way past the second floor, to the third floor where the bedrooms were. Once there, he would jerry-rig some sort of pulley system and hoist us all up for the night. It would have been a brilliant plan, if we had actually had rope stashed away on the third floor in anticipation of such an event, and if Lester had been a trapeze artist. But we had neither nimble dexterity nor cordage. I could have said something, but I decided for once to keep my mouth shut. Protest was futile. There were larger forces at play and clearly they were all out of my control. And so it was that we watched Lester scale the flimsy aluminum banister, which promptly gave way, sending him plummeting, like a Flying Wallenda, onto the newly finished wet floor. He landed in a heap outside the kitchen. His body sprawled on the floor, like a gigantic crime scene body imprint. Whatever hopes we might have had for pristine hard wood flooring had been dashed.

"If we had been around instead of pissing off on vacation, this could have been avoided," complained my mother.

"If we hadn't been on vacation, we wouldn't have been able to have the floors done," I replied.

"And I wouldn't be out six hundred bucks!" said my mom. "See, this is what happens. Just like the Minoans..."

I didn't have the energy to listen to her go on and on about the sins of leisure. It went without saying that it would be a good long while before we ever went on vacation again. And so, like a rag tag group of newly conquered Minoans, we grabbed our bags, climbed over Lester's prostrate body, and trudged up the wet steps to bed.

5. tRUtH OR CONSEQUENCE

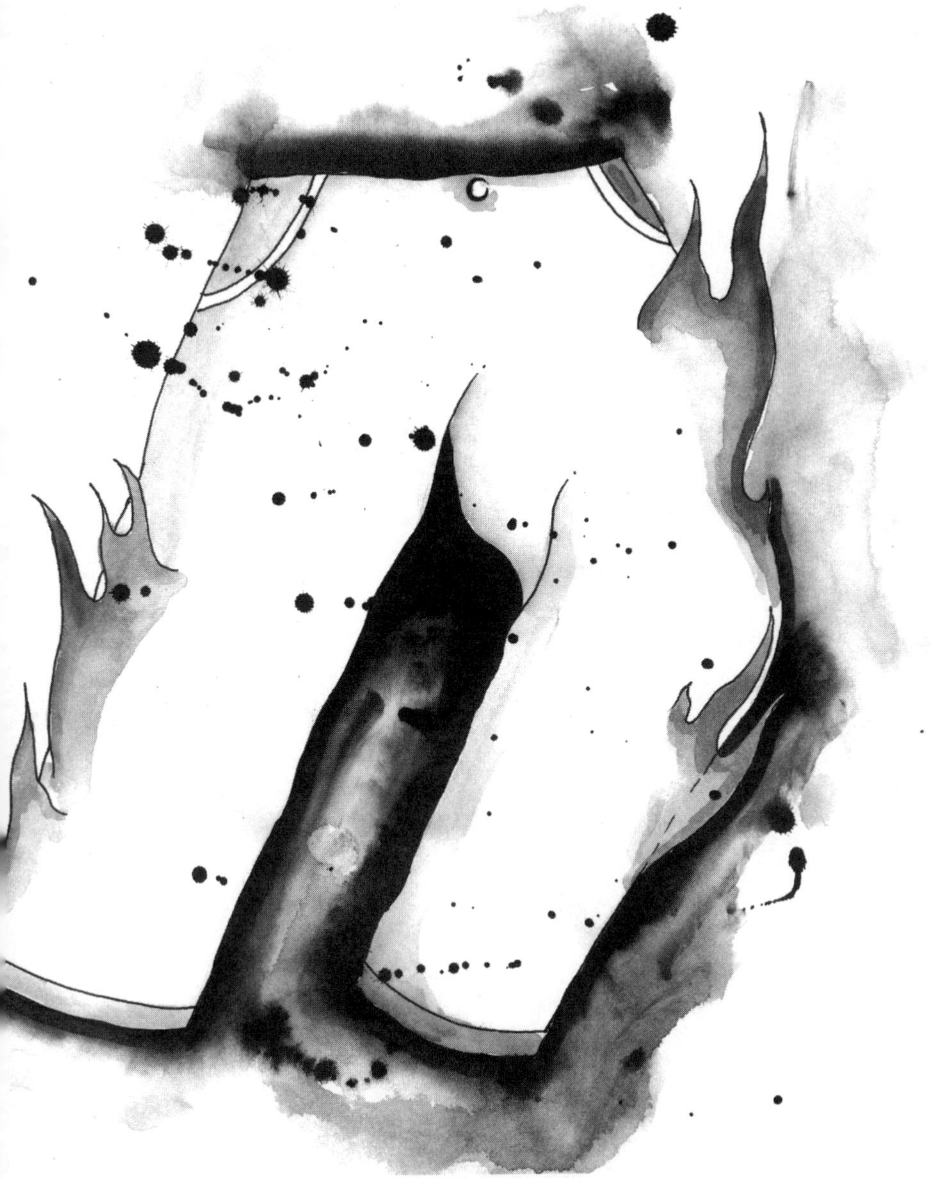

MY GRANDMOTHER, on my father's side, always maintained that she was French. It was a singular lie, perpetuated since her youth and one that she clung to until her last dying breath. Had her name been Anaïs Nin, Jean de Florette, or perhaps Camille Claudel, the French thing may have been a bit more palatable, but her name was Santa Maria Alimo Randazzo, and no matter how feverishly she swung her imaginary Gallic flag, it was a tough one to swallow. The only thing she had going for her was that she had been born in the then French-controlled city of Tunis, which incidentally embarrassed me to no end as a kid. *Tunis* bore an uncomfortable similarity to the word *penis* and when asked, "Where was your grandmother born?" I would always stammer nervously, "Northern Africa," and hope they didn't push.

My earliest memories involved my grandmother informing anyone who asked, and many who didn't, that she was indeed French. While I liked the idea of having a French grandmother, there seemed to be no evidence of this French past that she was so fond of pimping. Case in point, I had a friend who was Japanese and her house was filled with Japanese crap. Rice-makers, origami, kimonos on the wall; you walked into that house and without ever seeing a single member of that family, you knew Japanese people lived there or, at the very least, visited often. But this was not the case with my grandmother's home. Where was the little statue of the Eiffel Tower? Where were the matching prints of the Champs-Elysées and the Moulin Rouge? Why didn't she have a copy of *A Tale of Two Cities*, or a little mock guillotine, or even so much as a postcard with Napoleon's image? Why didn't she celebrate Bastille Day? And why, despite her love of bread products, was there never a croissant in the house? Surely, if she were going to pimp the French thing, she would've accessorized accordingly. It was perplexing indeed. I began to wonder if she were even really from Tunis, secretly hoping that she was really from a place called Springfield or Columbus. Any city that didn't sound like a male sexual organ would have done. But my mother verified the fact that my grandmother was indeed born in Tunisia, though the details regarding her early life there proved murky. According to legend, because at this point, it may be just that, my grandmother's mother Antoinette was from Spain. She had red hair and blue eyes and was by all accounts a bitch on wheels. So, this fiery red head, as I presume she must have been, traveled to Tunis to work as a tutor for some rich guy's children. The rich guy, whose last name was Randazzo, knocked her up and they ended up having three kids together. It's not certain that they were ever married, but what is certain is that he abandoned the three girls, Santa, Francis and Sarah, either en route to America, or once in America. And oddly enough, despite his disappearance, my grandmother maintained an undying love for him. Once in the States, my grandmother worked in the garment industry as a teenager and married my grandfather Joe, who was a truck driver for Schaefer Beer, which was the one beer to have, when you were having more than one. My grandparents had three children; two girls, Honey and Gloria and a boy, Joe, my father. And while my aunts were content to toe the proverbial Gallic line, my dad wasn't. My dad grew up in Weehawken, New Jersey, which was deep in the heart of Hudson County where you were either Irish or Italian or a little bit of both. Being French was something that didn't fly there, which might explain my dad's discomfort with his own mother hanging out the window screaming, "We're French!" to anyone who passed. He would argue openly with my grandmother about it every chance he could. This would have been okay, if the point was to reach a deeper truth, or to get to the bottom of our alleged ancestry. But the truth was, my dad was just looking for a better story; something sexier, maybe a little more interesting. As a teenager, he grasped at different origins, trying them on like one does a pair of shoes. Alsatian seemed too tight, German gave him hammertoes, Greek bothered his bunions. He never could find one that fit just right. Then finally, after watching Francis Ford Coppola's *The Godfather*, my dad decided he wanted to be Sicilian. After a little research, he learned that there was a small city on the slopes of Mt. Etna in Sicily named Randazzo. After more research, which was conveniently misplaced, it was learned that the town had been named after a former monarch who bore the Randazzo name. Armed with this certain proof, my dad proceeded to sell the Sicilian origin story. Not only were we Sicilian, we were also the descendants of kings. This was more than my poor grandmother could bear, especially at the dinner table. And she would almost always burst into tears, scream "We're French!" and then lock herself in the bathroom or bedroom depending on her mood. My father would just keep going, ignoring the fact that he'd actually made his mother cry. He would wax poetic about the Kings of Sicily and our regal bloodline and everyone in the family would sit on the edge of their seats, taking in the new, more exciting family history as if it were manna from heaven. My grandfather would just roll his eyes, as we all tried to ignore the muted strains of my grandmother's sobs.

Of course, I was always the voice of reason.

"There are about a million people named Randazzo living in the tri-state area and doesn't it seem sort of unlikely that we're all descendants from one king?" I'd point out.

My father wouldn't even bat an eye. "The original Randazzos were Jews and had blonde hair," he'd say.

"Now we're *Jewish*?" Considering the assortment of Jesus portraits adorning the walls, this was highly unlikely.

"No, we *were* Jewish, but we converted hundreds of years ago," he'd explain.

I'd have to strain to hear him over the din of my grandmother's wailing.

"Okay, but we don't have blonde hair and blue eyes," I'd point out.

"I was blonde as a baby," my dad would say. Which might have been true, but before the advent of color photography, it was hard to really put a label on the color of his hair, which was now jet-black.

"But you don't have blue eyes," I'd counter.

"Yes, that's because my father has brown eyes and brown is a dominant trait and therefore it would be statistically impossible for me to have blue eyes."

All my cousins and my aunts would glare at me. They liked the Sicilian royalty thing and hated when I'd argue about it.

"Couldn't it be that the people in the town of Randazzo, *took* the name Randazzo, in a way to honor the king?"

"This may be the case with the other Randazzos, but *our* family is directly related to the King," he'd say with the self-assured calmness of a pathological liar. Then he'd launch into some strange story that was sort of a combination of the Romulus & Remus myth and the film version of *Seven Brides for Seven Brothers,* which proved we were related to the former king of some two-bit Mediterranean rock heap.

But why the initial lie? Why the French story? What was the big deal? Sicilian, Italian, French, or not French, did anyone really give a shit which part of Europe we were from?

We were at my Grandma's one Sunday for dinner. While choking down her bad ziti and some cold, canned eggplant parm, I found myself looking around the table, pondering our origins. Lack of accessories aside, I didn't think we were French, mostly because no one looked like Catherine Deneuve. As for the Sicilian thing, I knew instinctively that we weren't descendants of kings. If we were, at the very least there would have been a royal family crest lying around somewhere. But on purely visual terms, I went to school with kids who were Sicilian and they didn't look like us. They weren't quite as dark and their features were different. They had longer noses and their hair was wavy, but not kinky like ours. Could we be Italian? That was a toss up too. All the Italian kids looked different as well. No, we were a strange looking bunch of people, dare I say exotic. Maybe Corsican? That could have explained my dad's dark skin and dark features, which, upon closer examination, bore a shocking resemblance to Bill Cosby. As I scanned the table, I found myself seeing that there were other resemblances that I hadn't noticed before. My grandmother was a dead ringer for Ella Fitzgerald and my two aunts looked like Cicely Tyson and Dionne Warwick respectively. Could we be black? Or at least part black? I decided to lob the question out there. After all, what could be the harm to adding my thoughts on the origins issue?

And so I asked, "Is there any chance that we're part black?" which brought an eerie, calm-before-the-storm type of silence to the table. I probably should've just left it at that, but instead I asked the dreaded question, "Maybe we could find a photo of Great Grandpa Randazzo," of which there seemed to be none, "and see what he looked like?"

The immediate result of this inquiry was a smashed plate of ziti and a smattering of eggplant parm on the wall. The end result was my grandmother locked herself in the bathroom and began sobbing uncontrollably and my aunts took over the bedroom for some sort of strange huddle that involved vehement whispers. My father moved back and forth between the bathroom and the bedroom, and my grandfather just smiled at me and said, "Nice work, kid," as he enjoyed a moment of peace at the dinner table.

Clearly, I'd touched a nerve. I scanned the wall of photos in the living room. My grandmother had a picture of every crone in the family, but not one of her beloved father. Why was this, I wondered? Could it have been that my grandmother's father, who was from *Africa,* might have been a rather dark skinned fellow? Could my grandmother have been the biracial love child of this man? Was it possible that Antoinette Alimo came to the U.S. looking for a decent life with her three biracial daughters and realized that having biracial kids was a very bad thing and first floated the "Tell them you're French" story as a way to keep people from looking too closely? Granted, they lived up North, but let's face it, being the biracial daughter of a red-haired, blue-eyed woman has never been a cakewalk in this country. I suddenly understood the source of my grandmother's lie and I felt badly for her. It was probably a lot for her to haul around and so I leaned against the bathroom door and whispered, "I know that we're French, Grandma. I was just joking."

After that I began to see that lying about who you are, was really about being uncomfortable with who you were. I saw that the unintentional result of my grandmother's initial lie was an overall feeling of inadequacy within the family unit. At this point, it didn't matter if we were Zulus, Canadians or Madagascans. We had morphed into a family whose defining hereditary trait was an inbred penchant for lying about who we were.

Like a cancer gene, everyone suffered from it. You could not go to a family gathering without being immersed in a free-for-all of reinvention where any number of varied personas could be tried on for size. You could reminisce about your days as a showgirl, or recall the brief period when you were considering going pro with the NFL. As long as there was a shred of a connection, say you once went to a dance, or you once attended a football game, it was enough to make it true. After her death, my grandmother, who was arguably the worst cook ever (a woman who felt rotten milk could substitute for buttermilk), was suddenly a gourmet chef. "Remember the sauce Mama used to make?" my Aunt would ask my dad. And my dad would shut his eyes and nod, as if his mother had been Marcella Hazan and not the woman whose idea of sauce was oil infused with tomato paste. My dearly departed grandfather, the Schaefer Beer truck driver, was now a former "brewmaster" for Schaefer. The truck driver part being a front, so that he could stay in touch with the likes of the "common man". My aunt, the alcoholic nightclub singer, was suddenly a misunderstood musical prodigy. Even the Sicilian King story was supplanted. It was the '80s and with the rise of white-collar crime, my dad opted for something with a classier feel. Something more in tune with the "banker as rock star" vibe of the times. The new legend was that we were the "Merchants of Venice" – not the Medicis of course, but the lesser-known Randazzos of Venice. What was most shocking was not the way in which he told the story, but rather, the ease with which everyone in the family believed it. As if they were born without so much as even a bullshit meter with which they could extrapolate fact from fiction. You could have said that we were related to Leonardo da Vinci, or maybe Christ himself, and not a single person would have batted an eye. The lies flowed like ketchup. And afterward you were left feeling queasy and confused, with the sneaking suspicion that you were surrounded by crazy people.

I told myself that I'd never be like them. Lying is a behavior, and like other behaviors it is learned. In order to break the pattern of behavior, it helps to understand the history and hopefully break the cycle so that one family's homicidal maniac can become the next generation's top criminal profiler. In my family's case, the hope was to turn the legacy of at least two generations of liars into another generation's paid writer.

But it's hard to fight genetics and eventually the right confluence of events merged and I told my first big lie.

It was a drizzly January afternoon. I was in fifth grade and we were stuck inside due to the inclement weather. We were bored and the lunch monitors were busy breaking up an orgy in another classroom down the hall. We were all tired of playing with the wooden tilt-a-labyrinth and so a few of the boys decided we should have a beauty pageant. I had good teeth and was tall, so while I abhorred the notion of a beauty pageant in the abstract, I was comfortable with one that I felt I had a chance of winning. After brief negotiations, where we refused to do a bikini round, it was decided that we would be scored on looks, smarts, personality and athleticism. Honestly, I really thought I had it in the bag. But a dark horse emerged and Kiki Brinkman was pronounced the winner. (I got second place and was able to fill in for her should she move or fall ill.) Kiki's win annoyed me, mostly because I felt she had won only because she was super tall. But Kiki added insult to injury by invoking the term "world peace" during her acceptance speech. It was a fifth grade beauty contest organized by a group of bored eleven-year-olds; the world peace nonsense seemed uncalled for and smacked of bloated largesse. As runner-up, I too would have to make a speech, but I was beginning to feel a lot of resentment and perhaps a touch of insecurity regarding my placement as runner-up. Never one to be happy with second best, I decided that at the very least, I'd be first place with my speech.

I was looking for a showstopper. Something that would not just make them regret not voting me number one, but something that would set me apart. Something that would make me special. I had always been a boy's girl rather than a girl's girl, which differs from being a tomboy in that I enjoyed looking and dressing like a girl, but I just preferred the company of boys. Wendy from *Peter Pan* was the classic example of a boy's girl. As a boy's girl you got to be little sister, big sister, confessor and flirt all wrapped up in one. And in that moment, I wanted to be *their* girl. I wanted it badly. I was already sort of there, but I saw this as a golden opportunity to seal the deal. Of course screaming, "I'm part black!" wasn't going to do it, only because it would've confused everyone. And it wasn't like I could have added, "And my dad's Reggie Jackson!" because even *I* knew that would've been a reach, mostly because the then Yankee designated hitter, Roy White, had a daughter named Lorena in our grade and she would've refuted my Yankee lineage. But I did have another ethnic card that I could play, one that I hadn't played before and one that was infinitely more interesting. I was the only person in the school with adopted siblings and although my brother Lee was in another school, everyone knew who he was, because he was Asian and therefore exotic. This was before the Korean Diaspora, when schools along the Eastern seaboard became filled with Chois and Kims and Parks. So, when it was my turn to speak, instead of thanking them for their second place vote, I decided to share a piece of my family history with them. I then told them my orphan brother Lee, a mere blue belt in Tae Kwon Do and a third-grader at the time, could stick a motorcycle spoke through his arm, hang a bucket of water from it, while standing on shattered glass, and then break a board with his bare foot. I had recently been to a local demonstration at Lee's Tae Kwon Do club, where his teacher, Master Bai, had done this very thing. And while Master Bai was a thirty-eight-year-old, ninth degree black belt in Tae Kwon Do, he had a round face just like my brother, so for a liar like me, it was really just a hop, skip and a jump to envision my brother standing in his stead. It made the Merchants of Venice lie seem quaint. But not only did the boys in my class believe it, they were impressed. They spent a great deal of the afternoon wrapping their heads around it, until a consensus was reached and it was decided that Lee's round face and almond shaped eyes had clearly imbued him with some sort of super-human, Shaolin-like abilities. Frankly, I could've told them he was the Buddha himself and they would've bought it. But my plan worked. They were my own personal Lost Boys and I was their Wendy. A few even pulled me off to the side on the way to gym, to tell me that there had been a secret revote and I had emerged in the first place slot. I smiled big, yet tried to act unassuming. I was *so* in. And I was filled with a warm fuzzy feeling that I can only describe as bliss.

I forgot about the whole story, didn't give it a single thought actually and life went on as usual. Another undercurrent during the time was my involvement in Swim Team. A few months BTL (Before the Lie), my father, in his infinite bat-shit-crazy, eye-of-the-tiger wisdom convinced me to join the swim team. The one caveat being, I didn't know how to swim. I kept telling this to my father but he never really seemed to acknowledge what I was saying.

The swim club where practice was held was near my house and I could walk to it, which was good since my mom didn't get home from the Bronx in time to drive me. My dad met me at the pool for my first session. We were introduced to Coach Joan, whose big claim to fame was a bronze medal in some junior Olympics of yore. Joan had the no-nonsense demeanor of a lesbian gym teacher and the shoulders of a linebacker.

"Are you prepared to be a Barracuda?" she asked.

I nodded my head, "Sure."

"'Cause everyone here contributes. We're a team. We move as a unit and we're only as strong as our weakest link."

I swallowed hard and looked around for signs of quadraplegics in the pool.

"What are your favorite strokes?" she asked.

My dad looked at me on that one. We hadn't discussed things like strokes. Mostly because I couldn't swim. And while I would have loved to have shouted out "Butterfly!" and then regaled Joan with tales of my mermaid-like swimming prowess, I just couldn't. And so, after much hesitation, I simply replied, "I can't actually swim."

This was the last thing that Coach Joan was expecting to hear.

"What do you mean you can't swim?" snapped my Dad.

"I've been telling you that for weeks!" I answered defensively. There was no way he was going to pin this on me, after all, the swimming thing had been his idea in the first place. He'd spent weeks plying me with that "eye of the tiger" bullshit of his and I'd fallen for it, but now that the moment had arrived, there was no way I was going down without a fight. There was an awkward silence and then my dad mused, "Well, she'll learn on the job."

Joan looked at me with a shard of pity and then placed me in the first lane (a.k.a. the slow lane), which was the aquatic equivalent to the short bus. At first I could barely swim a length of the pool, but eventually I got the hang of it and I began to move into better lanes. By the spring, I was in the fifth lane, right next to Danny Mayland, who was in the sixth lane. Danny was one of my Lost Boys from school. He was a great swimmer but he had webbed feet, which was sort of like cheating. He and I read *Uncle Tom's Cabin* together as an extra-credit assignment and I never spoke of his webbed feet, which I think he secretly appreciated. Of course, during practice we never spoke. Swim Team was a different world. Outside the safety of Mrs. Politi's classroom, we obeyed different social rules. Namely, we ignored one another.

One warm, sunny day I walked to practice and found a note on the club door that said PRACTICE CANCELED. It was short notice, but no big deal. If I got home fast enough, I could catch *Match Game* before my mom got back from work. As I was turning to head back home, I spotted Danny sitting by the bushes. Apparently, his mother had done a drive by and pulled out before he saw the sign. Since no one else was around, we greeted each other. It was awkward, but at this point we were like two marooned teammates, stranded on our own grassy front island. And instead of just moving off, after our quick "hey", I pushed the encounter and suggested that we walk down the hill together. Danny didn't realize that I'd lived in the 'hood and I was sort of mortified now that he mentioned it, but I quickly pointed out the Stevens house and told him about their deadbeat, publishing-tycoon dad. Danny seemed interested enough and things were good. I felt like we'd reached a new level of comfort. Who knew? Maybe we'd even start talking at swim practice, now that I was in lane five and all. Things were looking up. And as we reached the corner of Ware Road and I was about to turn off toward my house, leaving Danny to continue on back to his house, he suddenly stopped and asked if my brother Lee was home.

"Yeah, he's home," I answered. "Why?"

"'Cause I want to see him stick the motorcycle spoke through his arm."

There's a feeling you get right before you're about to vomit. It's a forty-second window, when you know that it's going to come up and if you don't get to a toilet, you are going to have an enormous mess on your hands. If you combine that feeling with the full-body heat rush you get when you pop ten niacin pills (on an empty stomach) and then couple that with the unbridled regret you feel as your car plows into an eighteen-wheeler and you realize you are not wearing your seatbelt, it might come close to describing how I felt in that very moment. And in mere seconds all that occurred, suggesting a myriad of responses which could have included:

"He's sick."

"He's in a coma."

"He's got leprosy."

"He's in a Shaolin Trance and can't be disturbed."

Instead I just said, "Sure."

As we walked the rest of the way home, I tried to figure out how I could make this situation work. Ever the optimist, I began to think I could handle this. All I needed to do was get a moment alone with Lee. I would quickly explain the pickle I was in and then have him say some Zen shit about how he wouldn't perform on command (make it a principle thing). If he preferred, he could make up some crap about how getting into an altered state could take hours, even days. Or, even better, we could make it a dietary issue; he had to lay off wheat for five days prior to jamming motorcycle spokes through his arm. Yes, there was a way out of this. I'd deal with the collateral damage later. Obviously, I'd have to get Lee out of town; perhaps military school might be a solution. If not, we could just sell the house and leave town. Either way, it was pretty clear I'd never be able to see Danny again, and though I'd miss him, life would go on. Most importantly, I'd *never* tell another lie again.

Unfortunately, my brother Lee was hard of hearing and my frantic, frenzied whispers (while Danny waited on our buckling, semi-scuffed, unevenly-stained wood floors), only made matters worse. Lee kept saying, "What?" and "Why are you whispering?!" thus proving that deaf people really need to be educated on the finer nuances of panicked whispering and its causes. I tried another route and jotted everything down on paper. But he read my frenzied missive and then blurted out, "I can't stick a motorcycle spoke through my arm!" Which again, was something I already knew and not something that really needed to be stated, but so often with the deaf, they enjoy hearing themselves speak.

Of course, there was no solution in sight. My brother, like my father before him, was refusing to toe the line. We were not French and he could not stick a motorcycle spoke through his arm. It was time to face the music. I emerged from the room, ashen, only to find Danny just outside the door.

"I'm telling everyone that you're a liar," he said.

Which was what I deserved, but was so incredibly horrible that I still felt the need to do damage control. With nowhere left to turn, I promptly called my classmate Nancie McDonnell. I had hired her to write a short story for my mother's birthday. Nothing said "I love you Mom" like a short story written by an eleven-year-old girl you didn't know. But Nancie enjoyed the freelance work, and as she wrote, I would chat, occasionally glancing at pages, making suggestions, (e.g., make the oldest daughter thinner, make the younger brother more Zen-like). I'd recently confided in Nancie that it was my secret desire to become the first female manager of the New York Yankees. I made her swear not to tell Lorena White mostly because I didn't want to be accused of nepotism when I actually got the job, years down the line. Nancie had kept the secret and therefore she was the first one I turned to in my time of need. Nancie was a nice person, she made smiley faces above her "I's", she would understand. And much to my surprise, she did.

"The boys are such jerks," she said. And I agreed, because what else was there to do? But then she said, "None of the girls believed you, we thought you were just goofing on the guys because of their stupid beauty pageant."

There was silence on my end. My pathetic brain whirring at the sudden emergence of this new information. If I wanted to, I could take the chicken-shit route and get out of my impending mea culpa and the subsequent humiliation that would follow. There was a light at the end of this tunnel, but I would have to pay a price; I would have to forsake my Wendy-hood for this. I'd have to become a girl's girl and leave the comfort of my Lost Boys for God knows how long. Maybe forever! I didn't want to go, but what choice did I have? The threat of humiliation was too much to bear and I decided to take the hit. Better to be pegged as a callous bitch than a big fat liar. And so, I agreed with her. "That's *exactly* what I was doing! I was goofing on them, because seriously, they'll believe anything! And who were they to objectify us like that?"

The next day, the boys listened in stunned silence as Nancie explained the collective female rage regarding the beauty pageant and how I alone had dared to stand up to the insanity, by fooling them all into believing a lie so epic, only a pack of morons would have fallen for it. The girls all nodded their heads in agreement, while the boys stood there looking angry and feeling used. They stopped speaking to me, but the girls stood by me and we became a class divided. Our poor teacher, Mrs. Politi, was at a complete loss as to what the hell had happened in her classroom.

I just fell into auto-mode and pretended that I didn't care. That Friday, I was invited to a slumber party at Nancie's house. After being forced into a group sing-along to Cher's timeless hit, *Half-Breed,* I endured a viewing of the Robby Benson epic *Ice Castles*, where I guessed that the Lynn-Holly Johnson character was going to go blind, and inadvertently pissed off all the girls who felt that I'd ruined it for them. After that, Nancie took us up to her room and proceeded to give us a French-kissing tutorial. "Being able to kiss a boy properly is super important," she said. All the other girls agreed heartily, but I felt that they were somehow betraying their own feminist cause. And while all the girls squeezed their eyes shut and made out with their pillows, I just stared out the window, hoping against hope that the Lost Boys might miraculously appear and take me back.

6. RIdICULE

FOR MOST OF US, grammar school classroom locale was our first foray into real estate. Some classrooms had great views; others had lesser ones, but made up for it with added perks like built-in cubbies, or in-class water fountains. I'd always done well in the classroom real-estate department. In fact, I couldn't remember a time when I didn't have the equivalent of southern exposures and soaring park views. And despite the fact that the odds dictated that I was going to end up with a windowless stink-hole at one point or another, I never really thought it would happen to me. Thus, the placement of my sixth-grade classroom came as something of a shock. If there had been a corresponding real estate ad in our school paper, it would have read something like this: *Fixer-upper, limited light, needs work, will sell as is.*

As if being in the worst classroom wasn't bad enough, I was surrounded by the biggest group of rejects my school had to offer. It was a mélange of loserdom and I suspected that my inclusion in this squalid mix had karmic ties to the dreaded Motorcycle Lie of the previous year. It was the only way to explain why I was now trapped in the Ninth Circle of Hell, reserved for traitors to their kindred.

I took my new status as an outcast as well as I could, but struggled to find some greater meaning within the situation.

I needed a ray of hope. Something to hang my despair on. Luckily, I managed to catch *Quadrophenia* one night and the movie spoke to me in a way that I don't think it would have had I been placed in a class with soaring southern exposures.

Set in Brighton, England, the film told the story of a group of Mods, as they club-hopped, took amphetamines, intimidated vacationers and rumbled with their chosen rivals, the leather-clad Rockers. I found myself drawn to the character of Ace Face, the coolest Mod, whose shameful secret was that he was a hotel bellboy by day. The parallels between my life and Ace Face jumped out at me from the screen. We were both misunderstood hipsters, we both harbored shameful secrets and we both enjoyed Ska music. And though, for whatever reason, the powers that be tried to relegate me to the last class in the hallway, filled with ugly kids and a few smelly ones, I knew that somewhere, somehow, I would be redeemed. I knew this because, quite simply, I was the Ace Face of Sixth Grade and my poor classmates were the misunderstood Mods. There was Dick Cox, whose name could have only been worse had it been Dick Hertz. There was Glen Summers, who breathed with his mouth open due to a deviated septum. There was Mike Gorsky, who was obsessed with the *TV Guide*, and Peter Wellford, who was the resident hypochondriac, and pale, frail Jill Smyth, the resident crier. We also had the Wardell Twins, who thought Europe was a type of shoe despite the fact that their father was a globe-trotting pilot. There was Beth "Over-A-Ton" Overton and our very own resident genius Yumiko Yokoi, who rebelled against her innate brilliance by having the messiest desk in the history of grammar school. There was also an assortment of boys with names like Shane, Chad and Bryce, all of whom had penchants for blowing up toilets with M-80s. And no class could be complete without the token exotic. In our case this void was filled by Smitta, the Indian girl whose parents owned hotels all along Route 17. Smitta was like a *Welcome To The Dollhouse* version of the hot babe from *Mississippi Masala*. And while there was a chance that in the distant future she would hook up with a young Denzel Washington look-alike (sending shockwaves through her community, though since he was so hot, they would ultimately see her point, acquiesce to her wishes and then buy him a colorful tunic and embrace him), Smitta's life of the present involved unfashionable Indian garb and curried food. The end result being, that in addition to looking strange, she stunk to high heaven of garlic and cloves. Sitting next to Smitta meant breathing with your mouth open all day. I often wondered if this was why Glen had been placed in the class in the first place.

But just as seating arrangements had been worked out and our teacher Mrs. Giarattana was beginning to remember our names, she broke both hips. The poor woman was out for the year and we hadn't even made it to the end of September.

After her fall, we were sort of adrift. There was a flurry of subs, none of whom wanted to be a part of our dismal world. It got so bad that for a full week they actually put our hallway custodian, Jim the Janitor, in charge. Jim loved to talk. And his tale was an interesting one and unlike any we'd ever heard before. Originally from Nutley, N.J., Jim had spent a great deal of time living in the rural South where he picked up a thick Southern accent and an inordinate amount of colloquialisms. This was of particular interest to me at the time because my dad had taken to wearing cowboy hats, riding horses, speaking with a Southern accent and listening to Tanya Tucker 8-tracks. Deep down, I secretly hoped that Jim could bridge the gap of my lack of understanding regarding my father's sudden obsession with all things Southern.

It turned out that Jim had left home early because his mother was "crazy as a shithouse mouse." From there he fell in with some gangster types, none of whom he could trust because they were all "slipperier than a witch's tit." With nowhere left to go, he joined the army. He claimed the recruiters sold him a lie. "They were so full of shit, their eyes were brown," he said. But since he "didn't know his ass from a hole in the ground," he enlisted. Trouble was he had flat feet, which meant he could only stay on the base and load trucks. He was sent to some crappy outpost in Macon County where he met a pretty girl. And despite the fact that she was "two sandwiches short of a picnic," they fell in love. They ended up having four kids, but she never lost the weight and now she was "so ugly, you had to hang a pork chop around her neck to get the dog to play with her," and as a result things were not good on the home front. Jim was at a crossroads. He needed to keep his job because he needed health benefits for his sciatica, but the truth was he wasn't in a good place. "I'm so confused I don't know whether to scratch my watch or wind my ass," he often said.

We felt Jim's pain. We were confused too. While the other kids were learning Ancient History, Science and Math, we were The Forgotten at the end of the hall. And while Southern colloquialisms slipped into our vocabulary (my favorite being "A horse that shits fast don't shit long"), we couldn't help but wonder if there was going to be more to sixth grade than this, and if not, could we at least get a copy of the Iowa Achievement Test so we could bone up.

Finally, by mid-October, we were told that we would be getting a Permanent Sub. The words sent shockwaves through our class namely because it meant that someone inept would be assigned to actually teach us. But instead of bringing in some unsuspecting rube, the school went cheap and designated Mr. Heenahan, the maniacal, hirsute, assistant gym teacher for the job. Heenahan was a frustrated jock, with a hatred for kids and a penchant for screaming. He lived to berate kids who couldn't climb a rope in ten seconds, or those who didn't know the finer points of the lay-up shot. And while the other kids quaked at the thought of Heenahan, I found the entire situation to be amusing. In fact, the day he walked into our class I promptly raised my hand and asked, "What makes you think you're qualified to teach us?" The other kids eyeballed me nervously as Heenahan's face began to turn red. Unlike them I could climb a rope in ten seconds and though I didn't know much about a lay-up shot, my sister Jenny was friends with the son of Knicks great, Bob McAdoo, which I figured bought me at the very least a modicum of name dropping clout. Heenahan narrowed his gaze and barked, "Do you have a problem with me teaching you?"

With nothing left to lose at this point, I paraphrased the great Woody Allen and said, "It's just that those who *can*, do, and those who *can't*, teach gym. So where does that leave you?"

Of course I thought he'd get the Woody Allen reference; in fact I figured everyone would, but they didn't. And Heenahan turned all red and screamed, "I'm in charge here!" with a little too much desperation in his voice. The rest of the class looked at me, and in that instant, I became the leader of my own rag-tag band of misfits.

The class quickly grew to loathe Heenahan, mostly because he screamed a lot and hated teaching us, but I was quick to remind them that it would have been much worse had we gotten Dick Fyzle, head of Physical Education. In addition to having a glass eye that wandered or "free-floated" as he liked to say, Dick had a serious penchant for giving all the girls neck and shoulder massages. Dick would later go on to be accused of sexual harassment (allegedly), but back then Dick was still living the halcyon days, copping every feel that he could. It wasn't the unsolicited back rubs that bothered me about Dick, as I'd always been a whore when it came to massage. What bothered me were his hairless legs and his tight gym shorts. Heenahan could be handled, but

Dick Fyzle's camel toe was more than we would ever be able to bear.

The class agreed and sucked it up.

The first thing Heenahan did was to establish a daily rotating seat arrangement. No one was going to get too comfortable in this class. Bonds would not be forged and as a result there would be no threat of mutiny on our part. The only upside to this innovative form of daily musical chairs was that no one had to sit next to Smitta for more than a day. The other big move was the establishment of time zones. There was "my time" and "your time." During "my time," we were not allowed to speak, think, fidget, laugh, or ask questions. We could breathe, but Deviated Septum Glen ran into trouble because his open-mouthed gasps were distracting. "Your time" meant going to the bathroom and eating lunch.

When it came to the actual teaching part, Heenahan didn't feel a need to review the Ancient History text that seemed to occupy most of sixth grade. He was winging it. And the results were disastrous. He confused Persia with Sumer and Ur with Canaan. The Nile was somewhere in Africa and a mummy was what Brits called their mothers. He was so out of his league that when we pointed out that Smitta's people were Hindus from India and not Persians from Canaan, he became sullen and irate. "Fine!" he screamed. "Teach yourselves!" And so we did.

While we did our reading and answered our questions, Heenahan listened to Neil Young albums on the portable turntable in the back of our classroom. Ever efficient, we cut our work-time down to a manageable thirty minutes, leaving us countless hours of "your time," during which we would pick ourselves apart as depressed outcasts often do. We became like nightclub comics, sitting around the Carnegie Deli, insulting one another and anyone else who came within our sights.

We also enjoyed word games and spent countless hours playing our own version of *Match Game.*

"Smitta is so smelly?" someone would begin.

And we'd all yell, "How smelly is she?!"

"She's so smelly that when she goes to the zoo, the pigs ________?"

From there we'd go around the room shouting out answers:

"Faint!"

"Barf!"

"Cry!"

"Stick their heads up their asses!"

"Gag!"

"Choke!"

"Try to kill themselves!"

"Hop into the oven happily!"

"Roast themselves!"

All the while, Neil Young would be playing in the background. His high-pitched, whiny voice seeping into our psyches, getting under our skin, until one day we couldn't take it anymore. Who was this Southern Man and what was all this talk about the gold rush? Strangely enough, Heenahan needed very little prodding on the subject. Instead of screaming at us, he prattled on quite happily, explaining how Neil's songs echoed Dylan's poeticism, but how his imagery was uniquely his own; how Neil, unlike other rockers, combined the seemingly disparate elements of mysterious psychedelia and razor-sharp observations on culture, politics and love into a cohesive and hummable whole. We listened to songs like *Cortez the Killer,* a retelling of the Spanish conquest of South America from the viewpoint of the Aztecs. Heady stuff for us sixth graders. We analyzed the verses of *After the Gold Rush* and learned that lines like "burned out basement" were meant to evoke the image of urban decay of the late '60s.

More importantly, we learned that music wasn't just about music, it could also be about politics and emotions. And more often than not it was imbued with subtext and pathos. When Neil said, "Mother Nature on the run in the 1970s," it wasn't just the incoherent ramblings of a major pothead. This was Neil warning of the fate that was in store for people who ignored Mother Nature and destroyed the earth. Heenahan wanted us to see that it was important to fight the good fight. He wanted us to be like the Southern Man who didn't give up even when all hope was lost. Each day Heenahan would have us analyze another song, searching for signs of tyranny and injustice. After that, we'd spend a solid half hour on Ancient History and then it was time for verbal sparring, of which we could not get enough. It's safe to say, we lived for it. Sometime after Christmas, all substantive thought had been replaced by our endless games of witticisms, where a student's social standing became inexorably tied to their ability to master the art of the putdown, preferably in as acerbic manner as possible. We took on the personal and the political. And armed with our newfound understanding of Southern Rock, nothing was out of our reach.

Word spread of our Ben Jonson-like abilities and soon we were all "Ace Faces" in a sense. We may have been relegated to the end of the hallway, next to Jim the Janitor's shit sty, but they all knew who we were.

We had created a world where a clever wit could lead to fame or undoing. Yes, it was about humor, but it was also about power. Yes, we were the smelliest rejects in the grade, but no one crossed us because when it came to words, we could not be undone.

Then one day, Smitta returned from the girl's room, with a troubled look on her face. Had someone tried to spray her with air freshener?! We'd kick their asses! (It should be noted that Smitta, in a bold and brilliantly devious move, had gained standing in our crew by introducing us to Indian samosas, a.k.a. hot pockets, long before such a thing could be purchased in our supermarket freezer section. In addition to being sublime, delectable, fluffy pillows of potato and strange meat, they were loaded with garlic. Thus making us all smell and thereby causing what master perfumers refer to as Induced Temporary Selective Anosmia, which loosely translated meant we stunk and therefore could not smell her. Though others, throughout the school, could indeed smell us. We became further cut off from the rest of our world because of it and we came to see that to be shunned because of your smell was intrinsically unfair, especially when you yourself didn't notice said smell. It was especially disturbing when our science teacher kept a can of Lysol in her desk to rid her lab of our stench. Had we not been rushing to get back to our classroom for more hot pockets, we might have taken offense to the use of said aerosol product and the corresponding detriment to Mother Earth. But we had hot pockets to eat and verbal sparring to get to.)

But on this day, Smitta had not been the brunt of another Smelly Smitta joke nor a random aerosol attack. On this day, she had been approached in the bathroom because there was another cunning linguist in our grade. One who claimed she could take us. Her name was Machine Gun Anne. Though we did not know her well, everyone knew Anne's laugh which sounded like an AK-47 ricocheting off the hallways of the sixth grade corridor. Anne's laugh could wipe out entire villages in South East Asia, but it was still no match for us. Yet, despite our callous indifference and certain superiority, Anne was insisting on a duel.

Diane Randazzo, who was no relation to me or the former Sicilian King, was the neutral party who brought forth the initial proposal. Anne's only request was that the subject of our little verbal war be Mrs. Rathke, the aerosol-spraying science teacher. Negotiations following the content, the rules, and the judging were furious. We spent the better part of three recesses hammering them out. Of course, it was decided that *I* would be facing Anne in this bitter duel of wit.

The rules were finally agreed upon. Being a Lutheran, Anne wanted the contest to take shape in the form of letters. We negotiated that the letters could not be revised, though they could be considered mentally and then written in pen in one sitting.

The letters would be written under an assumed name (of course). In the letters, we would try to defame Mrs. Rathke and portray her in the worst light possible. The letters would then be sealed and brought to the spelling bee – the school's annual pointless contest where overzealous bibliophiles struggled to regurgitate Webster's unabridged. While those rubes were busy spelling onomatopoeia, the notes would be passed to Diane Randazzo, who throughout the entire process had somehow managed to remain neutral. Diane would judge on wit, level of humor, and ability to use original words or phrases. I felt confident that I could kick Anne's ass. She was the daughter of casserole-eating, thank-you-note writing Protestants. But I was, at the very least, half Irish, which meant I had the gift of gab running through my veins. Yeats, Joyce, and Heaney certainly trumped some zealot whose big claim to fame was that he left a note on a church door.

All at once, it was upon us. The day of reckoning. It was quiet in the classroom as they placed the paper in front of me. Jim the Janitor sensed something was afoot and was thankfully chatting up the hall monitors so they ignored us. I was just about to start writing, when a final message was delivered.

"Address the letters to Mrs. Rathke directly and sign them in your mother's name."

I was too mired in my thoughts to really consider this last minute addition to the rules. There was no time for negotiations. We had ten minutes to do this and get to the spelling bee in the gym. Weeks of careful planning would be out the window and so I agreed to this final adjustment.

I sat down and composed my letter. I laced it with as much profanity and ridicule that I could muster, until a vision was formed of my kindly science teacher that would make prisoners blanch. But there was also alliteration, syncopation, metaphor, and simile. Everything that had to be there was there. I wrote without lifting my pen as the rules stipulated, and when I was finished I signed my mother's name.

We walked in silence to the spelling bee and took our seats. Fyzle was standing down front, patrolling the stands, his wandering glass eye ever alert for signs of trouble or a girl looking for a backrub. And while he headed over to briefly fondle some seventh grader (allegedly), we passed the note down the line. It was all going according to plan. I can still see Diane Randazzo's smiling face at the end of the bleachers, as the note was passed, as if in slow motion. And for a moment, it seemed that we were almost there. And we *were*, until Tony Cotugno, a boy whose big dream in life was to break into the meat business, reached his hand down into our aisle and grabbed the note. It was an ugly intercept and one that violated all rules of note passing etiquette. But the kinky-haired bastard had it. Worse yet, he read it. And then, in what was the ultimate violation, he handed it over to Fyzle. Apparently the kiss-ass was trying to score brownie points because he wanted to be captain of the basketball team and saw this as his chance to get in Fyzle's camel toe.

I could only sit and watch in horror. All that work and not even a moment to bask in our glory. Anne and I were removed from our seats and brought to the dreaded Gym Office. Meanwhile, the boys attacked Tony with a flurry of insults and ridicule, mentally pounding him into submission. Fyzle had Anne and me in his office and was reveling in disgust. Then, in a display of incredible compassion and understanding, Fyzle, ever the diplomat, called Mrs. Rathke into the office and handed our notes to her. Mrs. Rathke of course, gentle soul that she was, broke down and wept.

Anne and I could only sit there, staring at each other, as Fyzle paced back and forth interrogation style, demanding answers. "Where did you learn words like *cocksucker*?!" he screamed, which only made Mrs. Rathke cry more. I was horrified, struggling to find a way to stop this, while Anne became sullen and defensive. I tried to explain that it was a contest. Mr. Heenahan poked his head in and I looked up at him with wide eyes. "Tell them about how we have contests with words!" but Heenahan wasn't going there.

"They're out of control," was all he said.

I continued to try to explain the situation and how it had evolved over time. I tried to explain to them the merging of Southern Rock, with *Match Game*, with the fine art of ridicule. But I didn't seem to be reaching them. "The French aristocracy did it all the time!" I cried out in desperation. "It was a depraved comedy of manners!" I continued. Fyzle just looked at me like I was insane and Mrs. Rathke was now rocking back and forth in her seat, weeping uncontrollably.

"It was a contest!" I kept repeating, but no one seemed to hear me. Instead they called in the big guns. Apparently the music teacher, Mrs. G, had a degree in child psychology. There was a brief huddle and when they emerged, the big question on everyone's mind was why we had signed our mother's names to the notes. They were convinced that the use of our mother's names was a cry for help.

"No, it was a last minute rule! Anne's Protestant. They do a lot with notes!"

Anne was acting like she wasn't even involved and I was like some crazy bag lady screaming about socialism outside Zabar's. But I was desperate. I needed to make them understand.

"We were bored because Mr. H just played Southern Rock all day! We made up word games!"

Nothing.

"Joe's wife never lost the weight after the third kid! Now

she's so ugly you have to tie a pork chop around her neck just to get the dog to play with her!"

Nada.

When Anne finally chimed in all she said was, "She came to me with it."

Which was a total lie.

I protested, "No, she came to Smelly Smitta!"

"Racist!" they cried.

"I'm not racist, my brother's Korean!"

"Yeah, yeah ...We know all about the motorcycle spoke," said Fyzle.

Which shut me up in an instant. Apparently, karma *had* been behind the entire year. I was paying for my sins big time and now I'd fallen into the Tenth Circle of Hell where they kept one-eyed gym teachers. I gave up trying to explain. We were bored and we had potty mouths. That's all it was. And now, much like Ace Face at the beginning of *Quadrophenia*, I was flying over the edge of the cliff, wondering how this was all going to end. I remember hearing the words "permanent record" before I blacked out and woke up at home.

The end result was that Anne and I were suspended for a week. They tried to keep us at home, but my mother argued that keeping me home would be a vacation and would defeat the purpose. My mother was disappointed in me for being stupid, but as a teacher, she felt that reading passed notes was a violation of privacy, and in her practice, all intercepted notes were placed in the trash unread.

Of course, the school demanded my mother come in for a meeting but she couldn't take off from work, so a conference call was arranged. My mom got on the phone with the vice principal just as a quasi-riot broke out at her school in the Bronx, so as my mother spoke to them, pretending to be appalled by my behavior, she was alternately covering the receiver and screaming, "Put the fucking desk down, Jose!"

The damage done, I accepted my suspension. I was

content to talk to the shrinks and apologize to Mrs. Rathke because I could say in all honesty it was never my intent to hurt her feelings. Mrs. Rathke even accepted my apologies and would wave to me through the office window as she passed by in the hallway. Anne was too pissed and bitter to cop to anything. Her family hated me, she hated me. She didn't have the balls to stand up and say she was as much a part of it as I was. But I did my time with a quiet dignity. The other kids could see me through the glass window and they'd wave to me. In fact, if there was any up side to this, many of them were my Lost Boys from fifth grade, whom I had forsaken the year before. It was as if they realized I'd been punished enough and now they were ready to take me back into the fold. Not only that, but I was breaking ground in school suspension. Before me, there had never been a straight A student and soccer player who'd been suspended. And this in turn led to a greater understanding on the part of Vice Principal Dursma, who saw that sometimes smart kids did stupid things too. His wife, who was the school librarian, began to pop in and we would talk about Young Adult Lit. I told her how much I loved *The Westing Game* and how I felt *Nancy Drew* was overrated. She in turn recommended Robert Cormier's *I Am The Cheese*, which ended up being seminal reading for me. It was all going smoothly, until midweek when it was decided that Fyzle would be on guard duty during lunch hour. At this point Anne and I had been separated. Anne was put in another room, because she still refused to apologize and they were trying to break her.

Fyzle came in a few minutes early, chatting up the secretaries. My heart was pounding and all I could think about was the woman-in-chains gem, *Nightmare in Badham County*, which was about two girls from the North, one white and one black, who get arrested for basically driving through the South, being friends, and looking cute in shorts. They get thrown into a women's prison on trumped up charges where they're forced to endure all sorts of atrocities until they try to escape. The blonde girl makes it out, but of course the black girl gets shot in the back while running. I could see the look of fear on Anne's face through the glass as the secretaries left for lunch. Fyzle was coming for both of us. We were no longer in New Jersey, we were in the backwaters of Mississippi and I was most definitely the black chick who was going to get shot in the back if I didn't acquiesce. I saw the hypocrisy in the system. I saw how authority bred a greed for power.

I saw all this as Fyzle hit my room first.

"I'd really hate to see this unfortunate incident end up on your permanent record," he said as he walked behind me, warming up his mitts (allegedly) for what was no doubt going to be a major grope.

"I guess not," was all I could manage to say.

"Maybe I could help you out. I know a few people, maybe put in a word with the superintendent," he continued.

My heart pounded and my blood boiled. He was trying to bribe me. If this wasn't tyranny, I didn't know what was. I thought of everything that I'd learned that year. I thought about Neil Young and Hammurabi's Code and how garlic can stay in your system for weeks at a time. But here was an even bigger lesson, one that was entirely unanticipated: While it's important to fight the law to overrule things like tyranny and oppression, going to jail for it was never a good option because prison guards would rape you.

Thankfully, I still had my cunning linguistics to fall back on and I shot back with the only weapon available.

"You lay one finger on me and I'm gonna tell the superintendent all about your penchant for giving prepubescent girls back rubs!"

Fyzle stopped in his tracks and from the other room I heard Anne cheer.

"Stay away from us, or we'll sing like canaries!" I continued.

Anne thought this was hilarious and proceeded to laugh that staccato machine gun laugh of hers. And I don't know if it was my threats, or the ear-piercing pain of Anne's laugh that sent him running, but I didn't care. I'd dodged a major bullet, but the next time around I might not be so lucky.

7. d0jANG BLUES

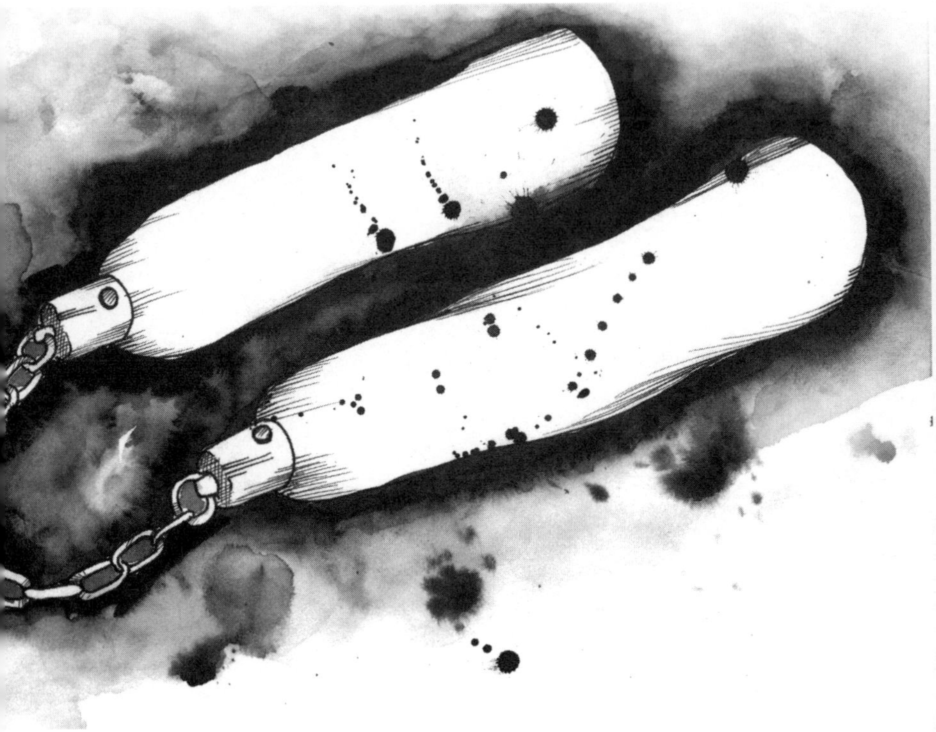

THE FIRST RULE of Tae Kwon Do was that there were eighteen rules that had to be rattled off before class could even begin. At the start of class, we would line up in front of our *sabumnim*, Master Bai (the real life inspiration for my Motorcycle Spoke Lie) and recite them from memory.

I had hoped for a more esoteric, Confucian, fortune cookie-esque set of rules: *Respect your enemy; Consider all vantage points before moving toward the goal; You will have great success at an early age; Never play leap frog with a unicorn.* But Koreans, being the pragmatists of the Asian world, had a far more grounded outlook. As such, the rules began with the following:

1. *No smoking in the DoJang at any time*
2. *No gum-chewing in class*
3. *No profanity in class*
4. *No jewelry is to be worn during class*

I guessed that these were meant to keep the DoJang from degenerating into a smoke-filled dump, frequented by gum-chewing, potty mouths, swathed in bling.

After these early rules, things heated up.

5. *Students are not allowed to belong to another DoJang*
6. *Never get a drink of water without permission*

I always found it interesting that Rule 5, (which forbade

inter-dojo practice) was so casually slipped in between 4 and 6, thus making it seem far more innocuous than it actually was, when the fact was that joining another DoJang was the worst thing you could do and therefore should have been the first rule.

Next came:

7 *Never lose your temper in the DoJang, especially while sparring*

This was really more of a safety tip than a rule.

8 *Never lean on the wall, or lay on the floor spread-out*

It was my understanding that the first part of this rule was a throwback to the days of rice paper walls, though I never confirmed it.

9 *Students must keep their finger and toenails clipped short and clean at all times*

Easy enough and sort of a no-brainer. Moving on, we then had:

10 *No horseplay or whistling*

According to this rule, horseplay begat whistling, though I'd never seen any evidence of that.

At this point in the daily Spouting of the Rules my sister Jenny would lie on the floor (in flagrant violation of Rule 8) out of sheer exhaustion. While Jenny lay there, we would all continue with the next set of rules, which dealt with the two heavy hitters of the martial arts world: Respect and bowing.

11 *When you see Sabumnim (Master Bai) you must bow to him*

12 *Bow to the flags before entering and leaving the DoJang and before leaving the office*

13 *You must respect your Sabumnim and always use the word "sir" when speaking to him*

14 *You must respect all senior belts*

15 *You must bow when asking questions*

16 *When fixing your uniform or belt, do not face your instructor*

17 *You must bow to all black belts*

18 *You must call all black belts "sir"*

The general rule of thumb on this portion of the rules was to build an extra ten minutes into your day to account for bowing and "sir-saying."

Once we finished these, Jenny would usually stand for the last and most dramatic rule:

19 *Always keep in mind that you are being taught a deadly art, treat it with respect and above all, never misuse it*

Parched from the lengthy recitation, we could get down with the business of Tae Kwon Do, which wasn't really all that hard to learn because it was basically a glorified form of kickboxing. The class was divided into two different sessions. First we'd spar, which meant pairing up with someone your size to fight. Sparring was all about flexibility and good body awareness, the main idea being to defeat your opponent and more importantly, not look like a 'tard when you threw a roundhouse. After that we worked on forms, which helped hone technique. There were about twelve different forms of varying degree of difficulty. The forms were all based on ancient battle plans and followed paths that various armies of Korean warlords had taken back in the day. You went right, you went left, you went forward, you went backward. As you did that you threw various kicks and punches. The focus was all on technique and each move had to be practiced slowly and methodically, while you envisioned yourself invading China.

My brother Lee was already a red belt when I joined. This was a boon to me, sort of the equivalent to having an uncle in the business. Every night after class, he'd teach me new moves, which put me ahead of the game (where I always liked to be). In fact, I came to see that my brother Lee was something of a martial arts prodigy and I was bummed that I had embellished to the extent I had, vis-à-vis the motorcycle spokes, because it kept me from bragging about the really cool things that my brother could actually do, like break boards and jump high into the air *Matrix*-style (before the advent of multiple-speed cameras). With my brother tutoring me, I began to get pretty good, which gave me a modicum of street cred at the DoJang. Jenny on the other hand had no interest in using our brother to further her Tae Kwon Do career. She hated Tae Kwon Do and wanted nothing to do with it.

"It's so stupid," she'd say. "And the place smells like crap."

"It's good exercise," my mom would tell her.

"What do I need exercise for? I play kickball at school, it's enough already."

But my mother liked the hour and a half of silence that Tae Kwon Do afforded her. It was a little peace before she had to deal with dinner madness and my stepdad's thermostat third degree. As such, she insisted my sister go. In protest, Jenny made a point of chewing gum during every class, and shortly thereafter also stopped clipping her toenails. My mother hoped Sabumnim could knock the defiance out of her, but even he was helpless. He told my mom that Jenny would do very well under interrogation. My mother felt this was a plus and not something that could be said about the rest of her children. So, while Jenny lay sprawled on the floor in the back of the DoJang, blowing monstrous Bubble Yum bubbles that she would pop with her talon-like toe nails, Lee and I worked hard to get good. Within a year and a half I'd managed to get my black belt and suddenly grown men were bowing to me upon entering the DoJang. Master Bai even added an addendum to the rules saying:

All black belts must be called "sir" or "ma'am."

I was officially a "ma'am" and I have to be honest, I dug the power.

My mom was very proud of the fact that she had two black belts in the house (Jenny was hovering somewhere around high turquoise after a bleaching incident). She felt that our double black belt status put us in a certain standing and that as a result, lower-ranking members of the school should have to drive us home after class as a sign of respect. While we didn't really want to take advantage of our ranking, doing so wasn't all that difficult because as black belts we could ask people to wipe our ass and they'd have to do it. Jenny smelled opportunity and turned into our own personal button man, demanding Charms Blow Pops from all the students as payment to keep us happy. Still, we felt sort of bad extorting rides from people, but our mom was tired, so Jenny arranged for us to get regular rides home from a guy named Allen. Allen was pushing thirty and still lived at home, thus making him perfectly suited for the job. He didn't pay rent, he didn't have a family and his mom still made him dinner. Forcing him to drive fifteen minutes out of the way to bring us home wasn't going to make a dent in his lifestyle one way or another. But we liked Allen. He was extremely funny, and yes, it was odd that he enjoyed our company (considering the fact Jenny, Lee and I were eight, ten, and twelve respectively), but we reasoned that he was making the best of the situation because after all, he didn't really have a choice. Allen worked during the day as a travel agent. He had previously been a road surveyor but he quit because he didn't like the hours. He then got into the travel business as a way to get cheap fares because he loved to mountain climb in Tibet. This was way before Richard Gere started pimping the Dalai Lama. Allen was a groundbreaker. He was humping to Tibet, back when all we knew about it was that it was the place where Indiana Jones' girlfriend drank herself silly and then beat up the locals. And when Allen wasn't dangling off a Himalayan slope, he could be found at our DoJang, working on his preferred weapon of choice, the nunchaku, which was the only nontraditional Korean weapon that Sabumnim allowed in the school. According to Chinese legend, after you practiced long and hard enough, your nunchakus would take on some of your spirit and character, which explained why Allen's had become limp and clumsy.

The DoJang became a home away from home. And like all homes, it possessed a dysfunctional family dynamic. The three most senior black belts were Jay, Rich and Hideki. Jay and Rich were still training under Master Bai, but Hideki had moved away, though his presence within our school loomed large. Jay was in his early twenties. He was very tall, with short blonde hair and blue eyes. In addition to being seriously handsome, he was from Hoboken and had a thick Hudson County accent, which made him deliriously adorable to my mother who would often linger in the front of the school staring at him. Jay didn't have a steady job. One week he'd be a janitor, another week he'd be selling shoes out of a van, and yet another he'd be working as a bouncer. One particular week he had found work painting, which led to the following conversation between him and my mother, who I really think was trying to bust a move on him.

"So, what do you do?" she asked.

"I paint," he said.

My mom's ears pricked up immediately. Conveniently forgetting that she was already married, she drifted into some sort of halcyon vortex and became, for an instant, Jill Clayburgh in her own personal remake of *An Unmarried Woman.*

"Really? Oils or watercolors?" she asked breathlessly, already imagining our sprawling downtown loft and openings at the Mary Boone Gallery. Sadly, Jay's answer was, "Houses."

Yes, despite his good looks, Jay was not what one would call a chronic overachiever. He would say things like, "Everybody loves the smell of their own farts, but no one likes the smell of other people's farts."

After a few moments pondering this, he'd then offer yet

another scintillating tidbit, "And yet no one likes b.o. Be it their own or someone else's."

We'd all just have to nod and murmur, "Fascinating."

The Yang to Jay's Yin was Rich, who was around nineteen. He had dark curly hair and was a dead ringer for Yankee Ace Mike Mussina. Rich was intense and cerebral, but in a bad, Unabomber type of way. One minute he'd be talking about how great Bachman Turner Overdrive was and the next he'd be screaming about how Reagan was destroying the country. You never knew which way the wind was going to blow with him. And while we found Jay to be sort of harmless, we feared Rich, mostly because he seemed like a wife beater in the making.

Then there was Hideki, the seventeen-year-old fatherless, half-Japanese kid who had since moved to California. Hideki was Master Bai's prize pupil. He had won more championships than anybody else and his pictures were all over the walls of the school. We would always hear news of his exploits, which included going to film sets to advise stunt coordinators and attending kickboxing matches with World Karate Champion and *Black Belt* magazine cover boy, Benny "The Jet" Uriquez, who incidentally was once sponsored by Elvis Presley himself. Hideki was a tough act to follow, plus he had the pan-Asian, fatherless thing going for him and as a result Jay and Rich, who didn't really agree on anything, would always bond together in their shared jealousy of Hideki. But when they weren't fighting over Hideki, they were fighting with each other. At least once a month there would be a blow up and one of them would violate Rule 5 and go train at another DoJang. This would be followed by the posting of a large grammatically incorrect sign, which would read:

YOU NO LONGER BE ALLOW TO BOW TO JAY
IF YOU TO SEE HIM

Rich would then run the show and teach the majority of the afternoon classes and we'd be subject to his unique brand of insanity. But after a few weeks, amends would be made and Jay would be brought back into the fold like the prodigal son and everything would be fine ... until the next blow-up. And thus the cycle would continue.

There was an undercurrent of tension between Lee and me and Jay and Rich. We were Sabumnim's new favorites, but we were also kids. Jay and Rich could whine about Hideki, but they would have looked really pathetic if they had complained about us. Still, it was obvious that they wanted us out of the picture. And every time Sabumnim stepped out, they'd terrorize us by forcing us to do squats and push-ups until we nearly threw up. Taking a cue from Sun Tzu, Lee and I formulated an unspoken plan to get rid of them. I had long since learned that it was best never to discuss secret plans with Lee because he had a tendency to shout "What!?" or "Why do you want to get rid of Rich and Jay?!" during inopportune moments, but I knew Lee well enough to know without ever asking that he wanted them gone too. And while Jay and Rich were busy with their petty infighting, Lee and I proceeded to take over the school. We signed up for every tournament; we offered to teach classes; we cleaned the school *and* washed Sabumnim's yellow Trans Am. We even scored invites to Sabumnim's house for dinner (on the grounds that Lee wanted to get in touch with his culinary roots). Of course, his childless wife was more than happy to have us and Jenny feasted richly. Another unexpected bonus for me was that due to the demands of our tournament schedule I stopped having to go to my dad's every other weekend. This was a relief because my dad had remarried a rather mixed-up woman who found me to be an affront to her existence. As far as she was concerned, it was me or her. And since my dad had to live with her, he didn't object to my absence. I was having too much fun to care. My life was the DoJang and crushing Jay and Rich. And pretty soon, the Friday night dinners became a regular fixture on our social calendar. Jay and Rich were too busy bickering with each other and didn't notice that we had begun to assemble a posse of sorts, bringing more people into our fold, including our personal driver Allen. Friday Night at Master Bai's became *the* place to be if you were looking to gorge on Korean food and watch Sabumnim get loaded and sing songs about the old country. Being deaf and as a result unable to carry a tune, Lee forced me to learn a few of the songs. My first was *Arirang,* which meant "fa la la" in Korean and was supposed to reflect the longing associated with having been jilted by a lover. The other big fave in my limited repertoire was a little number called *Palgaedal,* which was much more upbeat, though I had no clue what it was about. Pretty soon, due to my stellar phonetic singing skills, we started getting invites to the after-tournament parties. The only other student who had ever managed to gain access to those velvet rope events was Hideki and as such, this was a big coup. The parties were usually held in a Chinese restaurant where food would be served buffet-style. This delighted my sister Jenny to no end. She would become giddy at the sight of those metal vats, brimming with wontons. You could put ten in a bowl, sans broth if you felt like it! You could scarf General Tso's chicken and neon Sweet and Sour pork until you barfed! And after the eating, there would be singing and of course, Sabumnim, who would be half in the bag, would trot me up to the dais where I would wow everyone with my phonetic Korean vocal interpretations. We'd eat and they'd drink and when it was over, Allen would drive us home in his car. Though before we left the party, we'd bring our winning trophies to Sabumnim and bow down as low as we possibly could, then hand them over to him. We'd seen enough *Kung Fu* episodes in syndication to know that this shit was the way to a Karate Master's heart.

One day, as our trophies began to crowd the front window of the school, Jay and Rich suddenly realized that whatever foothold they had had in the school had now been reduced to a festering hangnail. Jay and Rich ganged up on Sabumnim, accusing him of favoritism because he had hired a professional photographer to shoot Lee and me for a series of promotional photographs for the school.

"Why can't we be in the pictures?!" yelled Jay.

"I kick higher than Lee!" argued Rich.

"It's for a children's magazine," sighed Master Bai.

"So, what? Why can't we be in it too? We were kids once!" Jay yelled.

"You did the same thing with Hideki! Just because they don't have a dad you have to treat them like they're better than everyone else," whined Jay.

"Like the time you bought Hideki new sneakers," added Rich.

Master Bai just shook his head. Lee of course couldn't hear a damn thing but I was rapt. It was amazing the way the entire conversation deteriorated. If I had known how easy it was to get rid of them, I would've made my move much sooner.

"And now those two come to your house for dinner and then there's the little one who lies down all the time!"

"*Enough*!" Sabumnim screamed, clearly worried about incurring the wrath of Jenny.

"But you have different rules for different people!" claimed Rich, using the all pigs are created equal *Animal Farm* argument.

"All b.o. smells the same, Sabumnim," added Jay.

But Sabumnim wouldn't hear it.

"Get out!" yelled Sabumnim.

This was Jay and Rich's cue to grab their stuff and leave and go train at another school for about a month and then come back like the Prodigal Sons, into the lukewarm embrace of Master Bai's smelly armpits. But Jay and Rich were so out of their minds, so filled with jealousy and rage, they did the unthinkable; they went to train at Master Kim's school in Lodi. Never mind Rule 5, this was the *ultimate* no-no because Master Kim had recently traveled to North Korea. As such, this made him an Enemy of the State of South Korea. This was back when South Korea was on shaky human rights ground. Chun Doo Hwan had just become president in a coup, following the murder of Park Chung Hee, and pro-democracy demonstrators were getting shot in the streets. Many Koreans in the United States, who had left family members behind in Korea, were being watched. As a result, socializing with a person who had been to the North could get your family into trouble. This was especially true for Sabumnim, who had been forced to work as a bodyguard for the now dead, enemy President Park Chung Hee when he had come to the United States. Even my mother said it was serious. Sabumnim went so far as to hang a large photo of Master Kim and under it he wrote, with his usual grammatical finesse:

YOU MUST NO TALK TO THIS MAN FOR EVER AGAIN

Master Bai knew that he would never be able to take Rich and Jay back after this. He spent a few days in his office punching his favorite cement block wrapped in rope. Lee and I were a bit worried that maybe we had gone too far, but Allen told us not to worry. This was a long time coming. Following the grieving by way of callous building, Master Bai went on a two-week fast. Lee and I took turns teaching the evening classes for him while Jenny lay on the lobby sofa, eating blow pops. At the end of fourteen days, Master Bai emerged from his stupor with news for the entire school.

"Hideki is coming back to New Jersey to live with me and train. You will all show him your most respect. He is like a son to me."

Lee and I looked at each other with bright eyes. Of course Lee missed the whole damn thing on account of a hearing-aid malfunction, but he knew from my face that this was good news.

"Hideki's coming back!" I mouthed.

"What?!" cried Lee excitedly as his hearing aid squawked.

"Hideki is coming back!" I yelled jubilantly.

Later, Allen told us how surprised he was by our reaction. After what happened with Jay and Rich, he thought that we would be jealous, but we weren't. Hideki was a legend to us. We had spent years staring at his photos wanting to believe that he was as brave and honorable as he looked.

Sadly, I spent the next six weeks serving my shared-custody, summer-vacation sentence with my dad. Lee was left to get in tight, but he did not fail me. Within weeks he had Allen driving Hideki everywhere. Hideki in turn took Lee under his wing, and each night my mother and Lee would call and tell me about all the cool things he had done with Hideki.

"What about Jenny? Is she okay with the situation?" I asked.

My mother replied for Lee since he couldn't hear on the phone. "She's not as lazy when he's around," said my mother, repeating Lee's words. Though she then added, "Your sister is not lazy."

"Mom, interpreters can't interject," I explained. "This isn't a three-way conversation, you have to remain impartial."

"I'm your mother and I can do whatever I want," she replied.

"He loves to eat submarine sandwiches and he's training for a fight in Paterson and he says we can go," Lee blurted into the receiver.

"You're not going to Paterson," she cried.

"We know the town like the back of our hand, Ma. Remember, Deeana?" I argued.

“But still, it’s not safe,” she said.

“Of course it’s safe. We’re with Hideki and he’s our bodyguard!” Lee shouted.

My mom couldn’t argue, because even she had bought into the myth of Hideki.

September finally came and though I was bummed out to have missed all the lazy summer days with Hideki, I was happy that my brother Lee had had fun. Once school started Hideki taught a lot of our classes. I was brought into the fold and everything was bliss.

We started blowing off Friday night dinner at Sabumnim’s in favor of Friday Night Fights in Paterson with Hideki. We met all sorts of interesting people, some who had even done time in jail and would offer us pearls of wisdom like “Don’t drop the soap,” and “You don’t need friends, you need alliances based on mutual self-interest.”

Wherever we went, there was someone who knew Hideki. He was a celebrity, a bodyguard, and a martial arts legend all wrapped up in one.

Winter came and tournament season died down, and Hideki started taking us to Kung Fu movies on 42nd Street. This was way before Quentin Tarantino started extolling the virtues of martial arts cinema. Back then most people had heard of Bruce Lee and that was about it. Hideki explained to us that the martial arts genre had begun in Shanghai in the late 1920s and that the first big serial to gain popularity was *The True Story of Wong Fei Hung*, which starred Kwan Tak-hing, who was best known to American audiences as Mr. Han (offender of Bruce Lee’s family and the Shaolin Temple) from *Enter the Dragon*. These early movies were all about authentic Chinese martial arts. There was no gratuitous violence in them and they promulgated righteous values, moralistic messages, and heroes who were the personifications of Confucian virtue.

By the ’70s, there was a loosening of the reins and directors like Lau Kar Leung began a new wave called Kung Fu films. Some argue that Lau Kar Leung's influence was greater than Bruce Lee's in pimping Shaolin Kung Fu. I personally think it wasn't, but that's only because I feel Bruce Lee had better hair than Leung. Regardless, he ushered in the new wave with plenty of gratuitous violence, comedic acrobatics, and heroes who were cute screw-ups. All the movies revolved around a similar story. Someone was thrown out of the school or town, and had to train for a while with some master in a wooded, mountainous area, and then return to the fold to avenge the people who drove him out. As a general rule, the films had titles that were formulated by combining various words from at least two of the following subgroups:

ANIMALS
Cranes, Monkeys, Snakes

BODY PARTS
Fists, Fingers, Feet

ADJECTIVES
Drunken, Angry, Screaming, Flying

The end result was usually something like: *Fists of Fury, Dragon Fist, Drunken Fist, Ten Fingers and Flying Sword, Flying Master, Flying Drunken Master, Fists of Monkeys, Flying Drunken Cranes, Drunken Monkeys of Fury*, etc. (*Chinese Connection* being the exception to this rule.)

But no matter what the title, you couldn't help but love the movies. They had a pulpy quality to them that made even the worst one a complete guilty pleasure. Not only that, but there was something for everyone. At the time, I was completely obsessed with Angela Mao who was the first great female action star. She was best known among Americans for her small role as Bruce Lee's sister in *Enter the Dragon*, but she was the star of many of her own movies. She took action to a new dimension and showed the world that a woman could be just as exciting to watch as any man. I was overwhelmed by her agility, grace, and athleticism. I yearned to be Angela or, at the very least, her sidekick, defending the Shaolin Temple in a fetching bright red uniform.

We'd spend every Saturday at the movies with Hideki, munching on sandwiches, the smell of pot wafting through the theater. I can honestly say I was never happier. I don't know that I had a crush on Hideki, as much as it was the first time, since I could remember really, that I felt safe. Hideki had our backs. We thought we could always count on that.

What we didn't count on was Hideki getting a girlfriend. Worse yet, unbeknownst to us, he had started dating a girl from school and Sabumnim didn't approve. Her name was Rebecca DeVry. My mother was the one who got this out of Master Bai and we were sort of hurt that Hideki had kept it from us. Still, something about the name sounded familiar.

"Why do I know that name?" I asked my mom.

"Because she's a Jackson White from Stag Hill. They all have the name DeVry or DeGroat," was her answer.

My heart nearly stopped.

"He's dating someone who's *inbred*?!" I cried.

"You don't know that she's inbred, that's just a myth. Although, she does have webbed feet and her ear lobes are connected to her neck."

"How do you know that?!" I moaned.

"Master Bai told me."

"Oh my god, she *is* inbred! Is that why he doesn't like her?" I asked.

"Stop with the inbred. Webbed feet don't necessarily mean inbreeding, it's just a ..."

"Sign of inbreeding!

"Calm down, don't get hysterical."

"But why doesn't Master Bai like her?"

"'Cause he thinks she's part black."

"But I'm part black ... I think."

"Yeah, but you pass for Italian and you have a white, middle-class mother."

"Barely," I scoffed.

"Don't push it."

"So, Master Bai is a racist?" I asked.

"He's not a racist, he's just Korean. And he doesn't want Hideki knocking her up."

"Knocking her up!?"

"Yes, it could happen."

"But then Hideki wouldn't be able to take us to movies," I reasoned.

My mom looked at me like I was nuts, "Well, people need to live their lives."

I wanted to cry. In fact, I believe I left the room and did cry. Didn't she see that losing Hideki would be like losing *my* bodyguard? This was not how that movie had ended. Clifford Peache didn't get blown off because Ricky Linderman found a girlfriend with webbed feet!

I told Lee what was going on and he admitted that Hideki didn't seem himself. Even Allen was sort of acting crazy and when I asked him why, he explained that he was in love with his stepsister Roxanne, but it wasn't going over well with his newly married mother.

Was the whole world going mad? Weren't Lee, Jenny and I enough to keep everyone happy and fulfilled? Why the need for inbred girlfriends and torrid affairs with stepsisters?

We decided we needed to make a grand gesture and invite Rebecca into the fold. It was the only way to hang onto Hideki. Though deep down I couldn't help but wonder if the presence of Rebecca was some sort of karmic retribution from the Jackson Whites in retaliation for my family's daily invasion of Stag Hill.

Regardless, we went forward with the offer, hoping the

gods would smile upon us. We were willing to embrace Hideki's web-footed honey if that's what it was going to take. We phoned Hideki to see if he wanted to get some Kentucky Fried Chicken and then go see Jackie Chan's latest opus *The Big Brawl*. Hideki agreed and was happy that we had invited Rebecca, the only snag was that Allen's car was in the shop. Hideki couldn't use Master Bai's car because he had told Master Bai that he was going to a tournament in Rhode Island, when in fact, he was spending the weekend with Rebecca at her father-uncle's house. As luck would have it, our parents were away for the day and there was a shiny, newly leased, Buick sitting in the driveway begging to be used and so *we* lied and said that our folks said it would be okay for Hideki to come and use it.

It turned out that Rebecca was very nice. And after some greasy chicken and a few laughs about Allen's latest nunchaku debacle, we headed to Paterson to see the movie. Things were good; we had the impression that everything was going to be okay. We enjoyed the movie and then came out, only to discover that we had locked the keys in the car. This wasn't good, because my parents were going to be home in about two hours and the car needed to be put back before then. Thankfully, Hideki was handy with a hanger and we got the door open, but not before being spotted by two undercover police officers that thought we were a bunch of delinquents stealing a car.

We headed up Route 80 for home, when suddenly this rusted Impala came out of nowhere! There was this crazy looking guy riding shotgun and he was screaming at us through the window. We couldn't understand what the hell he was saying. Allen figured they wanted to race and tried to change lanes, but they were on us like white on rice. Hideki thought they might be rival students from another DoJang who had followed us out of the theater and ordered Allen to lose them. Allen hit the gas and thus began our forty-minute, high-speed chase down Route 80, which ended with us cornered by three cars in the parking lot of Jade Fountain restaurant, where we had enjoyed many a good bowl of wonton soup. We sat there for a moment, out of breath, wondering what was going to happen next. All the cars staring at each other, like samurais in the rain. Suddenly, two guys emerged from the cars, holding up police badges, which came as quite the shock.

Hideki of course was furious. He jumped out of the car, "Why were you chasing us?"

"Why are you stealing a car, punk?!"

"I'm not stealing a car. It's their parents' car, we took it to the movies. I'm an instructor at Bai's Tae Kwon Do."

"Bai's, huh?"

There was a certain level of recognition in his voice.

"You know Jay Laughlin? 'Cause he's a good friend of mine."

Hideki had of course heard about the Jay and Rich Exodus but didn't realize we were behind the whole endeavor. I swallowed hard, sensing doom. But as luck would have it, Hideki was filled with anger toward Master Bai's refusal to accept his forbidden Jackson-White fever and unleashed all his frustrations upon the unsuspecting, undercover cop.

"Master Bai, he's a control freak. He tries to manipulate everything and I'm doing the best I can. I just saw Jay the other night and we're thinking of cutting out on our own together."

"You're *Hideki*, right? I saw you in *Black Belt* magazine."

"Yeah, I've had a couple nice articles."

They blathered on for some time, while Lee, Jenny, and I sat in the car with Rebecca, feeling sort of lost. If Hideki was going to open a school with Jay, we were most surely going to be left behind. I tried not to think about it. Maybe Hideki was just saying it to get us off the hook. Either way, the cops let us go and we all breathed a sigh of relief as we headed home.

"Did you really mean that stuff you said about Sabumnim and you and Jay?" I asked.

Hideki just patted my head, "Don't worry about that stuff. It's complicated is all."

Which wasn't the reply that I was hoping for, but still, I was just happy to be with him. Of course, I forgot that in the time spent unlocking the car and chasing the cops and then talking the cops down, my parents had since come home. And finding the car missing and us not at home, they worried. And whenever my mother worried, she called Master Bai, who discovered that Hideki was not home and phoned Rebecca's mother who informed him that Hideki had in fact picked up Rebecca from her father-uncle's in my stepdad's maroon Buick.

Pulling into that driveway was not a good thing. The sight of my parents and Sabumnim standing there was too much for my little heart to bear. As soon as Allen parked, I ran out of the car and locked myself in the bathroom. I just couldn't manage to take the hit for this one. Down below, from the window, I could hear Master Bai screaming at Hideki and Rebecca, and my stepdad berating Allen for being irresponsible.

"You're almost thirty, when I was your age, I already had three kids," he said in his typical, find the "biggest picture possible to illustrate your point" fashion.

"Lester, please, just give him a ride home," interrupted my mom.

Lee and Jenny headed inside, confident that while they had been a party to this madness, they were too young to be implicated any further.

Master Bai dragged Hideki and Rebecca out of there. Lester drove Allen home and I hid in the bathroom, not because I was afraid of getting in trouble, but because I was aware of the fact that I had just witnessed the end of an era. My bodyguard was no longer mine and once again I felt forsaken and alone.

The next week Hideki moved back to California. I learned later that Rebecca moved with him. The DoJang was never, ever the same without him. Lee and I took our cue from Jenny and began phoning it in. Just lying on the floor with uncut toenails, pretending to stretch, while we stared at the blank spaces on the wall where Hideki's framed photos used to hang.

.5. I AM tHE EGGPLANt

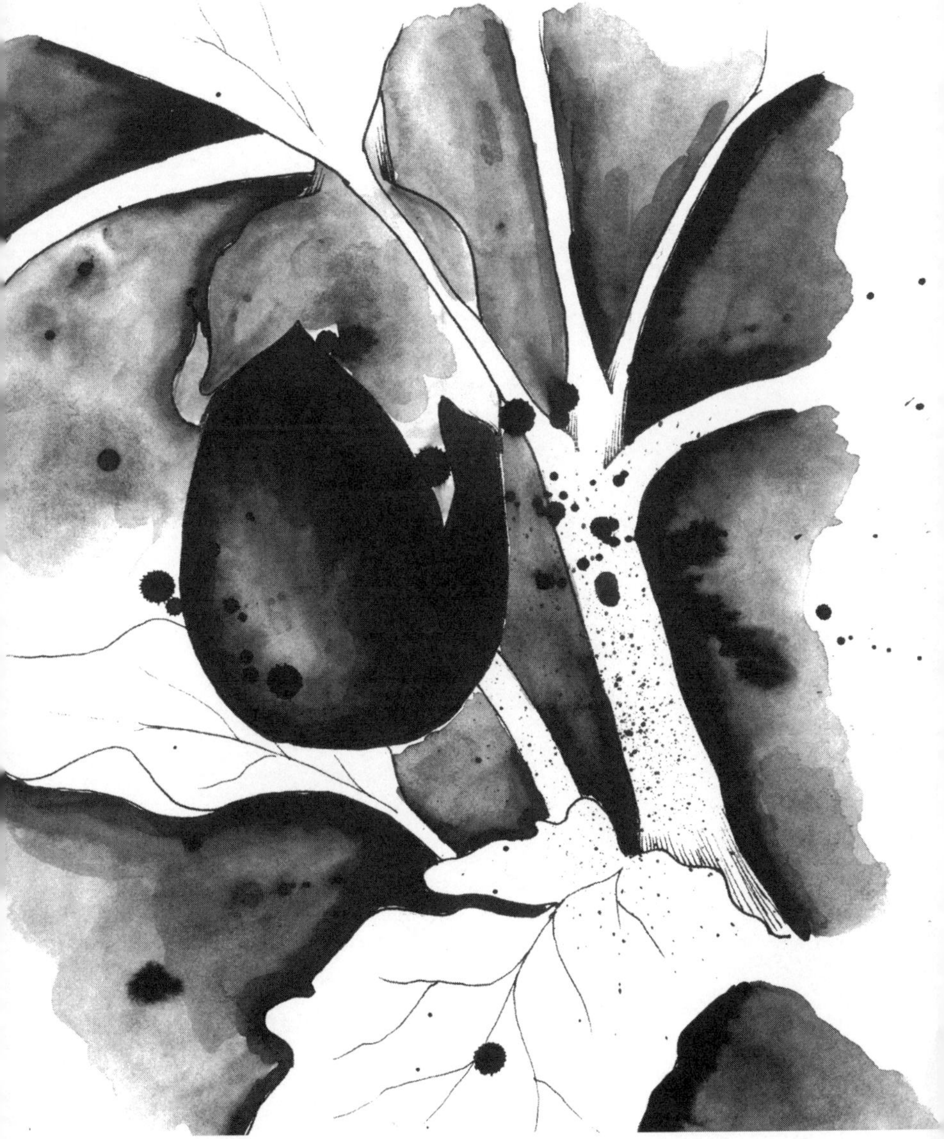

IT WOULD BE IMPOSSIBLE to grow up in New Jersey and not have a working knowledge of the mob. While we couldn't brag that any members of the famed Five Families lived in our town, we did have a big population of connected guys. My firsthand knowledge of the mob stemmed from a legendary shootout that occurred in my neighborhood. The Pizzolo family (name changed to protect my ass) lived through the woods behind our home, in a palatial, gated, white-brick estate. Their money was in supermarkets and they owned a chain that was popular among locals. The story goes that Mr. Pizzolo had pissed off one of the New York families, which earned him a nocturnal visit from some armed enforcer. Fearing for their lives, the Pizzolo children raced through the woods in their pajamas and banged on our neighbor's front door. The Gronlunds were Southerners and believed in all that hospitable nonsense and because of this the mom, whose name was Mimi, opened the door and gave safe haven to the fugitive Pizzolo children.

Mimi got major props for this, even from my mom, who would go on ad nauseam about Mimi's bravery and selflessness in the face of evil mobsters. Despite my mother's never-ending praise, I smelled Mimi's guilt in the equation. Mimi's father was the Supreme Court judge who cast the deciding vote that interned all the Japanese Americans during World War II. As such, I always felt that her harboring of the hunted mafia children was really an attempt to gain karmic brownie points. Irritating me even further, was the fact that Mimi got preferential treatment at the Pizzolos' local supermarket. She got the best cuts of meat, the freshest dairy products, and the middle-aged retarded bag boy, known to all as "Tard Man" (before the era of political correctness dictated that this was not a preferred nomenclature), would always help her out to the car, leaving the rest of us to fend for ourselves.

The truth was, it was no big secret that there were mobsters in our town. They never went to any lengths to hide their connections. In fact they tended to wear their affiliations on their sleeve. They all lived in ornately-decorated homes, where the favored color scheme was white on white or white on gold. Good furniture was always covered in plastic. Mirrors and fountains were the decorations of choice. The women wore their hair big and streaked, and the men relied heavily on gabardine as a fashion fabric of choice when heading to their jobs, which were almost exclusively in concrete, sanitation or harbor management. No one ever discussed why it was that Mr. Giordono's house had a fifteen-foot-high metal fence, complete with barbed-wire fringe, running the perimeter of his property. No one questioned Mr. Russo's fleet of trained German shepherds or the armed guard who would sit at the edge of his driveway, or for that matter the giant floodlights that graced the Cameraris' backyard. Like turnpike stink, you just pretended it wasn't there.

During this time, Reagan had just come into power. The country was in the shitter financially. Inflation was high and unemployment was even higher. Reagan's solution was to cut taxes and make government smaller. This was supposed to stimulate the economy and put more money in people's pockets. However teachers, small business owners, and lower-wage earners got screwed. That was reason enough to hate Reagan, but what bugged me more about the guy was that he was apparently cold to his children and seemed to have a serious hard-on for getting into a nuclear showdown with the Russians. Then he fired the air-traffic controllers, which didn't do anything to allay my fear of flying. My stepfather was a small business owner and my mom was a teacher, which made her union. It goes without saying that my family got poorer under Reagan's stupid economic reforms.

Fueled by the power of the American Dream, my parents pooled their formidable brain trust and came up with a plan to solve all our financial woes: They were going to write a Freight Term Dictionary. No, it wasn't Webster's, but it was a niche market and with some groovy cover art, we were cautiously optimistic that every trucker in the country was going to want a copy to peruse while resting at various *chew-and-spews* en route to *Shakey Town*.

Giddy over the prospect of what was without a doubt *the* get-rich scheme to end all get-rich schemes, my folks cranked out the tome in less than three months. Then, we all worked together to market that baby. This involved mailing out thousands of hand-printed fliers, which had to be folded into perfect thirds, placed in envelopes, stamped and sealed. The response could best be described as barely tepid. We learned that supply-side economics only works when you actually have a supply that someone wants. In the end, my folks broke even on the endeavor. Still, this left my siblings and me covered in paper cuts, our tongues permanently damaged from envelope glue and my parents still arguing about money, of which there never seemed to be enough.

I tried to stay Zen and not focus on money. This wasn't very easy to do, considering the fact that most of the people in Upper Saddle River had a lot of money. I reminded myself that we weren't like them. We didn't actually belong there and I tried to focus on the things we did have, like an enormous book collection and a working knowledge of septic systems. I'd almost fooled myself into submission when my classmate, Joe Ventigmelia, showed up at school one day in a Rolls Royce. Joe's dad, Joe Sr., was a barber who worked out of a small, dumpy shop in Nutley. There was no way in hell, even if he were cutting hair round the clock, that Joe Sr. could have swung a Rolls. I guessed he hadn't earned his extra cash writing a freight dictionary and realized from the white on white exterior/interior that the Rolls had been bought with mafia money.

All at once, it occurred to me that there was a financial alternative that we hadn't considered.

That night at dinner, I grilled my mom.

"Do we have family members in the mob?" I asked.

"Of course not," was her response.

"Isn't there someone, maybe on Grandpa Joe's side, since he's Italian, right?"

Treading into the nationality waters was always murky when it came to my father's side of the family, but I was fairly certain my Grandpa Joe's people were in fact from Italy.

"They're not connected. They came a long time ago and lived in Philadelphia."

"They have mobsters in Philadelphia," I countered, desperately clinging to some hope.

"Your grandfather was an honest man. You're not connected."

"What about on your side? The Irish mob? The Westies? We have to have a few of those.

"No such luck."

"What about Uncle Pete?" I asked. Uncle Peter was my mom's uncle, the youngest son in the family and a total eccentric, who carried a gun, smoked like a chimney, and never married.

"He could've been a Westie. He always carries a gun ...," I said.

"Uncle Peter was a merchant marine. He spent a lot of time in Burma."

My eyes went wide as I considered another possibility. "Chinese mob ties?"

"Will you stop it and eat your lima beans," was her response.

But my mind was whirring. Uncle Peter had to know someone who was connected, even if they were Chinese. What did I care? Just so long as we could get into the fray and make a little extra cash, and with any luck maybe score an automotive upgrade.

"I'm going to ask him next time I see him," I said.

"No. You are not going to ask him," she said in a tone that meant I better not.

We didn't have any organized crime connections in our family. It was hard to believe, yet true. Still, looking at my own blended family, it occurred to me that there were other ways to be a family, without being born into one. You could adopt, you could remarry, perhaps you could even horn your way in and become an annoying houseguest who never left. There were definitely options and lord knows I had the will; it was just a matter of finding a way. I couldn't discuss this with any of the mafia kids in my school. That would have been poor form and potentially dangerous for obvious reasons. Instead, I turned to the seventh grade's answer to *Pinky and the Brain*: Vinnie Mancini and his personal button man, Mike Pitti. Vinnie was a small guy with a serious Napoleon complex and Mike was his flatfooted sidekick who bore a striking resemblance to a platypus. But my sudden interest in them stemmed from the fact that they were obsessed with all things mafia. Vinnie and I weren't exactly friends, it was more that Vinnie and I had a certain simpatico because earlier in the year I had saved him from a potentially embarrassing gym class incident, when I pointed out discreetly that his left ball was hanging out of his shorts. He felt that I had shown great discretion in not sharing it with any of the girls but the reality was none of the girls had any interest in looking at his ball and I was tired of looking at it myself. After that, if I needed anything, like fifty cents for an ice cream sandwich or help opening my locker, which always seemed to stick, Vinnie would always oblige. This time what I needed was information about the mafia. Vinnie was half-Irish and half-Italian, thus barring him from full mafia entrance and relegating any potential role he might have to consigliore, at best. Still, he was more than happy to meet me on the playground for mafia talk. At our first meeting, Vinnie insisted on explaining the origins of the organization to me.

"See, there was this guy and he had a sister and she got raped by this other guy who was part of a rival family," he explained.

"Sort of like *Romeo and Juliet*, only without the love part," I responded.

"Who are Romeo and Juliet?" he snapped. Vinnie hated not being in the know.

"They raped the sister and then she went home and they totally freaked out. Screaming and yelling and beating their chests," he continued.

"What happened to the sister? Did she get pregnant?" I asked.

"Who cares about that?" Vinnie asked.

"I don't know, I just think it would be interesting to know if there was some sort of child that came from the relationship and maybe that's how the Five Families got their start."

Vinnie just stared at me. "Do you want to hear this or not?" he asked.

"Fine," I responded, annoyed with Vinnie's bossiness.

"So, the brothers yelled 'Ma fia! Ma fia!', which meant 'My sister! My sister!' and then they promised to avenge her rape, but since they waited a minute to do it, it was called a vendetta," he said.

"So, vendetta's different than vengeance because vendetta involves planning?"

"Yeah, whatever. That's not the point. The point is that they yelled 'Ma fia' and when you put it together quickly it sounded like 'mafia' and that's how the mafia began."

"You mean, that's how the mafia got its name," I corrected.

Vinnie just shot me a dirty look and his ever-present sidekick Mike laughed nervously. "What difference does it make? We have the mafia and that's all that matters," said Mike.

Mike was right and Vinnie and I decided not to get into a pissing match over our shared mutual interest. After that we'd meet a couple times a week on the playground to exchange interesting tidbits regarding all things mafia.

Vinnie's forte was recounting plot points from *The Godfather* movies.

"'Lucabrasi sleeps with the fishes' means that someone has been killed and dumped in the ocean," Vinnie explained.

"If I get another C in history, I'm gonna *lucabrasi* Mrs. Moratto," nodded Mike.

What neither of them seemed to realize was that *lucabrasi* was not a word but the name of the character Luca Brasi. I didn't bother to correct them because I was too focused on my own strengths, which involved memorizing facts. After a few marathon sessions at the local library, I was a wealth of pedantic information regarding the history of the mob.

"Did you guys know that the mafia's arcane rituals and much of the organization's structure were based largely on those of the Catholic confraternities and even Freemasonry? This in turn was colored by Sicilian familial traditions and even certain customs associated with military religious orders of chivalry like the Order of Malta," I explained.

"Of course I knew that," Vinnie would say.

"Yeah, he knew that," Mike would counter defensively.

"Did you know it was the duel that gave way to the vendetta?" I asked.

"Everybody knows that, right Mike?" Vinnie would say, rolling his eyes, no doubt secretly irked that he didn't know this stuff.

Both Vinnie and Mike were what my grandfather would call "knowers." And while it annoyed me to no end, that they could never admit to things they didn't know, I still needed them as I had no one else to talk to about these things.

One day, when Mike was being particularly dopey, I called him a *stugots*.

Vinnie perked up immediately. "What did you just say?"

"*Stugots*," was my response.

Vinnie was clearly intrigued, "What does that mean?"

"It means idiot," I responded. "You never heard of that?"

Vinnie shook his head "no."

"Doesn't your grandfather say words like that?" I asked.

"He's dead," was Vinnie's response.

"Which makes it hard for him to speak," Mike noted.

"Tell me more," said Vinnie.

I never even realized that there was any currency to knowing those words. My grandpa Joe often said them but I never thought anything of it. But now that I thought about it, I realized that I had an extensive arsenal of Italian words, which covered mental conditions, food choices, pejoratives and stomach conditions. There were loads of them: *oobatz, fanook, gabagool, bracciole, sfogliatelle*. Then there was *agita*, as in, "I don't know which gives me worse agita, your grandmother's crying or her cooking." And of course there was *mulignon*, which my grandfather told me meant black guy. This was long before Christopher Walken's stellar explanation in *True Romance*, where we as a culture learned that *mulignon* actually meant "eggplant" but it was one of those words that my grandfather could say, but I couldn't. Another one of those words was *puttana,* which meant slut, and then there was the much more palatable *chiacchierone,* which meant chatterbox and was the nickname that my grandpa had given me since I had the gift of gab.

Vinnie, Mike, and I started calling our classmates *oobatzes* and *fanooks* on a regular basis and laughing to ourselves over our lingual superiority. Then things took a turn for the better and Vin got his hands on the Mafia Pledge. This was mob gold and we were excited. The three of us tried to do it on the playground one afternoon, but none of us could manage to draw blood from our right index fingers. Finally, Large Marge, the chronically irate, whistle-blowing lunch lady, saw Vinnie biting my finger (with me screaming in pain) and broke it up.

But I was hooked. I wanted to be part of the mafia. I wanted to belong to a club that called itself family. I wanted to surround myself with people who weren't afraid to take matters into their own hands. People who would kill someone who crossed you and then serve you the best ziti dinner of your life afterwards.

Things took a bit of a turn when I made the mistake of confiding in Mike and Vinnie that I wanted to become a "made girl." Much to my surprise, they laughed at me, saying that girls couldn't get made. "Just like they can't become major league baseball managers," mocked Vinnie.

My face went white when he said this. My blood ran cold. Maybe it was all the mob talk that got me going, but I was incensed in a way that I'd never been before. The new reality facing me was that Nancie McDonnell had blabbed my deepest secret to everyone in the seventh grade. I had trusted her implicitly and she betrayed me. I wondered how long everyone had known and if they were secretly mocking me behind my back. It was a clear and direct violation of the Omerta, which was part of the mafia code of conduct and basically said you should never betray another person's confidence. Adding insult to injury, my associates, Mike and Vin, proceeded to tell everyone about my secret mob desires.

"Can you believe Kristen thinks she could actually become a made girl?" scoffed Vinnie in the lunchroom. Oh, everyone had a good laugh on that one. But they didn't realize who they were messing with. Not only did they fail to show me respect, they offended me. This stirred all sorts of feelings inside me, which I came to realize were the hazy, emotional formation of a vendetta. It was a slow burn. I had no desire to lash out immediately, but I knew that at some point they would all have to answer to me for their complete and total betrayal. To me they became *mezza morta*, living dead. I was done with them and in time, they would pay. After all, I knew a thing or two about waste management from the overflowing septic days of yore.

I wasn't daunted and I decided to ask St. Rosalie of Palermo for a little bit of intercession. After all, my desire to be a made girl was really about getting an automotive upgrade for my family. If Joe's dad was driving a Rolls and my mom was in a Chevette, surely the karmic balance needed tweaking. I promised St. Rosalie I'd be patient (I'd learned the hard way that badgering saints was never a good idea), if she could just make something happen. And, then, one weekend, my prayers were answered and Vicki Marinelli's family threw what would be the first in a long line of Friday night dance parties at their palatial, white-on-white, brick home.

Vicki lived in a house that would make Carmela Soprano weak in the knees. Everything was white or gold and entire walls were covered in mirrors, which made for confusion when trying to find the bathroom. There was a giant dance floor in the basement, complete with shimmering disco ball and strobe lighting and Vicki's dad, Victor, who was in waste management, oversaw the festivities with five of his business associates, who took turns making us virgin piña coladas, while Vicki's mom plied us with fish sticks on account of the fact Catholics couldn't eat meat on Fridays.

Vinnie and Mike were in attendance and I took a lot of pleasure in executing my plan in front of their very eyes.

My plan was to move in subtly, so on the first night, I stood next to Mr. M and casually asked, "Where's the gabagool? I'm starving."

The next week, when Vicki's mom brought out the cupcakes for dessert I sidled up to Mr. M and said, "Boy, a sfogliatelle would really hit the spot right now..."

Vinnie and Mike mocked me from a safe distance. But a few dance parties later, not only was there sfogliatelle in a small box just for me, but there was a vinyl-covered seat at the bar as well.

After that, I would sit with Mr. M and his associates and discuss Italian sports cars. This involved saying things like, "I really like Ferraris," and, "Ferraris are so cool."

I realized quickly that I was going to need to bring more to the table. My mom taught Latin and was an expert in all things Roman, so I began pumping her for information. Armed with copious amounts of knowledge I proceed to wow them with the history of waste management and concrete.

"Did you know that systems of waste removal didn't come into existence until the Greeks started it in about 330 B.C.," I offered one evening.

"You don't say?" Mr. M responded.

"Of course organized waste collection was associated only with state sponsored events, like parades and stuff. But Rome employed garbage men and for the most part their garbage was burned, which was why they didn't have trouble with plagues," I explained.

"Those Romans, they could run a city," nodded one of his associates.

"And did you also know that Rome made the best concrete in the world."

"That I did know," said Mr. M.

"But did you know that it came from Puzzuoli, which is just north of Naples? Apparently the clay there is the best in the world and it makes the best cement, which of course when mixed with stones becomes concrete."

"This kid is dy-no-mite!" exclaimed Mr. M as he poured me another virgin piña colada.

"The other great thing about Rome was that the sanitation was amazing. They had water continually flowing under the city and they were obsessed with bathing, so there were very few germs and because of that, next to no plagues. It was only with the advent of Christianity centuries later, when bathing was a sign of paganism and people stank, that all the plagues started."

Mr. M would stare at me with wide-eyed wonder. "How do you know all this stuff?" he'd exclaim.

Of course I didn't mention the part about my mom being a Latin teacher. Coming of age in a family of pathological liars enabled me to believe that I was in fact some sort of mafia princess who was imbued with this knowledge from birth. I even started pimping the Sicilian King story, not because I believed it, but because it furthered my agenda to become the first made girl, and eventually the first female don, at which point, (and this was after watching a few choice episodes of *Days of Our Lives* featuring the mythologically-influenced mafia warlord Stefano DiMera) my plan was to broaden our scope and crush Peruvian warlords.

Mr. M started asking me about my grades and complimenting me on my hard work. Meanwhile, Vin and Mike stewed in their own misery, realizing that they had seriously blown it by crossing me.

I was so close to being made it wasn't even funny. It was only a matter of time before things began to fall off the back of trucks outside my house. With any luck, maybe I could even score a new Ferrari for my mom.

Then came a sudden glitch in my proverbial plan.

The Gronlunds were moving away and Mimi decided to pass the "protect the Pizzolo kids" torch to my mom, who being the save-the-world zealot that she was, was more than happy to take it.

The worst part was that the Pizzolo children had grown up to be a bunch of spoiled, obnoxious brats.

"It was different when they were all little in their pajamas and their teddy bears," I explained, "but they're teenagers now and they're total a-holes!"

"Stop it, we help those who need help," she snapped.

"Yeah, but I don't see why we need to be responsible for a bunch of delinquents. Tony Pizzolo is flunking out of chemistry. Are you aware of that?"

My mother eyeballed me. "No, I wasn't aware of that and how would you even know that since he's in the high school and you're in middle school."

"I have people," was my response.

My mother eyeballed me, but I wouldn't let it go. "You demand good grades from everyone, but Tony P. can just phone it in and flunk his classes and then waltz right through our front door, putting us in complete and total jeopardy. It doesn't seem fair, ma," I countered.

"Life isn't fair," was her patented response.

I could see that there was no way to pass the torch onto another family on the block. No, we would be stuck harboring those ingrates in our dank basement. And what then? The cops would come, arrests would be made; there'd be a court case. My mom would describe how the kids ran from the killers. There wouldn't be enough evidence. The killers would go free and where would that leave us? Smack dab in the middle of the Witness Protection Program.

I had seen enough Movies-of-the-Week to know the drill. You were taken under cover of darkness from your home in an unmarked van and driven to Arizona, where you got stuck living in some bland apartment complex, with neighbors like former mobster Henry Hill. And despite the fact that the homes were fairly new and had pristine hardwood floors, the reality was that all the while the mobsters we betrayed would be hunting us down, until they found us, at which point we'd get whacked.

With each passing Friday night, I grew more and more uneasy. One minute I was eating zabaglione with Mr. M, the next I was potentially harboring mob children. It was a dangerous existence. My fear and paranoia only grew when there was a mob rubout on Saddle River Road and the Iceman whacked a crooked cop named Peter Calabro. The worst part was that I saw the parked car containing the dead guy as I drove home from school on the bus. In addition to the investigation, there were constant articles in the paper about RICO and I began to see that it wasn't a guy named Rico that Mr. M had been talking about but rather it was the Racketeering Influenced and Corrupt Organizations Act. Articles about the Witness Protection Program were everywhere. The code of Omerta was falling to pieces as mob guys decided to turn into rats on what seemed to be a daily basis.

I finally broke down, and weeping uncontrollably I told my mom about how afraid I was that I was going to be forced to enter the Witness Protection Program. I was looking for a little comfort, but instead she just snapped at me, "We'll miss you, but be sure to keep those cards and letters coming."

Still, my mom didn't understand how deep within La Cosa Nostra I had traveled. I couldn't risk it. I was breaking sfogliatelle with made men. It was too much to handle.

Without so much as an explanation, I started skipping the Friday nights at Vicki's. This infuriated Vicki mostly because her dad kept asking about me, which in turn made her jealous. Vicki began to snub me openly on the playground. Vin and Mike became her personal button men and my fear and paranoia went through the roof. I kept waiting for the cops to show up at my house and subpoena me to testify on the Calabro rubout. Finally my mom, who couldn't deal with the fact that I jumped a mile every time the doorbell rang, dispelled my fears. "About two hundred people saw that car parked on Saddle River Road. There's nothing to testify about, you didn't see the shooting, you didn't see the shooter, you saw a car parked on the side of the road. So did every other kid on your school bus. You don't think they're going to subpoena an entire busload of kids, do you?"

She had a point. And I began to feel better about the whole thing. I started going over to Vicki's again, only now it was Spring and it was all about parties in the heated pool and bouncing on the brand new trampoline that appeared in her backyard one day after mysteriously falling off the back of a truck.

Hopped up on sfogliatelles and virgin coladas I celebrated my re-entry into La Cosa Nostra by jumping like mad on the trampoline. It was all great fun, until I fell.

Mr. M and his motley crew whisked me off to the Valley Hospital where my dad worked. There was a huge line in triage and my ankle was throbbing. Mr. M tried to convince the triage nurse to move me to the front of the line, but she wasn't hearing anything of it. He came back to me in the chairs. "Sorry, kiddo. We're just gonna have to wait this one out."

But my ankle was killing me and I didn't appreciate having to wait for service so I decided to pull my Child of the AMA card.

"Go tell the nurse my name," I said. "She'll let us in, if she hears my name."

Mr. M looked at me kind of funny, as if I was crazy, but I wasn't. I knew that once they heard my name, they'd let me in, since they didn't want to anger my father. But Mr. M didn't know that. He didn't even know my dad was a doctor. Despite the fact that he thought it was a complete waste of time, Mr. M went over and whispered my name to the nurse, who promptly waved me through to the front of the line past the broken bones and gunshot victims.

Mr. M could not have been more impressed. If I had been in less pain I would have taken pleasure from this.

My mom still hadn't arrived so Mr. M and his guys stayed with me while I got my X-ray. He kept telling me to be brave and such, but I was comfortable in the hospital setting and kept reassuring him that I was fine.

"The heart on that girl," he kept muttering to his associates.

The technician took the X-ray and within minutes there was a group of doctors in the room, all gathered around in conference. They were so intense, I actually got nervous. They called in other doctors and soon there was a crowd of them staring at my X-ray. I started fearing for the worst. Maybe I'd done some sort of horrible damage. My mind immediately zoomed to a bad place. I was thinking amputation when I heard one of them say, "She's got an extra bone in her ankle."

Which was not what I was expecting them to say. I nodded to Mr. M to go over and find out more.

"What's this about an extra bone?" he asked.

But they were all too fascinated to respond.

"Isn't she Dr. D's daughter?" asked one of the residents.

"Yeah, she's his daughter," replied the intern.

"This is pretty remarkable," claimed the radiologist.

"Explains a lot, I guess," answered the nurse.

Finally Mr. M grew impatient, "What exactly does this extra bone mean?" he asked.

"It's just something you only see in blacks," replied the chief radiologist.

Mr. M moved in tighter, "You telling me she's a *mulignon*?"

The doctors looked at him, not wanting to go there. Even I was sort of surprised by his response.

"Well, it's indicative of black anatomy," corrected the resident.

The doctors moved off to the corner, as if I wouldn't be able to hear them as they tried to process this latest development.

"But I thought Dr. D was French," said one.

"I never believed the French bit," said another.

"I thought he was a Medici or something," mused yet another.

"Please, you don't honestly believe that shit do you?"

While they debated the origins of my people, as if I weren't even there, Mr. M and his peeps just sort of stared at me with a mixture of confusion and disgust. But I remember feeling strangely comforted by the news. I was an eggplant. I'd suspected as much for quite some time, but now I had proof. Now I knew who I was and there was something so freeing about it. It was there, on the X-ray and no amount of plate smashing or crying could deny it. There was comfort in the clarity. I was of mixed race; moreover, I was proud of it. And that was a big step for my family.

My mom finally arrived. I told her about the extra bone, but she was too mad about the fact that I had gone on a trampoline to really process the full implication of the situation.

Mr. M lost interest in me after that and the Friday night parties seemed to stop, although maybe I just wasn't invited. But I didn't really care. I knew who I was. Part of the puzzle had come into place and I felt more at peace with my surroundings.

Still, I had to admit that a bit of La Cosa Nostra stayed with me, in that I harbored a little vendetta against Mr. M for the eggplant comment. And on occasion, I'd sit at our front window, hoping against hope that the Pizzolos would piss off one of the Five Families and have a shootout, so I could be the first to unlock the door and let their kids in.

8. PEt PEEVES

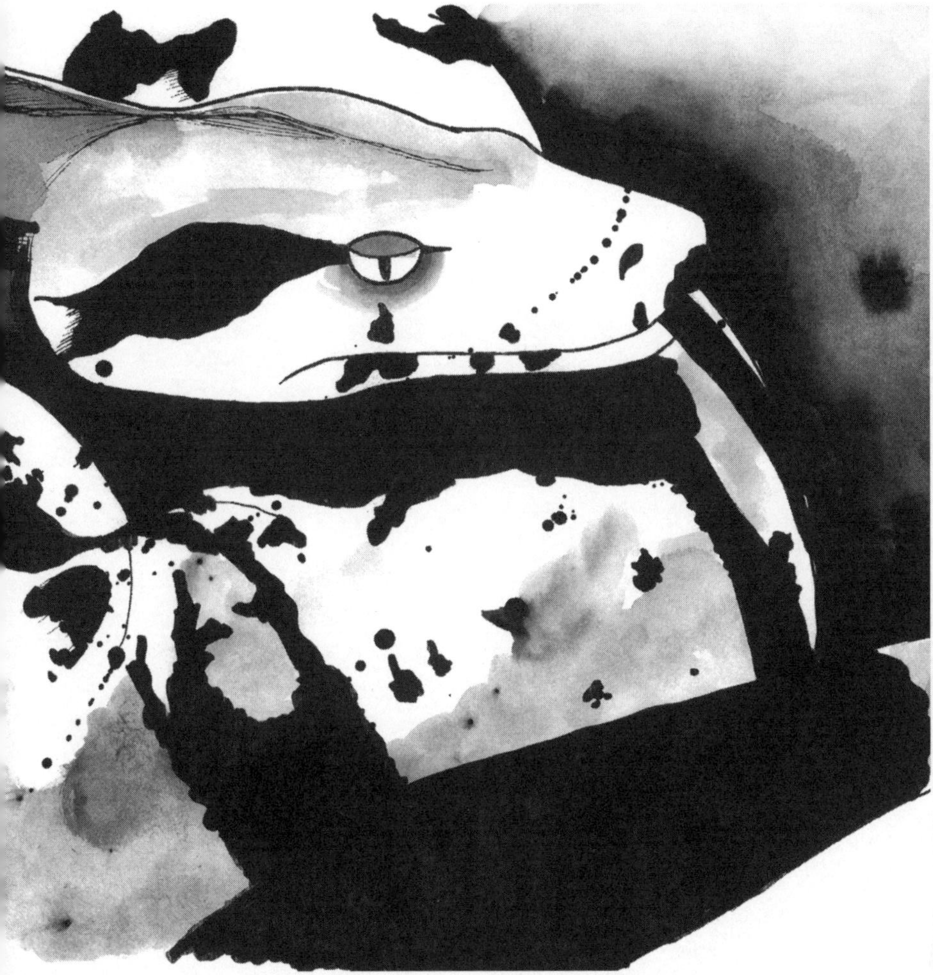

DESPITE THE FACT that I had long since done away with the "every other weekend visitation" stipulation of my parents' divorce, I still had to spend six weeks with my father every summer. This annual hellish sojourn usually spanned the latter part of July and all of August. I hated going to my father's house more than anything because my father ignored me and my stepmother brutalized me, but I never let my mother know the extent to which I was miserable. People have often asked me how it was that she didn't know, but my answer was always the same: She didn't know, because I didn't want her to know. Being born into a family of liars had its upside. Liars often have an easy time slipping into the sticky confines of a double life. It took some getting used to, but in time I became adept at shifting my perspective depending on the reality. Of course I could have told my mom about how my father ignored me and how my stepmother was cold, cruel, and abusive. But that would have made for trouble, and trouble was something I was looking to avoid. My mother's cross was very heavy, so I made a decision early on that a double life was to be mine. And while I did my best to carry it with a modicum of dignity, I often wondered why it was that my mom had married my dad in the first place. Perhaps it was rebellion that led her to my father. He was not like the other boys my mother knew. He was complicated and difficult, moody and strange. It was a departure even for my mom, whose own dad had never spoken harshly to her or been unkind. And yet she married my father, who could be unkind and who did speak harshly to her, and to me, and to anyone who did not view him within the prism of the larger-than-life character that he viewed himself.

What was it they saw in one another? Maybe it was a shared unspoken complicity. After all, my father had never wanted to be a doctor and my mother had never wanted to be a traditional housewife. Maybe this was the attraction. Yet once apart, there was so much displaced hostility and anger that it seemed to be the only defining trait in their relationship, of which I was the sole surviving product. And for this I suffered, on many levels. Still the biggest reason I hated going to spend the summers at my dad's house wasn't the fact that my father's new twenty-something wife loathed me or that my dad ignored me. It was that there was absolutely nothing to do.

With my dad at work all day, I did my best to blend into the woodwork. I became like one of those Wall People from *Flash Gordon*, trying to stay clear of my stepmother, Ming the Merciless. But summers without friends, activities, or pools proved to be quite challenging. There were really only two ways to kill time. The first involved daydreaming. I could eat up a solid two-hour chunk by imagining myself as Matt Dillon's love interest in *Over the Edge*, the cult classic film about urban planning gone wrong. While my body was sitting behind the ivy-covered detached garage of my dad's posh two-story Tudor, my mind was thousands of miles away, running through the streets of New Granada, with Matt's character Richie and all the other disenfranchised youths. I would add scenes, thus ensuring that Matt and I got more screen time together. These scenes would later appear as "out-takes" on the DVD release, with the director explaining that the scenes where Matt and I stare at each other dreamily over ice cream, or make out in the rec room, were ultimately not necessary to illustrate the overt chemistry between the two characters. And while I would've liked to have gone with a more upbeat ending, I'd always felt a certain degree of respect for a director's vision, so I never altered the pivotal burning-down-the-gymnasium scene. I suppose, deep down, part of the allure of Matt Dillon's Richie, aside from his bedroom eyes, his fabulous hair, and that rugged New Rochelle accent, was that he was doomed, which lent a deeper pathos to the entire endeavor. After all, how many times could you look at someone dreamily over ice cream?

If I were lucky, it would be lunchtime by the time the gym burned. Then Ming would hurl some food at me and I'd have about ten minutes to eat and get the hell out. This left me with a solid six hours to just pace around the backyard until my dad returned from the hospital. Thankfully, the day before I had to start my sentence, my mom would always take me to my favorite bookstore in Hackensack, Womrath's. In addition to having an amazing young adult section, Womrath's had a secret backroom where teachers could go to get textbooks and workbooks. Since my mom was a card-carrying member of the Teachers' Union, we were always admitted. Once inside this pedagogical candy land, I would pick out an assortment of workbooks, then we'd hit the young adult section where I'd stock up on Newberry Award Winners. It was bliss. I'd move down the aisles slowly, taking in the cover art and new book smell. No gnarly, dog-eared, snot-encrusted library books for me; these were my books to keep. The downside was that I would have to read them at my dad's house, but on the flipside, they staved off misery, so at least there was some cosmic balance to it all. We'd cap off the book buying with a meal at Hojo's on Route 17 where I would have my usual – Coke, fried clams and a scoop of mint chocolate chip ice cream for dessert. It was a last hurrah of sorts and it was an über important transitional day before I had to serve my time on shared custody row.

It was my sixth summer of shared custody and I was to ship out the following day. I woke up early and hopped into bed with my mom. While she stirred, I mentally prepared for our day ahead. How many books should I get? Should I focus on grammar or eighth grade algebra? Should I throw caution to the wind and order a chocolate shake with my fried clams? And as I dreamt of the intoxicating blend of salty and sweet, the phone rang. It was a collect call from my sixteen-year-old Floridian stepsister, Stacie. Stacie had barely begun speaking when my mother bolted upright in bed, as if she had just been shocked with a defibrillator.

"What do you mean you ran away!?" she cried out.

She instinctively reached for a pen and an index card, because in times of distress, nothing spelled potential solution like an index card.

"Who ran away?" I whispered.

My mother waved me off. A look of concern on her face, "Where are you now?"

"Who'd she run away from?" I asked.

My mother continued to ignore me. "Where are you right now?"

"What's going on?" I asked.

My mother covered the receiver and blurted out, "She ran away and wants to come live up here." Judging by the look on her face, my mom was completely perplexed by this sudden turn of events. But it was all pretty clear to me. Feeling very much like the disenfranchised youths of *Over the Edge* and tired of the fetid, bog-like conditions that Florida's weather had to offer, Stacie decided she wanted to leave. I grabbed an index card and scrawled *Send her a bus ticket, hang up the phone, let's go to Womrath's*!

My mother waved me off furiously because there was a slight caveat. In the angst-fueled, teen-empowered moment during which Stacie made the decision to leave home, she bolted to the airport in her mother's car. This so infuriated her mother that she reported the car stolen to the police, thus making Stacie quasi on the lam. I was happy with the idea of Stacie coming to stay with us, but her timing was awful. I had books to buy and Stacie, frantic, broke and, from what I could understand, barefoot at an airport, was really not working with my schedule. I tried to pry the phone away from my mother. I needed my books! How many hours of the day could a person walk around in circles around a backyard?! Desperation sank in and I blurted out, "Tell her to go home!"

My mother kicked me off the bed, but I wouldn't be stopped.

"Return the car and then send her money for a ticket!" I offered.

"Go to the beach and catch a bus when it gets dark!" I cried.

There were innumerable solutions, but we were in high drama mode and who was I to kill the buzz?

My mom and I raced to Western Union to wire Stacie money. After this, Stacie's mission was to figure out a way to pick up the money and make the plane before the cops found the car in long-term parking and nailed her. In the meantime, we did manage to get books in Hackensack, but only because it was near the Western Union place. Hojo's, however, was a wash because we had to go to Newark Airport to pick Stacie up, but her flight got routed to Atlanta due to a storm and she didn't end up arriving until the next morning. This was annoying to say the least.

The next morning I left for my father's. As planned, I killed time doing algebra, fantasizing about Matt Dillon, reading Elizabeth Enright novels, and playing a game that

I had invented called The Curious Silence. This was a new addition to the summer repertoire, but a necessary one since I had become something of a fast reader and the Enright novels were clipping by at an alarming rate. The Curious Silence was a very simple game: The object was to see how long I could go without saying a single word before my dad or Ming either asked me a question, or became concerned that I was not speaking. My record was five days. What was most interesting about playing it was that the quieter I became, the more I seemed to see. And the more I saw, the more absurd everything became, especially considering that my dad's obsessions of that summer revolved around the customization of a myriad of things. For example, vanity license plates: He chose RENAL and NURSE to grace his automobiles. Then there was the new flag for his sailboat: He labored over a hideous design that involved yellow squares and black arrows grouped in triangle-like formation. And then there was the car: a cherry red Cadillac that he transformed into a convertible. With so much on his plate, it was easy to see how my silence could have gone unnoticed.

Thankfully, August ended, and with my sentence served, I returned home to find that Stacie had managed to assimilate nicely into the fold. Her room was a mess, but apparently, this was known as self-expression. She even met up with lots of like-minded individuals at the local state park, who all seemed to revel in their shared love of leather moccasins, Southern Rock and pot. They were sort of like characters in a Richard Linklater film, but without the luxury of hair, makeup, wardrobe, and good lighting. But when school started, Stacie learned that there was a dark side to being in a burnout, because at our local high school, if you didn't do sports, you were considered a useless waste of protoplasm. Terrorized by gym teachers and overzealous budding lesbians (anxious for her to join the field hockey team), Stacie became moody and quiet. She'd come home from school, eat cold meat dipped in Polynesian sauce, and sleep for hours on end. My mom didn't know what to do, but tried her best to pretend that everything was fine. "She must be in the middle of a growth spurt," she'd insist. Stacie became a sort of sullen specter, who really just haunted our house. It was disappointing in the sense that it was as if she wasn't there at all.

Then something amazing happened that gave Stacie direction and purpose and filled her with a sense of unbridled joy. That something was the *MUSE NO NUKES* concert. *MUSE* stood for *Musicians United for Safe Energy* and they were a group of artists working together for a non-nuclear future. Among them were such luminaries as Bruce Springsteen, James Taylor, The Doobie Brothers, Jesse Colin Young, Crosby Stills and Nash, and Bonnie Raitt. But more importantly, at least for Stacie, was the fact that they were led by Jackson Browne. And while Stacie didn't know anything about nukes, she harbored an *undying* love for Jackson Browne and she demanded to go to the concert despite the fact that it was on a school night. In a bold, yet unexpected move, my stepdad swooped in to exert some power. Stacie was his daughter and there was no way he was going to let her go to New York alone on a school night. But my mom had never seen Stacie so animated and so she promptly overruled his kangaroo court ruling. Sensing opportunity I made a mental note:

Stacie – age 16
Allowed to travel to Manhattan Unsupervised
School Night

I tucked that one away in the file marked *Precedents* and went about my business assuming that, with the exception of a multicolored concert-T and a bumper sticker or two, nothing would come of the event. But I had misjudged the extent of Stacie's Jackson Browne love, because the next day, Stacie had effectively been reborn into a No Nukes, peace-loving, global disarmament disciple. Armed with just enough information to make her dangerous, she proceeded to fill my head with visions of nuclear Armageddon. Stacie's love of the bomb caused me an endless array of anxiety. I worried about the nuclear winter and if we had enough canned goods to survive. I wanted my mother to buy us all gas masks, after all, the Russians had them. I even floated the idea of a fallout shelter, but Stacie assured me that we lived so close to New York City that we'd be incinerated in the first round of attacks. I was a complete and total wreck. I knew the whereabouts of every fallout shelter in our town and occasionally, when a low flying plane flew over our house, I'd start screaming, "We're gonna die!"

My mother would just roll her eyes, wishing that the bomb would fall on me and shut me up, but Stacie was never happier. Living on the brink of destruction agreed with her. In fact, she was so happy that she and her friends Doozie and Clark, girls who later went on to do things like count elk in Greenland and teach deaf people to dance, decided that they were going to hold a no-nukes rally of their own. It was going to be just like Woodstock, only it was going to be in New Jersey. They'd get bands to perform and they would spread the word and people would come from all over. It was going to be the summer of love all over again and my sister would go on to be a rock promoter, or at the very least a groupie, and her life would be infused with meaning and accomplishment, and she could finally stick it to her guidance counselor who told my mom she was on the express train to nowhere.

Stacie, Doozie, and Clark donned their tie-dyed *kurtas* and got to work. Using their rather formidable burnout connections, they somehow managed to pull this thing together. They had decided to hold it in a park in the Ramapo Mountain Foothills. The Jackson Whites, hoping to make a better name for themselves, had agreed to act as security. And most importantly, bands were coming! They had commitments from Little Feat, The Doobie Brothers, and Bonnie Raitt, and of course, my sister's love object and MUSE spokesman, Jackson Browne. My sister was in a dither. Like all good producers, her biggest concern was turnout and so she took to plastering handmade signs all over the tri-state area. My mother was nervous that our house might take on some sort of mythic significance à la Yasgur's Farm and warned that if people started camping out front, she wasn't going to make them food. Still, in a show of support, she stocked up on Carnation Instant Breakfast. Knowing no one would camp out front due to our septic tank issues, I began hoarding the Carnation Instant Breakfast in the makeshift nuclear shelter I had set up in my bedroom closet. Screw those peaceniks, if the bomb hit, Jenny and I were going to survive.

As the date of the rally neared, Stacie became intensely focused. She, Doozie, and Clark burned the midnight oil making costumes for the event. Doozie was going to be the wind, Stacie the sun, and Clark was water. While this might have been on target for an Earth Day rally, I really thought the choice of costumes obscured their message. "Disarmament is about ending the Cold War, so shouldn't you guys go as dismantled warheads?" I reasoned.

"Shut up, Kris, you don't know anything!" barked Stacie.

It was semantics at this point. Stacie had a cause and she wasn't sleeping all day, so my mother told me to keep my mouth shut.

The three of them finished their costumes and my mother took photographs to commemorate the event. Shortly thereafter, we received the phone call informing us that Jackson Browne had been arrested for (allegedly) beating his wife.

Of course, Stacie lost her mind and completely freaked out, screaming that he had been framed and that the "pigs" did this to him. She just couldn't believe that her beloved Jackson could have anger management issues.

"Jackson is about peace and love," she cried.

"Actually, he preaches nuclear disarmament, so the alleged wife beating is really irrelevant within this larger context," I pointed out.

This only made Stacie cry more. I was ushered out of the room and my mother went into damage-control mode. She whipped out her index cards and got Jackson's representative back on the line. After hearing he had made bail and that he would be there on time, Stacie eventually fell asleep, though it should be noted that my mother already had him convicted and warned that he would not be coming back to the house for coffee and cake after the show.

Unfortunately, Jackson had done far more damage than just the alleged black eye, because he had made the mistake of mentioning that he was heading to New Jersey for a No Nukes Rally. This of course made the cops wonder what No Nukes Rally he was talking about. Being investigative by nature, the police sent out feelers and made phone calls. Ultimately the "pigs" got to the bottom of this No Nukes Rally and then, as is often their wont, they pulled the plug at the eleventh hour due to the fact that Stacie, Doozie, and Clark forgot to get permits for the event.

It was a dark day at our house. There was a lot of uncontrollable weeping. Stacie saw a bleak future ahead of her. She'd never get to be a rock promoter or a Jackson Browne groupie. More importantly, the jocks at school were going to be merciless in their humiliation and Stacie and all her well-meaning burnout friends would be back to the east corner of the parking lot, smoking Marlboro Lights, waiting for Richard Linklater to redeem them.

A dark cloud hung over her head and Stacie went back to sleeping for the bulk of the day. Of course, it was just depression, but this was before depression was stylish and words like Prozac and Zoloft were part of the vernacular. We were also Irish (at least half), and as such, we didn't discuss things like emotion. Yet, we all knew something had to give. Stacie was going to be lost in her room forever and drastic measures had to be taken. And so it was decided by my mom that Stacie needed a pet. Nothing cheered up a depressive like the unconditional love of a pet. We already had a dog, a cat, and a few fish, so my mom thought long and hard and ultimately decided that a boa constrictor would be the pet of choice for Stacie.

The snake was purchased and in an effort to show her understanding of Stacie's Jewish heritage, my mother suggested naming the snake after the legendary Queen of Sheba, whose big claim to fame was that she made Solomon answer riddles, then showered him with gifts and had his love child, who of course became the father of the lost tribe of Ethiopian Jews. It was a bold move on my mom's part, but the Queen of the Lost Tribe metaphor was lost on Stacie, who hadn't cracked open the Bible ever and probably thought Solomon was a guy who worked at the kosher deli. But still, one had to hand it to my mother for trying. Not many a stepmother would have brought a boa constrictor into the home just to try to cheer up a depressed stepchild.

We had high hopes for the snake, but for the most part it just sat in its big tank and stuck out its tongue. Occasionally you could hold it but then it would defecate on you, leaving an unpleasant warm liquid sensation running down your arm. The only remotely interesting thing it did was eat live mice. We'd spend countless hours waiting for Sheba to eat the damn, shivering thing. Then once she did, we'd all stare at the bump in her body as it moved down and then finally out; usually on one of our shirts. My brother Lee was the only one troubled by the snake. He was very concerned that Jenny was going to be devoured by it and began drawing graphic pictures documenting Jenny's demise. After weeks of crayon drawings featuring Jenny in various stages of death throes, Lee's teacher phoned my mother, a tad concerned, wondering if it were true that she had brought a massive anaconda into the house. My mother assured him that the snake was small and when it got big enough to eat Jenny, she had a contingency plan (at least mentally) wherein the snake would live on a reserve. Sadly, we never had to worry about Jenny's demise at the hand of our boa. In fact, Sheba never even graduated to rats because she came down with a horrible case of depression and stopped eating. I always thought she caught it from Stacie. All those hours spent in a cage watching Stacie sleep would've depressed even the happiest of snakes, but according to the vet, depression among boas was rampant. After all, what could be better than living in a warm cage the size of a postage stamp? Who needed the rainforest when there were suburban homes in New Jersey where nothing happened and strange pan-racial children would stare at you all day?

Sheba wasn't having any of it, which accounted for her hunger strike. Interestingly enough, this coincided with the Irish hunger-strikers and my mother wasted no time in educating us about Bobby Sands and the oppression of the Irish at the hands of the Ulster Defence League. Stacie would just glaze over – she didn't have any more energy for causes – but Jenny and I were enraged. How dare someone oppress the Irish?! After reading an advanced copy of Bernard MacLaverty's novel *Cal*, which chronicled the life of a young IRA operative trying to break the cycle of violence (which later became a film that featured Helen Mirren's incredible ageless tits), we decided that we too would go on a hunger strike. But we couldn't go longer than an hour without eating and what was life without food? So, we went on an eating strike instead. We weren't going to stop eating until Northern Ireland was free. Sadly, before we were able to accomplish our task, Sheba died.

We had a funeral on a gloomy March morning and buried her in a shoebox out in the woods behind our house.

My mom put a cross up on the grave, although I always felt that in keeping with the Lost Tribe theme we should have gone with a Jewish star.

We trudged back into the house and stood by the now vacant tank in which she had once lived. The only sign of life inside was the deliriously happy white mouse who, in avoiding certain death, had now inherited the mother-lode of mouse habitats. He had a beatific grin on his face that said prime real estate was now his. But my mother wasn't having it. The tank was perched on Stacie's dresser and my mom was worried that over time it would warp the wood. She made us stick our furry white tenant back into the mouse holding pen, which was really just a small fish tank in Lee's room. There was another mouse already living there.

"They can bond over their good fortune," my mother said.

Lee liked the idea of having two pet mice, mostly because he knew they could never eat Jenny. There seemed to be a silver lining of sorts after all.

We stuck the big tank in the garage and got back to our lives.

One Saturday morning three weeks later, my mother had taken Lee to Paramus Park Mall to get shoes and I was home alone with Jenny. Stacie was staying with a friend and my stepfather was away on business. I was right in the middle of a really great dream involving me and Matt Dillon and an alternative ending to *Over the Edge* that involved the two of us escaping in a dirigible (over the strains of *Cheap Trick*), when my sister burst into my bedroom and screamed, "You need to come fast!"

Like my brother Lee, my sister Jenny wore hearing aids. I glanced up from my pillow and saw that she wasn't wearing them, which would have accounted for the decibel of her voice, but the look on her face smacked of trouble.

I bolted out of bed, irked because I hadn't gotten to

the part where Matt and I kiss. It was all very unsettling and unsatisfying and I mumbled, "This better be some big goddamn problem to be dragging me out of bed at 10 am on a Saturday!" although I'm certain that she didn't hear me. We headed into Lee's room and she pointed to the tank. My face went white, my blood ran cold. It turned out that Lee's pet mice were not both boys as we assumed. Apparently, they had *bred* and *had babies*, and now the father was *cannibalizing* the babies, who resembled bloody pinky toes, and the mother was *howling*. Honestly, my first reaction was the Dog Poop Rule; just shut the door and pretend we didn't even see it. But the howling of the mother was so loud, my sister, sans hearing aids, had been awoken by it. And the father was vicious and awful, not just killing the babies but attacking them by biting at them, then retreating back into his corner where he would look around all shifty-eyed like a demon from hell. I did the only sensible thing and screamed like a girl, while my sister eyeballed me like an asshole. Jenny may have only been seven, but screaming like a girl was never her preferred method of dealing with any type of crisis.

"What should we do?!" I screamed.

"You need to get a spoon and take the father out," she explained.

After scouring our inventory of spoons, we settled on a ladle. But when we tried to remove the father, he climbed up the ladle and tried to attack us, which did make my sister blanch ever so slightly, though there was still no screaming on her end. I, however, was like an insane banshee.

Jenny and I left the room and regrouped over a bowl of Cheerios. When in doubt, our modus operandi always involved eating. Settling the stomach helped the brain think. While we were thinking, hopefully the mother would kill the father and this crazy Cronos-like rage of his would end and we could get those kids out of there.

Thirty minutes later, it was still on.

The cage had basically become the Roman Coliseum and something had to be done. Had we been stronger, we would've reached in and gotten them, but they looked like bloody, Shrinky-Dink pigs. We needed to get my mother on the horn and since my sister couldn't hear on the phone, it was obvious I would have to make the dreaded call to the Paramus Park Mall to have her paged. This took about forty minutes, because the mall had a policy that it would only page people if it were a serious emergency. You couldn't just have mom phone home to see if you should defrost some chop meat for dinner, it had to be big stuff, i.e. death and/ or dismemberment. But if a cannibalizing mouse eating his young in front of their mother wasn't an emergency, then dammit I didn't know what was.

The page was issued and my mother phoned home within minutes, with a nervous tone in her voice. Jenny and I were clinging to each other at this point because one of the babies had been split in half.

"Mommy, the mice had babies and the father's eating them!" I cried.

My mother, thinking that the emergency page was really a message telling her that one of her children had died, flew into a rage.

"You paged me about goddamn mice!" she screamed.

One would have thought there would have been relief in her tone, but instead she became incensed that no one was dead or dismembered.

"Yes, it's like the Coliseum. The babies are the Christians and the Dad is the evil gladiator, or maybe the lion, I don't know, it's a toss up!"

There was silence on the other end and I mistook it to mean that my mother was formulating a plan. I waited with baited breath for her response, but it was thus, "They're mice and you're a smart girl. Deal with it." Then she hung up.

If things hadn't been so harrowingly bad in the cage,

I would've been upset that my mom was mad at me, but things were so beyond our control that I didn't even care. My sister was losing patience. I had to do something. I gazed out the back window and into the woods behind our home. All at once, a solution presented itself to me. The way I saw it, had Sheba lived, both mice and their corresponding eggs and sperm would have been dead at this point. They would have been digested by Sheba and would now be resting within her rotting intestines. I reasoned that the mice should never have been relegated to that tank, they should have been food, thus fulfilling their role in the life cycle. Or if not, they should have been freed to live out their lives in a natural environment. There, they could have returned to a state of nature, kept their promises, honored their obligations, and lived a mostly peaceful, good, and pleasant existence. We had tampered with the natural order and the only solution was to free the mice and let them duke it out on their own. It was survival of the fittest time and it was also time to get the damn mother out of the house, because her keening wail was *so* bad that had Jonathan Demme heard it, he would've named the movie *The Silence of the Mice*.

My sister and I grabbed the tank and stumbled over the snow-covered grass into the woods behind our house. We then hurled its contents, ran back into the house, locked all the doors, and re-paged my mother at the mall to tell her that we had indeed handled the problem. She was eating when she phoned back and from the sound of the alternating crunch and slerve, it was pretty clear she had just pilfered a handful of free samples from the cheese shop.

"We dumped the tank in the woods. This way they can figure it out themselves."

"You did what?!" she yelled.

As she snacked on wasa bread slathered with Brie, I continued, "It was Hobbesian, Mom. We had to return them to their state of nature, to the place that they had come from."

To which my mother replied somewhat angrily, "They came from a pet store!"

"But they're back in a state of nature now," I cried.

"Go out there right now and try to find them," she said.

Clearly my mother had never seen a baby mouse, because finding a baby mouse in the woods was like trying to find a severed penis in a rubber factory. It wasn't going to happen.

"Mom, it's over. We're letting nature take over," I said.

"Nature my ass! You threw them away and you let them die!" she screamed.

"They were bloody and gross, and the dad tried to attack us!" I argued.

"It was the size of your finger!"

Which was true, but she hadn't been there.

My mom was pissed and Jenny was suddenly back pedaling. She grabbed the phone and yelled, "The whole 'throw 'em in the woods' thing was Kristen's idea!"

I grabbed the phone back, "I had no choice! Jenny didn't help!"

"She's seven!" my mother countered.

And while my mother continued to rip me a new one I glanced over and saw that Stacie had just returned home from what was clearly a night of debauchery. While my mother droned on about common sense and responsibility toward all living creatures, Stacie pulled out her beloved Polynesian sauce and a plate of cold leftover meat. Convincing my mother that I had done the right thing was futile, so I remained silent and just watched Stacie, as she stood over the kitchen island eating her own personal breakfast of champions.

My mother's voice rang out through the tinny receiver, "You've got blood on your hands, missy!"

Yet, Stacie seemed unfazed. Sensing my defeat at the hands of something bigger than myself, Stacie handed me a chunk of cold chicken, dripping in Polynesian sauce. And even though I found the confluence of textures and flavors to be disgusting, I have to admit, I really appreciated the gesture.

9. tHE EXtERMINAtOR

BY THE TIME I WAS THIRTEEN, my dad had moved to South Jersey and was in the middle of his Country Doctor meets Equestrian Tycoon phase. This trumped the Pimp My Ride meets The Old Man and The Sea phase, yet seemed tangentially related to the Tanya Tucker/Cowboy-hat-wearing phase, which had transpired several years earlier.

I was sweating the fact that I had to go down there for my summer sentence, for the usual reason (i.e. Ming) and also because the backyard was literally a training track and the stench of horseshit wafted through the house all day long. But as they say, timing is everything, and just as my sentence was due to begin my mom made a rather startling discovery: Lee and Jenny had a twelve-year-old brother still in Korea. His name was Nak Ho and he lived in an orphanage in the southernmost part of the country. An expert in the art of the excuse, I promptly told my dad I couldn't come because I had to help my mom spring an orphan from the grips of Southeast Asia. I expected a bit of a fight on his part, but for whatever reason, he didn't protest. I should have probably been hurt, but I was too preoccupied with the fact that my mom had been on a secret search for Nak Ho for quite some time.

Apparently my brother Lee had told her years earlier that

he had another brother in Korea. My mom had not forgotten this and after Lee and Jenny became citizens, she began to search for their brother without the fear that any surviving members of their family might try to take them back. It took years, but finally, one summer afternoon, a letter arrived detailing Nak's existence. Nak was the third child in a family of seven. After the death of the mother, the extended family took the four older children, but the three youngest children were placed in an orphanage. The ultimate tragedy was that the orphanage did not tell my mom about Nak because they feared she would not take Jenny and Lee. The irony was that had she known there were three kids instead of just two, she would have taken them all in a heartbeat. In the thirty seconds it took to read the letter and process the information, my mom informed my stepdad that another child would be coming into the fold. As she said, "The minute I saw his name written on that letter, he became my son."

It was not up for discussion; it was the only thing that could be done. It was her duty to Lee, Jenny, and Nak's birth mother, to reunite those three forsaken children and restore some cosmic order to the horror that had befallen their family after her death and the subsequent death of her husband, who was rumored to have been mentally ill.

My mother wasted no time in arranging for Nak's adoption. And while she haggled with the orphanage and bribed every Korean diplomat she could find, we speculated about our newly found brother-to-be.

The general consensus was that he was a Korean version of *Pony Boy* from the S.E. Hinton classic *The Outsiders*. We pictured him as a tall, leather-jacket-wearing, cigarette-smoking survivor-type, who wrote poetry and "stayed gold" while he fought turf wars with rival orphanages for power and respect. So what if he was only twelve? Life in the orphanage must have made him wise beyond his years. When a letter finally arrived from Korea bearing photos of him, we gathered around excitedly to see if we were right. There were three black and white photos that featured Nak standing at attention in front of a cement wall. He was dressed in some sort of quasi-military uniform, festooned with a lot of shiny brass buttons. We were barely able to mask our disappointment. Honestly, we had been hoping for a little more James Dean circa *Rebel Without a Cause*, or Elvis circa *Jailhouse Rock*. But the photos were nothing like that. They had a stoic Cold War vibe to them, which led us all to believe that Nak was really being held prisoner by Chinese Communists.

"Judging from the yellowish teeth, he's definitely a smoker," noted Jenny. We all nodded our heads, clinging to the some last vestige of our Pony Boy fantasy.

Eventually, Nak was sprung from the orphanage. Visas were secured, flights were booked, and Nak was flown to JFK to reunite with his long lost brother and sister and his new sisters, Stacie and me. And once again, I found myself standing in an airport, waiting to meet a new sibling. Jenny and Lee were both very excited, mostly because they had deluded themselves into believing that the quasi-military uniform had been a costume and that Nak would emerge in a leather jacket with a tattered copy of Robert Frost poems tucked under his arms.

And so it was a great shock for all of us when Nak stepped off the plane, barely four feet tall, wizened, skinny, nearly bald and encumbered with major dental issues.

"Where's his leather jacket?" Jenny cried out in disgust.

"How come he's so short!" yelled Lee because as usual, he had forgotten to turn on his hearing aids. My mother, of course, shushed us all.

"He doesn't speak a word of English," said Stacie.

But my mom pointed out that, much like our dog, "He can understand tone!"

I can't imagine what Nak was feeling, but I suppose it's safe to say that overwhelmed barely came close. I figured he was having some sort of epiphany about family and life and the randomness of fate. But when I asked him about it years later, he said he was just so overcome by the stench of cheese in the air that his main focus was not hurling.

When we finally got home, Nak climbed the stairs to his bedroom. At the sight of his new digs, he smiled a huge, beatific grin, which caused my mom to blurt out in horror, "My god, the teeth!" She had been too emotional at the airport to notice.

"Watch your tone, Mom!" we all shouted in his defense.

After that he proceeded to stand on his bed. And we all just stood there, unsure of his reasons. Was this some sort of Korean tradition? Then he handed us a small suitcase. Inside were a bunch of traditional Korean dresses. Jenny and I were thrilled. How considerate of Nak to shop for us before arriving and even though they weren't something we could wear on a daily basis, it showed that at the very least he had a sense of decorum. Nak looked like he was about to kill himself (this was because there had been a mix-up and the other older girl orphan on the plane had absconded with his suitcase which contained books, comics and candy), but we didn't care, the dresses were nice. In keeping with the pan-Asian feel of the night, my mom rang up Kung Pao Delight and ordered copious amounts of Chinese food while the rest of us showed Nak the bathroom. Nak turned on the faucet and stared at the water for a few moments and then relieved himself with the door open, which was unnerving, though not as unnerving as his refusal to flush. Lee took the bull by the horns, went in and flushed, and Nak jumped back from the toilet nervously as if he had broken it. We hustled him out of there and then spent a few minutes in his room staring at one another. The food arrived, thankfully, along with our Tae Kwon Do instructor, Master Bai, who was serving as our translator for the evening.

Of course, Nak didn't touch the food, which in retrospect was sort of like ordering French food for a Portuguese orphan. "It's all European," one could argue, but kimchee and lamen probably would've gone over better.

Nak sat at the table and pushed his food around, while my mother asked him questions that Master Bai would translate. Master Bai, we would later learn, was uncomfortable with the whole situation because Asians in general are not big fans of orphans, whom they find to be dirty and low class. But we were too busy trying to pump him for info to see the ill effects of classism at play.

My mother asked Nak what he liked to eat and he answered rice. She asked him if there was anything he wanted to try food wise. My money was on lasagne, but he surprised us all with chicken.

And finally, she asked him what he would like to be when he grew up and he replied, "A priest," which made us all groan in unison. Though my mother remained upbeat, saying, "No worries, we'll knock that out of him."

My mother asked if there was anything Nak wanted to know, and he asked Master Bai two pointed questions: "When is the driver leaving? And why is he eating with us?"

We all wondered for a moment who he was talking about and then my mom realized he was referring to our stepdad. Master Bai politely explained that Lester was not the driver but rather his new American father. My mom found this to be hilariously funny. My stepdad wasn't quite as amused, but dealt with it. Nak arrived on a Thursday and started school the following Monday. I was really freaked out that he was going to start telling everyone about his deep desire to become a priest and coupled with his diminutive stature, I foresaw a long line of ass-kickings in his future. I was in the eighth grade and he was in the seventh and I spread the word through my Lost Boys (who had long since forgiven me for my trespasses) that anyone who picked on my brother was dead meat. At least once each class, I would get up to go to the bathroom and run to the seventh grade wing to make sure they weren't persecuting my dentally impaired, pious, urchin brother. Strangely enough, there were never any signs of trouble. In fact, he was usually surrounded by classmates, who would stare excitedly while Nak performed sleight of hand games that bore a striking resemblance to Three Card Monty. I heard him say "fuck" constantly but this would only elicit smiles from his teachers, who were so delighted by the fact that he could read Korean above his grade level, they had no problem with his burgeoning potty mouth. In addition, Nak began teaching the kids Korean phrases, the big favorite being "*manjee bajee*," which loosely translated meant "horse penis," although I think Nak told them it meant something more along the lines of a ninny. After that, his teacher would often say, "Oh, what a silly manjee bajee I am," which of course would set the entire class into hysterics. Despite his size, he was adept at muscling lunch out of other kids and was feasting daily on meatball sandwiches, homemade cake and Yoo Hoo. I sensed something was going on, but I couldn't put my finger on it. Each day, we'd walk home from school together and I'd ask, "Hakio, okay?" which meant "School, okay?" in Korean. He'd nod his head yes and say, "Hakio, good." And that was pretty much it. But I had been living a double life long enough to know a phony when I saw one. I wasn't buying the innocent urchin schtick. My suspicions extended into the home, where there was a sudden influx of candy, comic books, Matchbox cars, and Bic pens. I saw that Jenny was often running around, fetching things for Nak and when she emerged from his room, she'd have a dollar in her hand, or a Hershey bar. In addition, Lee seemed to always have packs of Lifesavers in his pocket. *Where was all this swag coming from?* I wondered.

I began to watch Nak closely, tailing him when we went to the store. Lo and behold, I found my answer. Much to my delight, I learned that in addition to being a stellar shoplifter,

Nak was a skilled pickpocket. It was great news because the thought of having a brother who was a priest (unless of course he was of the Marxist variety à la Oscar Romero) had filled me with dread. I told Nak that his secret was safe with me. Even Jenny was delighted. "He really is like Pony Boy!" We wanted to know more and forced him to explain what was going on. Though his English was broken, we managed to piece it all together. Before he had left for America, the higher-ups at the orphanage had explained to him that Americans expect their orphans to behave in a certain way. It boiled down to a list of bullet points that went something like this:

- *Act stupid and innocent.*
- *Stand on the bed as if you don't know what to do with it.*
- *Don't flush the toilet. When asked why, explain because you think you might break it.*
- *Never admit that you want to eat the dog.*
- *Tell everyone you meet that you want to be a priest when you grow up.*

Nak had tried to toe the line, but he had an intense disdain for authority. Keeping up the undernourished, orphan routine just wasn't his thing. And while he did his best to keep my mother convinced, he let it all hang out with us and wasted no time in telling us that he, in fact, wanted to eat the dog. We made him promise not to kill her and he said he'd wait until she died of natural causes to do the deed, which we appreciated. Of course my mother had no clue. She was too busy juggling five kids to really have a feel for Nak's double life and we were awash in candy and anything else he could fit in his pocket and didn't want to blow the groove.

But Nak was still the newest baby and as such, he was reaping the rewards of showing up six years late with basically just the shirt on his back. Once a week, my mom would take him to the Korean market in Fort Lee, where Nak would buy jars of kimchee and bags of salted tilefish. Then they'd head to NYC to the Korean equivalent of Womrath's bookstore, where Nak would play the "I've got nothing" card and my mom would indulge him and overbuy. Nak became quite the discerning consumer. Suddenly, he refused to wear Wrangler or Lee jeans; it was Levis or nothing. And he had to have the $70 pair of Pumas because last season's half-price Adidas that were suitable for us, were way beneath him. As his consumerism grew, so did his love of American pop-culture. He was obsessed with the *Rocky* movie series, Eric von Lustbader novels (in Korean of course), Bo Derek, and strangely enough, Jethro Tull.

As Christmas time rolled around, I began to think that maybe I could ride the wave of Nak's consumerism. Preppy was in at the time and the Lodge at Harvard Square, with its fabulous selection of wide-wale cords, was like heroin to me. I figured if I could get Nak on the bandwagon, I had a shot at getting a few extra pairs during their after-Christmas sale. And so I splurged and bought him the *Official Preppy Guidebook* by Lisa Birnback, who would later go on to infamy when she was fingered by Alex Kuczynski as the nasty Mrs. X of *The Nanny Diaries*. (Interestingly enough, I would later work for Alex's friend and then for Birnback's then husband, thus proving that my entire life flows with the circadian rhythm of a *Seinfeld* episode.) I even brought him to the Lodge, but his response was something like, "Only a fucking loser be caught dead in that fucking shit," thus dashing my dreams of an after-Christmas-sale pillage.

Nak seemed to love all things American, but the one thing he couldn't get used to was calling people by their given names. In Korea, they have always had huge issues with names and in an effort to create some sort of pecking order that's somehow related to Confucian hierarchy, people don't refer to one another by their given names. As a result, Nak didn't feel comfortable with the American world of casual name use, so he began making up names for people.

The kids on our street were renamed Fat Lip, Banana Head, and Death Breath. Friends from school were Pumpkin, Steak, Porky, Geek, and Fly. At home, my mom was Don Quixote, I was Sludgy, Stacie was Large, Jenny was Shorty, and Lee was Peanut. Even my stepdad's eighty-year-old aunt was not immune. Nak renamed her E.T. In fairness, she bore an incredibly striking resemblance and we often wondered why we hadn't noticed it sooner. The name stuck, even my mom and my stepdad used it. But poor E.T. had been in an altercation with an ice cream truck (in which the truck emerged as victor) and wasn't working with a full deck. No matter how many times my stepdad tried to explain Nak's presence, she just couldn't wrap her head around it. To add insult to injury, Nak loved to act like he was a retard whenever E.T. came over. We'd sit in the living room while my mom made dinner and Nak would do impressions of the mentally challenged while E.T. eyeballed him nervously. During dinner, she'd always lean over at some point and ask about "the little Chinaman," and while my mother attempted to explain the situation for the millionth time, Nak would pretend he had epilepsy, scream "manjee bajee," and fling himself off the chair. My mother would ignore this behavior, but it was becoming increasingly clear that the rube in the woods orphan schtick was just that. Nak may have been a country bumpkin, but rather than being of the toothless inbred ilk, he was of the Huck Finn variety. And like Huck, Nak had had many adventures in his short life. He told us all about the orphanage and how he was set apart from the other kids because his parents had died, rather than given him up. This distinction enabled him to keep his surname, which bought him a certain level of respect from the staff and the other orphans because he was the real deal. According to Nak, the orphanage was a rough and tumble place, filled with mean older kids who took advantage of the younger ones, but as he got older, he became part of the hierarchy and ran things his own way. Interestingly enough, the orphans were big on pranks, the favorite being the time honored "stinky melon" trick, the veritable *Dirty Sanchez* of fruit pranks. For this prank, a party was sent out in the middle of the night to steal a watermelon from one of the neighboring farms. A small hole would be placed in the side and the contents of the melon pulled out by the younger kids. Once they finished, the older kids would take turns crapping inside the melon. When it was full, the hole would be plugged back up with the rind. Then the melon was placed in the staff kitchen, where it would be served with the next day's staff breakfast. My brother said nothing had filled him and his fellow orphans with more joy than hearing the screams from the staff dining room, as they sat eating their bowls of shitty, bug-laden brown rice. And even though they'd get beaten for it, my brother said it was well worth it. Plus precautions would have been taken and they'd pad their pants with books so that when the stick hit them, they felt no pain, though they would have contests to see who could pretend to be in the most pain during the beatings, with awards given for best dramatic performance.

He told us how he'd create diversions in order to steal food and how he learned to pickpocket when he had run away to Seoul at the tender age of seven. We begged him to teach us and soon we all got in on the action, though we stuck to shoplifting because it was easier. Within weeks, there was a raging stolen swag ring going on in the house. My mother found out what was going on and was horrified, but decided not to make too big a deal out of it. She gave Nak an allowance and watched him like a hawk in stores, but he could still manage to come out with something. He was just that good. Ultimately, my mom felt he had to make the choice himself and after a run on Rolaids and a bout of serious constipation, his thieving ended.

*

Of course, as all of this was going on, my folks had made arrangements to redo the kitchen *and* fix the roof. Given our past history with home improvement, I found their naiveté to be a bit annoying. By week two, the contractor had disappeared and by December, the pipes had frozen. This was an enormous problem because we were suddenly unable to let any water go down the pipes, though I've never really been able to ascertain why this was so. The end result was that we had to put buckets in the sink to wash the dishes. When the water in the bucket became too funky to use, we had to carry it through the dining room, onto the porch and throw it over the railing, down onto the backyard. Had Nak not been here, we might have crumbled, but he rallied us all and developed an ingenious bucket passing method that we used for months.

During this time, we also had torrential rains. Our lawn was transformed into a swamp and our roof sprung numerous leaks. Once again, Nak came through. Not only did he rescue many a deliveryman from the yard, he could move the Scandinavian sectional and insert water-catching trays, in a matter of seconds. But while he was handy and unafraid of the elements, he began to pepper my mom with questions about our surroundings.

"Why this fucking house so much a fucking dump?" he'd ask.

"Why you fucking no lease a fucking Saab?" or "Why we have no big fucking TV?"

My mother would roll her eyes and blame Nak's newfound quest for upward mobility on the power of advertising. But we were happy to have him asking the questions that were on all our minds. Nak's issues didn't just end with the house and the car; he had problems with my sister Jenny. In his opinion she was lazy and spoiled. "She fucking needs a fucking kick in the ass," he'd say. My mom would try to explain that Jenny's feisty personality was what enabled her to beat smallpox and that we had to embrace everyone in the family for who they were, not who we wanted them to be.

"She's fucking rude, ma. Never pays attention, fucking have to tell her things ten times," he'd grumble.

"She's not rude. She's hard of hearing and she misses things."

"It's bullshit, ma, she's faking it. If she fucking deaf, how come she doesn't sound like that fucking lady from *Children of a Lesser* fucking *God*?"

My mother would sigh and then explain how Jenny and Lee both had low frequency hearing loss and because of this they did not speak with any guttural inflection. And it was for this reason that people often mistook their cluelessness for rudeness.

"Totally fucking faking, ma," was his typical response.

Ultimately, my mom got to the true source of Nak's anger and figured out that the big issue he had with Jenny was that she called him by his name. This of course was a big no-no in the Korean world. Younger sisters were to respect their older brothers and call them "Hyung" which means "Older brother." My mom asked him where Don Quixote fit into the respect pyramid, but he argued that Don was a quintessential fictional hero and that his name for her was indeed a term of endearment and respect, although he said it something like this, "He's fucking cool, ma, fucking great fucking book and fucking funny too and fucking classic." My mom told him to get over it and reminded him that there were a lot worse things you could be called than your name. Nak stopped complaining about it, but when spring came, he began going on long walks. He'd disappear for a few hours, then come back noshing on fruit. It all seemed sort of innocuous, but what we didn't know was that Nak was doing recon work, scouting the neighborhood for fruit trees in what was to become a larger master plan to break Jenny. Once his recon work was done, he began waking up Jenny in the middle of the night. The two of them, armed with just a flashlight and a hefty bag, would then pilfer fruit off all the trees in the area. After a few weeks, the local fruit ran out and they moved on to nearby farms, clearing out inventories of cherries, apples and the occasional zucchini, which Nak liked to eat raw. Jenny resented being Nak's workhorse. Exhausted from hauling back massive green garbage bags filled with fruit, she began lobbying hard for Nak's return to Korea.

"Send him back!" she'd yell. My mother wouldn't have any of it. "Don't be ridiculous, we're not sending him back. He's part of our family."

"He can come back for holidays, we'll buy him plenty of gifts and it'll be fine."

"Stop it Jennifer!"

"The Chinaman must go!"

My mother was puzzled by Jenny's newfound hatred of Nak, mostly because she gave no explanations. I always suspected that it was her love of free produce that kept her from spilling the beans about the fruit (which was hidden in the crawlspace in the basement) though it was hard to say. Still, Nak continued to torture Jenny, dragging her out night after night, until finally some sort of Stockholm Syndrome kicked in. She became his minion, waking *him* up nightly, even suggesting they branch out to local greenhouses. Nak felt that his work was done and pulled the plug on the fruit raids, but this drove Jenny mad and with nowhere else left to turn, she finally admitted her dark secret to me. Suddenly, I understood why all the fruit trees in the neighborhood were barren. My mom ended up finding the bags of rotting fruit, but rather than being angry, she found Nak's raiding to be endearing. She even bragged to her friends about his stellar agrarian skills. Her friends would stop by and marvel at the sight of the bags of fruit that were heaped in our crawl space. They would say things like,

"Clearly, this must be the first step in the canning process," and, "The cool basement temperature must act as a natural refrigerator."

My stepdad was sort of delighted because he was always getting mad at us for our copious consumption of fruit. At the time, Lester had merged several diets into one mother of all colon-blow diet, which he was convinced was going to be the ultimate answer to his weight loss struggles. The diet was fairly simple and involved the exclusive consumption of fruit, diet soda and vats of air-popped popcorn.

"These kids eat too much damn fruit!" he'd yell.

"They could be mainlining heroin! Let them have their fruit!" my mom would yell back. In an effort to maintain his diet, Lester began hoarding fruit in his sock drawer, which was a major deterrent as there was no way any of us were going to eat a pear that had touched one of his black nylon stocking socks. But here was his new son, contributing to the fold. Money didn't grow on trees, but fruit did. "Steal away!" he'd yell as he fired up the air popper. "Finally, someone in this family's looking to save me money!"

But Nak wasn't looking to can peaches or save money; he was trying to make moonshine. The only problem was that he couldn't remember the name of the key ingredient, namely yeast. And without it, the fruit began to rot. The explosion of fruit flies probably should have been our first clue that it was time to clear out the bags, but we followed the First Rule of Dog Poop and ignored it. Of course the stench was completely drowned out by the smell of kimchee, so none of us realized that we were sitting on a serious time bomb, until we started to notice strange gnawing sounds emanating from the walls throughout the house. And we soon realized that we had rats.

Mired in denial, we removed all the bags of fruit and put them in the garbage cans in the garage, thinking this would somehow remedy the situation. Then we went back to our lives, hoping to live as one with our rodent friends. It didn't help that Jenny kept referencing *Mrs. Frisby and the Rats of Nimh*. Soon enough, we deluded ourselves into thinking that the rats had built a library inside our walls and were working hard to save a single-mouse mother and her kids. We envisioned a certain warped simpatico. With any luck, this breed of super genius rats would be kind to us and maybe even fix our kitchen. Sadly, the only thing they did was crap on our kitchen floor while we slept. Eventually, my mother's fear of Black Plague won out and an exterminator was called in. Rich the Ratman showed up in his yellow rat-van around dinnertime. He took a quick look around the house and then went into the garage where he found an entire garbage pail full of dead baby rats.

Moments later he screeched out of our driveway, shouting, "You're on your own!"

My mom later phoned Ratman's wife and partner to complain. Mrs. Ratman explained that from what the Ratman had seen, we had the worst case of rat infestation in the history of Northern New Jersey. And while other people might have been mortified, we were actually impressed. Still, we were all alone. Even the cat sensed her own mortality and moved out.

And so began our personal battle against rodents. We didn't just jump in. We did what any family facing the worst infestation in history would do: We went to the library and boned up on rat history. Friends at school became alarmed by our sudden interest in rats, as we spouted recently acquired facts and statistics, in what was an effort to avoid the inevitable fight ahead of us.

"China is where the rat originated and where you can find it on restaurant menus," I pointed out in Geography class.

"Rats have eaten cadavers in the New York City coroner's office. They've also attacked and killed homeless people sleeping on the streets of Manhattan," my sister Jenny explained during second grade Current Events.

"There are more rodents currently infected with plague in North America than there were in Europe at the time of the Black Death!" Lee shouted out during gym.

Nak took it to another level and turned into Quint from *Jaws*. Each day he'd regale his minions with rat anecdotes gleaned from his copious rodentia studies. "Rats that fuckin' survive to fuckin' four are the fuckin' smartest creatures on Earth," he'd tell them. "A trap don't mean nothin' to them. They'll fuckin' kick it around until the fucker snaps, then they eat lotta bait. And they fuckin' know it's poisoned, man. Fuckers can fucking read."

All the kids would be hanging on the edge of their seats. Nak would pause, take a piece of salted tilefish from his pocket, for dramatic effect no doubt, and continue.

"A fuckin' sniper with a fuckin' night-vision scope, that's the only way to kill a fuckin' rat."

Sadly, we weren't able to get our hand on night-vision goggles. Though the truth is, when waging a personal battle against rodents, it is important to remember that you are dealing with an animal that is capable of crawling, climbing, and chewing its way into your home. They can flatten themselves out and squeeze through the smallest of openings, even under closed doors. If the hole is not big enough, they can easily chew it or gnaw it to a large enough size so that they can get through. Generally, if a rodent can squeeze its head through an opening (most rodents' heads are the size of a quarter or smaller), it will eventually get through. This is why any strategy for rat control always starts on the outside of the structure. This meant there was only one solution: Much like the sixth century Christians had done with oversexed girls, we were going to get medieval on their asses and wall them in.

Step one was to shove copper wool into every crevice.

Once that was complete, we cleaned the inside of the house to within an inch of its life, so that there was no place to hide. Then we were ready to get down to business. Our arsenal included a wide assortment of glue boards, rat traps, and bait sticks. We had shovels of various sizes, ranging from the garden variety to those reserved for horse manure. Nak had also fashioned an array of homemade weapons and traps, most of which were lampshades attached to broom sticks. We were scared, but we had Nak and even though he was partially responsible for our predicament (although one could argue it was Jenny's fault for getting Stockholm Syndrome and thus enhancing our crop of fruit bags), we knew that he could lead us out of it. We had one final meeting before we began our battle. Nak reminded us that whenever we saw a rat, it would be a weak one, forced into the open to look for food, because the strong ones stayed out of sight. It was time to fight. In the immortal paraphrased words of General MacArthur, Nak rallied us, "When you fucking get in there, you'll fucking know what to do!" And everyone knew their role. Jenny was the visual lookout. I was the aural lookout. Lee was Nak's first mate in charge of caring for all weaponry. My mother, armed with a pair of yellow rubber gloves and a shovel, was clean up. And Nak, of course, was the exterminator. Lester chose to sit this battle out and remained holed up in his bedroom as a sort of surviving witness in the event the rats won.

And with that, we got to work.

We'd lure the rat out with bananas and water and then wall it off with Nak's patented steel wool fence of death. Lee would move in with the lampshade and trap it. Nak would move in for the kill and bonk the rat over the head with a rolling pin, then my mom would scoop the thing up, dump it in a garbage bag and just like that it was one down. We had traps everywhere but we mixed it up, never letting the rats get too comfortable – glue traps, light traps, rat houses, poison water. But they were good. They sensed a worthy adversary and made us work. A few even tried the *Tom and Jerry* move, during which they would run under the carpet, trying to see if they could out duel us cartoon-style. Nak and Lee would follow the moving bump and then – *BLAM* – sock it with a blunt instrument, no doubt causing the impish rodent to see stars and small orbiting circles over its head, before collapsing in a heap. Jenny and I would lift the carpet and my mom would remove the funny little bastard.

This went on for months. We fought the good fight together. Digging in, fortifying the hatches, and not telling a damn person outside the inner circle of the family what was really going on. We understood our enemy; we knew where they would run and how they would think. We were like Rat Profilers and Nak was the rogue assassin. *Rambo* became his personal hero. He started whispering, "I'll give you a fight you won't believe," before beating various rats into submission. This went on, until finally, the rats were defeated. With nowhere left to run and nowhere left to hide, the surviving few packed up their library books and hit the road.

The only collateral damage, aside from the fact that we needed new carpeting, was that some of the rotting fruit in the garage had spawned a colony of large white moths. As part of the walling-in process, we had placed plastic over the garage doors and the result was a greenhouse-like warming effect that made the moths grow in size and number until the garage was nothing but a blur of fluttering wings. Of course, we had bigger fish to fry and so for months, we chose to ignore the Hitchcock-like swarm festering in the garage. But now that the rats were gone, it was time to do something about them. Tired and exhausted, we gathered together on our driveway to formulate our next plan of attack. It was a beautiful, clear November day and nearly a year since Nak had come from Korea. As such, my mom turned the floor over to him. He had led us so brilliantly against the rats; surely he would have some idea what to do. "Let's burn the fucking house down," was his first suggestion. But my mom felt we wouldn't get a good deal on the insurance. We stood there, eyeballing the frenzy of activity through the garage window, when Jenny spotted a group of Jehovah's Witnesses heading up our block. And all at once it came to us. In a moment of familial synchronicity and lapsed Catholic self-preservation, we tore off the sheets of plastic covering the garage doors and yanked them wide open. We crouched down as the moths flew out in a sea of white, heading toward the Jehovah's Witnesses, who saw the approaching storm of pestilence and began to run screaming. And as Jenny, Lee, and I embraced in a giddy, pest-free hug, Nak turned to our mother and cried happily, "Only in America, Ma!"

10. JENNY WREN

WHEN A CHILD NEARLY DIES, something strange happens to the mother–child dynamic. Basically, the surviving child becomes a most favored child, one that can really do no wrong. Ever. I almost achieved this status with my mother. When I was four, she and I were in a terrible car accident in which an eighteen-wheeler, being driven by a drunk, sleeping driver, careened into our orange VW wagon, which was stopped at a red light just in front of a gas station. Moments earlier, I had climbed out of my booster seat and was waving to the driver of the car just behind us. My mom told me repeatedly to get back into the seat, but for some reason I didn't feel that following her advice was prudent. Seconds later, the eighteen-wheeler struck our car, with my now empty seat being the point of impact. We spun into the gas station, narrowly missing the pumps, and when we finally stopped, the car had been totaled, my mom's back was broken and I was trapped beneath the backseat. It was very harrowing. The firemen came with the Jaws of Life; a priest was called for last rites. Everyone thought we were both dead. But alas, we were not. In disobeying my mom I had survived, but it sort of took away from the "most favored" glory of it all, because I hadn't almost died as much as I just cheated death. As such, life moved on and my status didn't change. But my sister Jenny was a different story. She won the coveted most favored slot on account of the fact that she contracted smallpox en route to the United States. Coupled with a case of severe depression, which was not unusual for orphan babies, she was literally on death's door upon her arrival. My mother had lost her first child, my sister Mardy, and there was no way she was going to lose another. It didn't matter that the doctors, including my father, told her in no uncertain terms that Jenny was going to die.

"I'm giving Death the finger," she told them all as she marched out of the hospital with my sister in her arms. And in her usual unorthodox fashion, my mom did not seek out a second opinion, bang down the door of immunology specialists, or consult with religious types; instead, she turned to Joan Collins for inspiration. During one of her many Sundays spent perusing the entire Sunday *Times* (in her bathrobe), my mom had read a story about Joan Collins and her daughter who had been hit by a car and was in a coma. The doctors felt it was hopeless, but Joan never left her daughter Katyana's side. According to Joan, the "power of touch" was responsible for bringing her daughter Katyana out of the coma. My mom felt that she could take this Collins technique and put it to use to save Jenny. But since Jenny was not in a coma and was rather small, my mother vowed quite simply to never put her down. Jenny became a veritable appendage. My mom bathed with her, slept with her, went to the bathroom with her, ate with her, even drove with her. Jenny was like a little monkey, clinging to my mom for dear life. Knowing that my mom wasn't going to budge, Death eventually gave up the pursuit and left. And with each passing week, Jenny grew stronger and healthier. The doctors were all amazed and spent a great deal of time patting my mom on the back for her efforts, but true to form, my mom gave all the credit to Jenny's foul determinism. For years afterwards, when Jenny would get in one her moods and steal my food, or sneer at me, or kick me for no apparent reason, my mom would always stick up for her, "My little Jenny is a fighter. That's the spirit that kept her alive. So don't knock it."

And while we were all fighters to a certain degree, I tended to identify with larger than life characters like Alice Roosevelt and Joan of Arc. But the heroic character that Jenny most identified with was Jerry the Mouse. Like Jerry, Jen was an impish schemer, always happy to mind her own business until cornered, piqued, or generally provoked. And though she was small, she packed a serious punch, both physically and mentally. Coupled with this strong physical presence was an underlying disdain for the bourgeois suburban lifestyle. Jenny liked the yard big and wild. She had no interest in joining the tennis club or having a fancy house. She didn't care about hardwood floors or matching towel sets. In fact, the more outlandish it was the better. All that mattered to her were books, the rest was superfluous. It was all about having a rich life of the mind for Jenny, who fancied herself a cross between Harold Bloom and some long lost member of the Glass family. Moreover, she had a litany of complaints against suburban life and all that went with it. Riding bikes was for losers. Organized games like Tag, Hide and Go-Seek and Red Light-Green Light smacked of bureaucratic authoritarianism and she would have no part in them – unless of course she was put in charge – in which case she ran things with an iron hand. But coupled with this disdain for typical childhood pleasures was a strange affection for nature. She renamed trees, ponds, areas near ponds, and the groups of pebbles congregating around said ponds. The Trees That Look Like Fishing Rods. The Sweaty Bog. The Mossy Netherland. The Lumpy Pile. While other kids wanted to run around and play, Jenny preferred to spend her free time on a giant boulder located at the end of our street that she liked to call The Peaceful Hump.

Back in my day, kids roamed the streets like wolves and

no one really worried about things like pederasts or kidnapping. The scariest thing ever was the Son of Sam, but he never hit New Jersey and I was the only who ever really lost sleep worrying about him.

On most days, Jenny, who was nine at the time, could be found on the Hump, playing with her eclectic assortment of bric-a-brac that she dragged around with her in a small red wagon. This assortment included tarnished candlestick holders, rusted scissors, a small wine glass, a cracked ashtray or two and a small African fertility statue that was missing a hand. She also spent hours reading her tattered copy of *The Far Side,* chuckling to herself over the twisted irony. If anyone suggested that she get off the Peaceful Hump and come play hide-and-seek, she would yell, "Simple pleasures are for simple minds!"

Jenny's best friend in the neighborhood was a boy named Fat Lip (so named by Nak of course). Jenny's idea of friendship meant bossing people around and Fat Lip was her willing slave. She would often make him sit on the Peaceful Hump and peruse old photo albums. Jenny would ask, "Wasn't I adorable?" and Fat Lip would have to agree, somewhat enthusiastically, or else Jenny would hit him. Fat Lip also allowed Jenny to dress him in girl's clothing, complete with hair and make-up that would have put many a 10th Avenue tranny to shame. There was a nice mixture of friendship fused with fear between them and they were inseparable. I think Fat Lip understood Jenny in a way most kids didn't. He would often say to my mother, "She's a really good person deep down." We were too scared of her to argue.

My mother found Jenny's brand of insouciance to be delightful, except when she did things like lose a single shoe on the way home from school, which happened on more than one occasion. She'd arrive home with the single shoe and not even say anything about it for days until finally, the school would phone my mother and ask why it was that Jenny was coming to school in a single shoe, and my mother would lose her mind and start screaming. But instead of being upset, or frantically searching for the shoe (that was my job), Jenny would just shrug it off, head over to the Peaceful Hump, or The Mossy Everglade, or the Lumpy Mound of Turd-like Pebbles and read some Elizabeth Barrett Browning poems.

Jenny's big dream, aside from moving into a ten bedroom pre-war in Manhattan, was to have a pet of her own. Everyone knew this, but we already had dogs, a runaway cat, and a dead snake. The menagerie seemed to be big enough. But when Fat Lip suggested to my mother that she should buy Jenny a few rabbits, which I'm certain Jenny put him up to, she couldn't say no. After all, what mother could refuse an eight-year-old boy in a purple ball gown, nattily accessorized with fake pearl clip-on earrings?

It was nearly Easter and the stores were brimming with rabbits. Of course I warned my mother that rabbits could not be trusted and even suggested that she read the bunny-centric epic, *Watership Down*, but her mind was made up.

"Little Jenny Wren is getting her rabbits," she said.

The man at the store suggested a cage, but my mother wouldn't have it. Rabbits in a state of nature did not live in cages, why would ours? We brought them home in a large shoebox. There were two of them. One grey, the other black and they were welcomed into our family, where the hope was that we could live together in peaceful harmony. Flying in the face of family tradition, Jenny named the rabbits Pookie and Odie, after the *Garfield* characters. It was a decidedly lowbrow move on her part, as we normally named all pets after great historical figures.

"You're allowing these substandard pet names?" I asked my mom. "Next thing you know we're going to have a dog named Spot."

"She's going for irony, don't you see that?" snapped my

mom, who was unwilling to see anything negative when it came to her youngest and most favorite child.

Odie and Pookie were moved into Jenny's room and, judging from their uncontrollable shaking, seemed ill at ease with this new cage-free approach to living. Stressed out and of the same sex, they proceeded to do the other thing that rabbits do best; they shat everywhere. My mom found the firm turds manageable, but after a few hours, the rabbits walled themselves into Jenny's closet and refused to come out. Apparently the free-range life was not for them. Even Jenny seemed disappointed with the whole endeavor. And sadly, the rabbits were dead within days. According to my mother, the pet store was selling diseased rabbits and she made a big stink about the whole thing. Meanwhile, while Jenny was not a believer in the Immaculate Conception (her theory being that Mary was hit over the head and didn't remember having sex, which, it should be noted, she blurted out quite loudly during the rather solemn Mary, Mother of Jesus exhibit at the Met), she was sort of intrigued by the notion of rebirth, so she decided that the rabbits should be buried with their heads sticking out of the ground, so that they could resurrect. We all told Jenny she was insane, but she didn't pay any attention. She forced Fat Lip to dig two very shallow graves and proceeded to stick the rabbits in each one, careful to leave their rigor mortis heads above ground. My mother felt this was Jenny's way of coping with the loss and allowed the dead rabbit heads to remain sticking out of the front lawn. But they were dangerously close to the walkway and for the better part of a week we were tripping over them as we carried groceries into the house or returned from school.

My mother finally had Nak remove the rabbits, under cover of darkness. The next morning, Jenny saw the empty holes, thought the rabbits had in fact resurrected and was insufferably smug insisting that we were all morons for not believing her in the first place.

Jenny was at peace with the loss of the rabbits, but my mom felt that she was still getting the short end of the stick. But there didn't seem to be much that Jenny wanted. Around the same time, there was a technological advance that promised to improve Jenny's life in ways she could not have begun to imagine. Closed-captioning boxes had just come out for mass-market consumption. This was a huge boon to deaf kids all over who could now spend countless hours watching TV and actually understand the dialogue. But television to my mother was literally Satan. We had grown up being told that it would rot your brain, put hair on your palms, and cause all sorts of debilitating illnesses. My mother would rather have us vivisect small animals in our spare time than watch TV. To prove her point, she had taken the only TV in the house and stuck it in her bedroom, where my stepdad held it hostage. He hid in his bedroom all night watching his favorite shows, while the rest of us could only dream of regular TV access. The beauty of closed-captioning was that the dialogue was printed at the bottom of the screen. This meant you weren't in fact *watching* TV, as much as you were *reading* TV, and this was something my mother could get behind. Jenny got her closed-captioning box; a new TV was purchased and promptly placed in my mom's bedroom. We got the old TV, but were too delirious with joy to even care. The only caveat was that we had to watch with the volume off. The house was small and my mom hated the noise. We were fine with the rule, after all, who needed volume when we had closed-captioning?! It was a brilliant move to gain access to television and we assured our mother that our reading scores on the Stanford 9 were going to be through the roof. And after getting her not so enthusiastic blessing, we began our new life as regular TV viewers.

We started with *Happy Days*, because word on the playground was that it was a popular show and we wanted to see what all the fuss was about. According to our closed-captioning, the show was really called *Harp Be Daze* and it was about a guy named Fong Zee who lived with the Cunning Ham family. The Cunning Hams had a daughter named Joe Knee, who was always sent to her room and they had a son named Rich He, who was sort of the nice guy everyone liked. We were confused by the quasi-Chinese names on the American kids and wondered if they weren't all related somehow to Arn Old, the Chinese owner of the local hangout. We were also puzzled why Fong Zee would always say, "Ehhhhhhhh," and we suspected that he might be Jewish. But Fong Zee had a super cute cousin, Cha Chi and in one episode, Fong Zee had to go an entire day without a piss to save Cha Chi's soul. It was all very confusing and we thought that there was some sort of Eastern religious metaphor that we were missing. We consulted my mom's tattered copy of the *Bhagavad-Gita*, but there was nothing in there about refraining from urination to save a soul. Nor was there any explanation why Fong Zee always wanted to "piss" the girls. It was much too confusing for us and we became concerned. Perhaps we weren't as smart as we had originally thought, because if all the other kids at school understood the subtle nuances of Harp Be Daze, what the hell did that say about us? We quickly turned to other shows, but found that often we would have the same problems. Especially confusing was when Michael Jackson was named Popeye Doll of the Year during the Grammys. What exactly was the Popeye Doll award and why didn't it involve any mention of Olive Oyl? We pondered the theme song to *Wonder Woman*, which went, "In your sad tin tights, fighting for your kites." What were these secret kites she was fighting for? When would the kite subplot be revealed? And when the 4:30 movie played *Moby Dick*, we gathered around the television, eager to read *Moby Dick* in its more palatable filmic version. We sat rapt, as Richard Baseheart stood alone on a hillside before starting his valley descent toward the sea. His voiceover declamation of Melville's first line "Commie

Ishmael" had a haunting resonance. We marveled at Melville's foreshadowing of the Cold War. How he knew the Communists would have such power and the fact that he had the foresight to make the Captain a communist impressed us greatly. But when we mentioned this to our mother, she just looked at us like we were idiots and said, "What the hell are you talking about?"

We smiled smugly to ourselves. What she didn't know was a lot. Television was heady stuff and we felt ourselves growing smarter by the day.

Soon the Olympics rolled around and we sat by the TV eager to read Jim Kay's brilliant commentary. The caption read, "Jim Kay reporting from the XVI Ol' Limp Pigs!"

"Ol' Limp Pigs!" we screamed. Was nothing sacred?! When had this name change been instituted? More importantly, why the folksy apostrophe? It wasn't as if the Olympics had been invented in Georgia. My sister was appalled and in a disparaging letter to the editor of the school newspaper, she drew a convincing trilateral connection between the Miss Teen Beauty Pageant, the renaming of the Olympics and the end of civilization as we knew it. The principal called my mother regarding the article. My sister's display of quasi-anarchist behavior was a bit of a red flag and after my suspension, they weren't taking any chances. My mother decided to get to the bottom of things and joined us for a round of television. Unaffected by the captioning kryptonite, she figured out the problem immediately.

Our brains were scrambled from the captioning, which was riddled with typos. After a bit of research, she learned that captioning was done phonetically, by non-English-speaking listeners. And though the TV and the Caption Box were removed from the house, we still suffered the lingering effects of phonetic bastardization. My brother Lee wrote a paper about Black Angus Cows, but entitled it Cows Named Black and Gus. Our mother's friend Sue

Gasteyer became Sue Gas on Tire. It took us months to get our fluency back. But when it did return, Jenny was still left with the proverbial short end of the stick. First the rabbits had died, then the captioning was a futz. The solution was simple; we were going back to animals. It was decided that she would get two cats of her own. They could shit in a box and it would all be great. My mother took over, adopted two cats of Jenny's choosing and after a family meeting that rivaled any Asian naming ceremony, it was decided that the cats would be called Vanessa and Vita. Vita was after the legendary lesbian and professional hat-wearer, Vita Sackville West. And Vanessa was after Vanessa Bell, Virginia Woolf's first cousin, gal pal to Alfred Lord Tennyson and a talented artist in her own right. With names like these, we were sure to avoid any early demise that went along with having a lowbrow pet name like Odie or Pookie. The cats settled in and everything was going swimmingly until "Nessa" fell off the porch. She never seemed right after that, but we didn't pay it much heed.

A few months later, I was roused from freshman algebra and told that I had to call my mother immediately. My math teacher, who was a very nervous man, made me wait until the end of class. Obviously algebra was more important than anything my mother could have wanted. But after class, I made my way to the pay phones and phoned home. My mother was frantic, talking a mile a minute, her Hudson County accent ratcheted up way high, which often happened when she was stressed. It was loud in the hallway and upperclassmen were jostling me.

"Kristen, you need to come home right after school," she said.

"But I'm supposed to stay after for math."

"No! Right away, I want you home. Lesta is dead."

My heart began to pound and my face turned white. My stepfather was dead?! How could this be? What had happened? And what would become of our yard?! I wasn't going back to a state of nature, dammit!

"What did you say?" was all I could manage.

"There's no time to explain. I've got to get to the city to meet Lou for dinner."

I tried to process. Lou was my mom's best friend and they often met in New York for dinner to discuss their work. Lou was working on a book about Virginia Woolf and my mother was in the heat of her dissertation, regarding the politics of poetry in Northern Ireland.

"Don't you think you should maybe skip it?" I suggested.

"I haven't seen her in weeks. I won't skip it," she answered.

I admired my mother's ability to prioritize. She always said men shouldn't be that important in the big scheme of things and she was putting her money where her mouth was. Why let a dead husband stand in the way of a good meal and scintillating conversation? Clearly he wasn't going anywhere.

"I've got 'em in a box in the backyard."

What kind of box? A refrigerator box? I was so confused. But my mom was growing annoyed by my questions.

"Just listen!" she yelled, growing impatient, "I don't want your sister to come home and find it."

I assumed that her use of the pronoun "it" was an attempt to distance herself from the death. She was, in effect, dehumanizing the corpse.

"Okay, Ma," I stammered.

"You get home and make sure she doesn't go out back. She'll be upset."

I remembered my mother's angry words to the Winnebago dealer, "My mother died and I never inconvenienced anyone!" and while I appreciated the sentiment at the time, I really felt that this was going too far.

"Well, what about me?!" I yelled. "You think I want to go home and pretend that Lester isn't dead in a box in the backyard?!"

My mom began to laugh hysterically and I really thought she had lost it, in the way that grief does funny things to people and all that.

"Not Lester – Nessa! The *cat*, you dumb-ass!"

I was ready to vomit from the stress, but my mom, who thought this was the funniest thing she'd ever heard, promptly hung up on me to call all her friends and Lester to have a good laugh.

I crawled back to math class and informed my teacher that I couldn't stay for extra work because there had been a death in the family. Of course, what my mother forgot was that I got home *after* Jenny and when I returned home, I found Jenny and Fat Lip (in a pink princess dress, complete with tiara and white patent leather mules) standing on the front lawn with the box. Inside was little Nessa, all stiff and dead-cat like.

I actually felt bad for Jenny and so I approached her and put my arm around her.

"Are you okay about this?" I asked.

Jenny just sneered at me. "Of course I'm okay you dumb-ass. The cat died, big deal. It's gonna resurrect in a few days and that'll be that. Now get your paws off me and start digging!"

I looked over at Fat Lip who smiled weakly and handed me a small spade.

And with that, I proceeded to dig the shallow grave.

11. GYPSIES, TRAMPS AND THIEVES

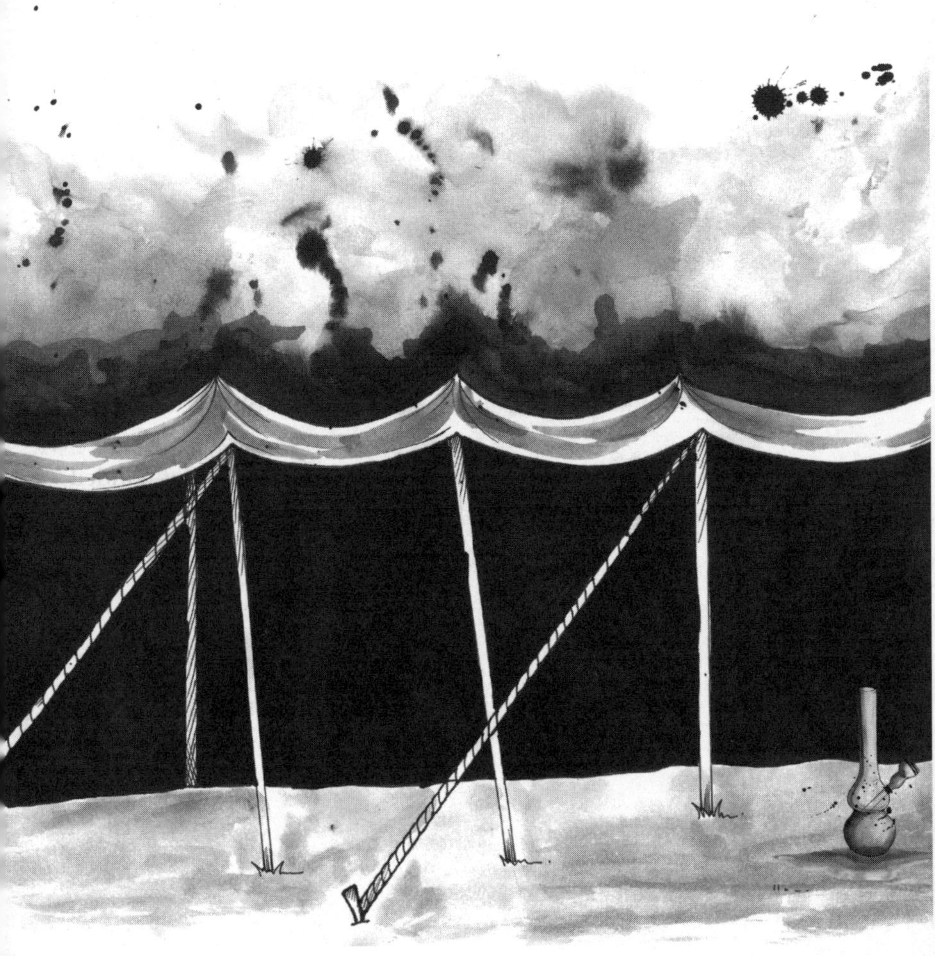

STILL REELING in a cycle of depression from the No Nukes Debacle of '82, and fresh from the first anniversary of Nak's arrival, Stacie decided that having an orphan of her own would be just the thing to pick her up. Luckily for her, Stacie knew a guy named Rob Schwab who was able to be of some service in this matter. Schwabie, as he was known around town, was a hybrid variety burnout, more Jarmusch than Linklater, with a touch of Capote thrown in for good measure. He had a huge pool, scads of money, smoked apple bongs exclusively, and never went anywhere without a martini in hand. Schwabie, being the social animal that he was, knew a girl named Becky, who had once lived in Upper Saddle River, but had moved to Wake Forest, Illinois, during grammar school. As luck would have it, Becky had run away from her cold, *Ordinary People*-like parents and was now living in a boarding room in Ramsey, New Jersey; a town famous for being home to the Ramsey Outdoor Store, as well as character actor Danny Aiello. According to Schwabie, Becky had been forced out of her home because her parents weren't down with her pot smoking and sleeping habits. They wanted her to burn her NAOT sandals (with the *Steal Your Face* insignia on the buckle) and shave her legs. Faced with this type of intolerable oppression, Becky had no choice but to leave. Schwabie was about to continue with the *Ballad of Becky*, but Stacie held up her hand and cried, "You had me at hairy legs!"

A meeting was arranged at Harriman State Park, the Northern New Jersey capital of Burnoutdom. Of course, it was really serendipity because the day that Stacie met Becky also happened to be the day that Becky had been sexually assaulted (for the tenth time) by her housemate, who was none other than the enormous, 165-pound chimp, Mr. Jiggs. Jiggs had gained fame for his numerous Polaroid commercials during the '60s and '70s. He had traveled the world, made *Mike Douglas* appearances, and ate only the finest Costa Rican bananas money could buy. But upon retirement, Jiggs, who it turned out was a female, had become a hard-living, coffee-swilling, timbale-playing lesbian with a penchant for runaways from the greater Chicago metropolitan area. Stacie smelled gold (and rightly so) and immediately brought Becky home to meet my mother.

My mom had lost both her parents at a young age, and knew what it was to feel alone and forsaken. In our posh suburban town, her kinship to the dispossessed didn't help her status as resident oddball. But her sense of duty, which stemmed in part from Catholic guilt, superseded any need to impress the neighbors. If someone needed help, she was more than willing to offer kindness, broiled chicken, and career counseling. No one was ever turned away. But more often than not, my mom's good intentions couldn't undo the years of damage done to most of these people. After a while, she'd grow frustrated, and begin to feel as if all her work was for naught. Then she'd lose her mind and start screaming because she couldn't find her scissors. It was always something small, but the anger would be so palpable, that we'd drop everything and tear apart the house looking for the missing scissors. Of course, we knew it wasn't about the scissors, but that's what my mom wanted it to be about, and that was more important. What it *was* about was the injustice of it all. The fact that people often treated one another like shit; that people let one another down; and that no matter how hard you tried, sometimes you couldn't save the ones you cared about the most. What made things worse were the multitude of housewives in our town with their cloying smiles and their perfectly coiffed hair. They would see my mom at the store and say, "You're such a good person," or, "You are a true hero." But my mother didn't want to be heralded or even noticed. She just wanted us to be able to realize our dreams. Ironically, all we wanted was to blend in and be like everyone else. But in our cookie-cutter, suburban town, we were the equivalent of East Village squatters, and as such, fitting in was not an option. And now here we were, with yet another wayward youth in need of a home.

We all stood around the kitchen eyeballing this greasy-haired, freckle-faced gypsy of a girl, as she told her tale of woe and intrigue to my mother. Nak, of course, couldn't resist jumping onto the counter and grunting like a chimp, which made Becky cry. The resulting waterworks brought out my mom's not so latent maternal impulses. She couldn't rest knowing that Becky was in harm's way and promptly accepted her as our newest orphan. Becky and Stacie moved into the basement together, and we all celebrated the fact that we had a new English-speaking orphan/runaway to hang out with. I don't think my mom bothered to explain the situation to my stepdad because the house was already filled to capacity, and bringing another stray into the fold would have surely raised his ire. Luckily, Lester was in the midst of an all-liquid diet and was sort of delirious from hunger. Still, on occasion, when he would ask about the girl in the basement, we would just be vague. I would usually respond by saying something like, "What girl are you talking about? Because there are a lot of girls in the house, and unless you're more specific, I don't really know how to answer."

If that didn't send him packing, the general rule was to change the subject to baseball. "Why do you think Winfield always seems to stop hitting in October?" was always a good one, as it would almost invariably lead to the "Twenty-three million dollars, the guy better start hitting!" rant, which was just the thing to get his mind off hunger and strange girls in the basement.

So while my stepdad remained in the dark, we got to know our newest family member.

There was a lot to like about Becky. She was very sweet, and spoke with a lilting Southern accent, cultivated from watching hours of *Green Acres*. To this day, the mere mention of her name elicits the phrase, "She was so nice," from everyone in our family.

And even though she smoked massive amounts of pot and slept for entire days, she was just so damn lovely to be around. She liked Cyndi Lauper and the B-52s, and she had no problem with jocks, or anyone else who was different. "It's all groovy, man," she would say in that fake Southern accent of hers. This giddy, fun-filled, pot-induced worldview began to rub off on Stacie, who became decidedly more cheerful during her waking hours. She and Stacie also shared a love of art, and suddenly color began to appear in Stacie's paintings. Giant, multicolored American flags began to be superimposed over the grotesque, bleeding, black penises that had been her favored subject. Still, next to Becky's work, it seemed suicidal, but it was hard to compete with fields of butterflies and puppy dogs on sleds. Becky would even make cartoon sketches on demand for Jenny and Lee, which in turn took some of the pressure off Nak, who was growing tired of his role as orphan du jour. My relationship with Becky bordered on cult worship for two very simple reasons: She had been an extra in the movie *Ordinary People* and she knew John Belushi. At the time, being an extra in a movie was as cool as being a star of a movie. This was before I came to realize that extras were just people who enjoyed sitting around for long hours, eating craft service, and pretending to talk while they crossed streets. As for the Belushi of it all, Becky was so tight with him that she called him "Johnny." There were other amazing things about Becky. She could do a dead-on imitation of Jefferson Starship's Grace Slick singing *White Rabbit*. She was also very into Genesis (before the Phil Collins coup that produced such horrors as *Invisible Touch)* and had managed to get backstage on more than one occasion to meet Peter Gabriel.

As far as I was concerned, Becky was a full-fledged celebrity, right on par with that fat kid with the red hair who ate ham on all those commercials, and Stacie won major points in my book for bringing her home to be our newest orphan.

Becky settled in nicely, attending William Paterson State College with Stacie, smoking copious amounts of pot, and shuttling me all over the tri-state area to see my favorite band, The Police. I had become obsessed with The Police in 1981, which was when I pulled my precedent-setting "Stacie got to go to the No Nukes Concert on a school night" card on my mother, and was allowed to go to NYC on a Monday night to see The Police. Of course, it was Madison Square Garden, and the GoGos were opening, and it was for me a seminal moment, as I was completely overwhelmed by the power and the spectacle of the event. With the advent of MTV roughly the same year, I became a rabid fan, obsessed with all things Sting, which was probably a natural course of events given my earlier involvement with Sting vis-à-vis his portrayal of Ace Face in *Quadrophenia*. As a result of this, I pulled the ever open-minded Becky into my web, and the two of us traveled all over the tri-state area chasing the blonde power-trio. Becky was with me when I became so overwhelmed with Sting love that I nearly killed myself jumping from the second tier to the first at Shea Stadium. Then there was the time in Atlantic

City when we were nearly suffocated by a crush of fans at the foot of the stage, and in a moment fueled by depleted oxygen and my desperation to live, I threw my wallet on the stage and actually hit Sting in the face. The moment was captured on the massive screens hanging over the stage and security moved in to save us. Becky began hugging me and jumping up and down, screaming, "YOU'RE *SO* FAMOUS!" over and over, because everyone knows that hitting a rock star in the face with any object, even an empty wallet, is as good as having sex with said rock star. The fact that it happened during the *Synchronicity* tour only heightened the intensity of the moment.

My mom was working on her PhD at the time, because in addition to having a million kids and a full-time job, she needed something to call her own. As a result, we could have been making pipe bombs in the kitchen, and she really wouldn't have had a clue. Under Becky's tutelage, I began to drive on a regular basis. Despite the fact that I was fifteen, and had no license, I could often be seen behind the wheel of one of our cars joyriding around town. Things seemed to be going well. Even the neighborhood seemed to change, in that it no longer felt like such a dark corner of the universe. There was safety in numbers and there were a lot of us. We were happy, content, and – dare I say it? – almost cool.

Then one day Midge Tyler moved in next door. Midge was a realtor. She had one child, a daughter, and a husband who was an estate planner. Midge wore Chanel suits with tops that allowed for a great deal of cleavage, which disturbed my mother to no end. "It's like she's got a baby's ass in there," she'd complain.

The first order of business, before her moving truck was even emptied, involved the installation of a large flagpole at the end of her driveway. After that, Midge forced the movers to hang a giant Technicolor flag featuring a very regal looking Dalmatian. This was before flags became an outdoor décor fashion statement. Back then, the only people who hung flags were cops and poor people. But judging from Midge's massive flag collection featuring Dalmatian dogs, she had a certain proclivity toward the breed. Between the one perfect child, the flags, and the Chanel suits, we couldn't help but wonder what the hell Midge was doing in our neighborhood. With her realtor connections and her husband's stellar salary, surely she would have been a better fit in one of those Waspy developments across town, where people with monosyllabic names could interact comfortably. My mom felt that Midge's cleavage was the issue. She suspected a hidden tramp-like dimension to Midge that forbade her from interacting with her own kind. Adding to the injury of Midge's arrival, was a stray dog named Spanky. Months earlier, Becky had brought home this horrible, hyperactive mutt who, judging from his behavior, had been abandoned with good reason. Spanky was un-trainable in every way, and my mother hated him with a burning passion. Spanky seemed oblivious to my mom's hatred, yet always managed to raise her ire by constantly shitting on Midge's lawn. With all the kids in our house, there was always a door left open, and Spanky would waste no time running outside, across the cul-de-sac, and onto Midge's lawn. My mom was in the throes of her dissertation, and had taken to wearing a yellow bathrobe and a pre-Ugg prototype boot as her writing outfit of choice. While this ensemble did wonders for Al Pacino in the movie *Author, Author*, my mother in a bathrobe smacked of "crazy lady." No matter how immersed she was in her work, she had an eerie sixth sense regarding Spanky. The minute he got out, she was up, bolting out of the house in her full-length robe screaming, "You fucking dog get back here!" We would quiver collectively, because we always knew that Midge would come out of her home and get involved. We knew this because Midge was a helpful person. She was the type of woman who made cookies and was involved in charitable organizations.

But the juxtaposition of my mom in her bathrobe and boots screaming, "Get back here you motherfucking dog!" against the soft-spoken Midge, in her Chanel suit, plucking the offending turd with a Kleenex, was more than we could bear. Nak thought maybe we could put a bullhorn on the roof, and as my bathrobe-clad mom bounded through the bushes to Midge's house, we could issue a warning, "Thank you Midge for your help, but please return to your home, and we will handle the situation." This was the dream really, but when we told my mother about it, she was very dismissive. "Putting a speaker on the roof will make holes. We've already got enough leaks as it is."

As a final research requirement for her PhD, my mom had to go to Ireland and unearth some old soggy texts regarding British Imperialism in the Trinity College Library.

Figuring there was safety in numbers, she and my stepdad left us to fend for ourselves as they journeyed to the Emerald Isle for two weeks of research, rest, and relaxation.

After all, what could go wrong?

On day one I got drunk on cheap red wine, vomited all over Jenny in her sleep, and then clung to her helplessly. Becky had the wherewithal to wash the sheets, but not rinse them, and as a result we were picking dried food off the sheets for weeks. Indeed, it was a lesson learned.

On day two, Becky and I almost burned down the house while watching a particularly hilarious episode of David Letterman, featuring the long forgotten swinging doorknob bit. The basement was always chilly, and even though it was summer, we decided to start a fire. Within minutes, smoke began to fill the room, but Letterman was so damn funny we couldn't be bothered to find the source of the problem, which, as it turned out, was the closed flue. Becky suggested that we get low, since hot air, a.k.a. smoke, rises. It was a wise decision, because visibility was becoming something of a problem. Still, for Dave we persevered, until Stacie came home, and opened the door, and started screaming, "We're gonna die!" which explained the flames shooting out of the fireplace and our difficulty in catching our breath. Forced out of our asphyxiation stupor, we grabbed a flexible flyer-sled out of the garage, nudged the flaming log onto it, and then dragged it up the steps, and out the front door, where it burned on the lawn for a few days before going out.

Lesson learned; always open the flue before starting a fire.

Other than that, things were going beautifully. A few bumps in the road of life never hurt anyone. Besides, I had the Grand Union card, a dish full of blank checks, and the car keys to my stepdad's brand-spanking-new Cadillac, which we had affectionately named The Pig. Every day I'd drive The Pig up to the Grand Union and shop 'til I dropped. Lobster bisque, Pop-Tarts, Stouffer's French Bread pizzas, it was one big free for all and we were loving life. Until the second week, when there came a knock on the door. Typically, Nak always answered the front door because he had no problem frightening off the Jehovah's Witnesses. But Nak was in Iowa attending wrestling camp with thirty of his best friends. Stacie and Becky were out, and there was just Jenny, Lee, and me to fend off the proselytizing Witnesses who were determined to save our souls. I didn't move at first, hoping Lee or Jenny might deal with it, but they pulled the old "Hey, I think my hearing aid battery just went dead" routine on me and I was stuck with the job. I headed to the front door, armed with my "We're Catholic, so fuck off!" speech, when I opened it and found the Deever Family standing there. The Deever patriarch was a guy named Ron, who had one of those bloated, pregnant man-bellies where the navel distends and sticks out through the shirt. Ron was a "transportation specialist" whose vast knowledge of intrastate tariff freight rates scored him a big job working as a salesman for my stepdad at his company. Ron was new to the fold and we hadn't gotten a feel for him or his man-belly. His wife Nellie had the bug-eyed look of a miniature bulldog with a thyroid condition. She was also very into Amway and was constantly pimping products, which annoyed my mother who was happy with her Ajax. Nellie and Ron also had two sons, who were both in their early teens, but they were of the "seen but not heard" variety. They always seemed to be wearing matching waiter outfits that consisted of khakis and blue polo shirts.

"What are you doing here?" was about the best I could muster.

"We told your folks we'd stop in to check on you," blabbed Ron, as he walked right into the house uninvited, his pod family following behind him.

"We're fine," I blurted out as I chased up the steps behind them.

Jenny and Lee sensed trouble and ran to their rooms, just as Stacie and Becky returned from some marathon pot-smoking session at Harriman State Park.

"Well, how about we take you kids out to dinner?" offered Ron as he grabbed the keys to The Pig off the counter.

Truth was, I had just purchased forbidden shrimp cocktail and was really looking forward to eating them in front of the television while watching *Dallas*. But Stacie and Becky were way too stoned to turn down the offer.

"That sounds cool, man," offered Becky.

Next thing I knew, we were sitting at a giant round table in the Allendale Bar and Grill. Without Nak around, I felt like we were prisoners. It was like *Red Dawn* without Patrick Swayze. We didn't know what to do. I found it hard to believe that my stepdad had authorized this type of debauchery, but Ron seemed so utterly confident, I joined in the fun and began ordering up a storm. If he was going to play the role of big shot freight-rate specialist, who were we to blow his groove? We ordered apps, main meals, had about five refills on our sodas, and even got dessert. This Ron guy was great! We ate until we felt sick, and then we ate some more. When the bill came he eyeballed it carefully, double-checking to see that we had been charged for everything. Then he pulled out my stepdad's credit card. The one that had been under the dish containing the blank checks, with the note wrapped around it that read "FOR EMERGENCY USE ONLY." Ron handed the card off to the waiter, while the rest of us just stared in fear, wondering if my stepdad had really okayed this. Looks were exchanged, but without Nak around to voice our every thought, we kept silent. It didn't matter. They would drop us off tonight and be on their way, and we'd inform our folks of this bizarre event upon their return, careful to point out that had we known Lester was paying, we wouldn't have ordered the fried zucchini. But it didn't end there. Ron filled the car up with gas, using my stepdad's card as well, and then informed us that he and his lovely family were going to be staying with us for a few days.

We got back to the house and watched as they erected a tent in our backyard.

"They'll be out back, we'll just pretend they're not here," reasoned Stacie.

"They're here. They're fucking staying in our yard," I argued.

"Man, we're judging and we shouldn't judge," offered Becky as she slathered Nellie's Amway body cream all over her arms. "Besides, when was the last time anyone let us order appetizers?"

"I don't think that dinner constituted an emergency!" I pointed out.

"You don't know that. It may have been an emergency in the sense that we were all hungry and Ron didn't know where the grocery store was," said Becky.

Stacie looked out the window again and caught the eye of one of the sons: "Fuck, he just gave me the evil eye."

I looked out too, and both of them stared back at me with a crazy look reserved for zealots and pod people inhabited by aliens.

Before we could say anything else, Ron and Nellie were back in the house. Nellie saw us all in the kitchen and smiled her saccharine Amway smile, "Okay kids, your tent is ready, just tell me where you keep your sleeping bags and I'll get you all zipped up." Ron nodded his head and added, "Better put on the flannels though, it's a bit damp out there." We were too stunned to speak. Too weak to resist. We were led out of the house, and into our new home, the tent in the backyard. Our only light a half-dead flashlight.

Reduced to whispering for fear of being heard, we bemoaned our fate.

"How the fuck did mom and Les do this to us?!" I hissed.

"Those fuckers! What the hell? This was supposed to be our vacation too and now here we are in the backyard with no running water!" groaned Stacie.

"We're sleeping on top of a goddam septic tank! I can smell the shit!" cursed Lee.

"Why didn't mom buy that brownstone back in 1970 when she had the chance!" lamented Jenny.

We poked our heads out of the tent, careful to avoid detection and watched as Ron, Nellie, and their waiter sons sat inside eating my shrimp cocktail and watching *Dallas*.

There was no way to reach our parents because they were on a particular leg of the trip that involved driving hundreds of miles and staying in some sort of backwater inn that boasted indoor plumbing but no phone. The only number we had was the hotel in Galway, but they weren't going to be there for another three days.

My mom said if there was an emergency we were to call Midge across the street, but before we could even consider such a thing, Midge walked over to our house, knocked on the door and proceeded to spend the evening chatting with

Nellie and Ron. The next morning Stacie and Becky fled to Schwabie's, while Ron dropped Lee, Jenny, and me off at the movie theater and bought us tickets to see a *Friday the 13th* marathon, featuring the first four installments. While Jenny wasn't scared of anything, allowing me to see those movies and then forcing me to sleep in a tent, was really not a smart move. For the next few nights I woke everyone up with my blood curdling screams and insane weeping because I was convinced Jason was going to find our tent and kill us. By the time morning came, I was so exhausted I spent most of the day sleeping in some sort of sweaty stress-induced fog, then night would return and with it, my terror. Meanwhile, Midge, Nellie, and Ron became fast friends, under the pretext that Midge wanted to sell them a house, but we all knew that this was Midge's revenge for the Spanky shits. After days and days of this, they finally left. Becky woke me up mid-afternoon to tell me that they were gone and that we could once again move back into the house. Shocked, bitter, and completely turned around time wise, we proceeded to get our revenge on our parents by throwing a huge blowout keg party.

We asked Schwabie to be the MC and he happily accepted. The entire tri-state area was invited. Schwabie made martinis and grilled shrimp, and our home throbbed with the strains of the B-52s. We partied all night, and then slept in for most of the morning. By noon we got up. It was time to clean up, as our folks were coming home the following day and we had to pick them up at the airport. Everything was going smoothly until Spanky escaped. En route to Midge's yard, he was struck by a car. We immediately moved into crisis mode, which meant Becky, Stacie, and Schwabie took The Pig to the vet in order to try and save that horrible mutt.

I was ordered to remain at the house cleaning, which seemed sort of convenient. I was about a half hour into the job when the phone rang. It was my mother on the other end.

"Where the hell are you?!" she yelled.

"I'm at home!" I yelled back. "Where are you?!"

"I'm at JFK waiting to be picked up!"

The words sent a chill through my spine. She was back, yet she wasn't supposed to be back until tomorrow. I tried to process. Surely, there must have been a mix-up.

"But you weren't coming back until the eighth," I tried to reason.

"It *IS* the eighth!" my mom screamed.

I looked at the calendar. She was right, it *was* the eighth, and yet somehow I couldn't wrap my head around this. How could we have made such a blunder?

"Well, Stacie isn't here right now," I said.

"You better get your ass to Kennedy and pick us up!" she screamed.

"Ron Deever and his wife stayed for days!" I yelled back, but she had already hung up by this point.

Two hours later, Stacie returned. The phone was ringing off the hook, but I pretended that my hearing aid batteries were dead, and just kept vacuuming.

"Why aren't you answering the phone?" she yelled at me.

"'Cause mom and Les are at the airport," I said.

Stacie looked stunned.

"What do you mean they're at the airport?" she asked, trying to wrap her head around the reality much as I had done two hours earlier.

"They're back. It's the eighth. We're in deep shit. They've been waiting for hours."

"Why didn't you go get them?" she asked

"Because I don't *actually* have a license," I pointed out as I pulled on my shoes. "Come on, we gotta go."

Stacie swallowed hard. I'd never seen her so troubled. "Becky and Schwabie have The Pig, 'cause they took Spanky to another hospital..."

My eyes went wide. "How the fuck are we supposed to pick them up then?"

"We'll have to take the Beetle," she said.

The VW Beetle had a hundred thousand miles on it, ripped seats, and reeked of gasoline. There was no way. But the phone wouldn't stop ringing. And so, we ventured to JFK in that old shit heap. Traffic was horrible, but we finally made it, though we went to Departures by mistake and walked around for about a half an hour, completely indignant because we couldn't find them. Sensing our stupidity, my mom thought to look for us in Departures. When she found us she threw two Irish sweaters in our faces and I believe muttered the word "assholes" under her breath. We drove home in silence, my stepdad behind the wheel of the old bug, Stacie and me jammed into the backseat. I decided to break the ice with the Deever story, but my folks only exchanged a look, and I didn't know how to interpret this, so I continued, "They made us sleep in a tent out back." Nothing.

"They forced us to eat appetizers at the Allendale Bar and Grill."

Zip.

"They drove your car around for days and Midge was with them."

"We get it! They're crooks. You can shut up now!" was my mom's response. Stacie and I exchanged a look; clearly the Deevers had not been invited by our folks. I suddenly realized that our folks had not been in on our torture at the hands of the Deevers. This, in turn, meant that our revenge party, and the subsequent mess (Spanky getting hit by a car, and us missing the fact that today was the day that we were supposed to pick up our folks at the airport) was, in fact, entirely our fault.

My mom eyeballed me in the rearview mirror with her patented "I Blame You" look. I just nodded my head. This one was on me. I should've known better than to think that my mom would have allowed an Amway rep to sleep in our house while she was away.

As we pulled into the driveway, we were relieved to see that The Pig had been returned and Becky had the smarts to hang a WELCOME HOME sign across the front door, though under it, there was a smaller sign that read, "I need $300 to save Spanky from certain death."

My mom just shook her head, took out her checkbook and threw it at Stacie. Then her gaze turned to the remains of the charred log lying on the front lawn.

"What the fuck happened here?" she asked glaring at me. And while I considered telling her about David Letterman and the hilarious swinging doorknob routine, and the fact that there really should be a sign reminding people to open flues before starting fires, the only thing I could manage to say was, "They made us sleep out back in a tent, Ma..."

My mom looked like she was going to rip me a new one right then and there, but instead she took a deep breath, grabbed her suitcase and just muttered, "Serves you right," as she headed inside.

12. BESt LAId PLANS

AS I ENTERED HIGH SCHOOL, my obsession with the band The Police festered like an open flesh wound sans Bactine. Over a period of two years, my room had become a de facto shrine with every inch of every wall covered in posters, European import album covers, and concert swag. It was my refuge, my haven, my safe space. Around the same time, I came down with a bad case of Plantars warts, which limited my ability to do sports. This meant that I was not getting the requisite amount of aerobic activity needed to maintain sanity and because of this, I went a little loopy. The end result of this strange confluence was that I came to believe that The Police and I were connected by some magical power that was fueling my creative life force. I was more than happy to tell this to anyone I met, which completely irritated my mother, who would just roll her eyes and mutter, "I don't know how she got so fucking crazy." Of course, I didn't feel that I was crazy. Like Sting, I had become a student of Jung, and so my obsession with The Police made perfect sense when viewed within the prism of Jung's Theory of Synchronicity. According to Jung, matter and consciousness, far from operating independently of each other, were in fact interconnected in an essential way, functioning as complementary aspects of a unified reality.

As legend has it, Jung was in the middle of a therapy session with some pent up broad who was telling him about a dream in which she was given a golden scarab beetle. Jung immediately racked his brilliant brain until he found the section containing the full text of *The Egyptian Book of What Is In The Netherworld,* which described how the dead sun god transformed himself into a scarab beetle before being reborn as the sun god in the morning sky. No sooner had he jotted down the words "scarab=rebirth symbol" in his secret shrink notebook than there came a tap on the window. Jung turned and saw a scarabaeid beetle (which is like the cousin of a golden scarab and, as they say, close enough for jazz) knocking at the window.

Jung opened the window and the beetle flew inside. The woman took one look at the bug and was suddenly reborn, trading in her overly rational, quasi-depressive worldview for one that allowed greater freedom of thought and feeling. The scarab beetle in her head had merged with the one at the window and voilà, she was a new person.

Jung began to think that the universe was working in mysterious ways. He even turned to astrology and in a stupid move wrote a note to his mentor Freud that said, "I often make horoscopic calculations in order to find a clue to the core of psychological truth. I dare say that we shall one day discover in astrology a good deal of knowledge that has been intuitively projected into the heavens."

Freud, of course, thought he was bat-shit crazy. He told Jung that his theories were "sheer bosh" and that he was drowning in the "black tide of occultism." But like most teenagers drowning in suburban angst, Jung's black tide was my river of gold. Jung imbued my every waking dream with new meaning. After all, if matter and consciousness were in fact interconnected aspects of a unified reality, then it was only a short hop to believing that the *Every Little Thing She Does is Magic* music video that came on just as I was thinking about Sting, was all part of a unified reality in which I was no mere bit player. This was *my* kind of reductionism and, coupled with the fact that out of 50,000 screaming fans, I was the only one to hit Sting in the face with my wallet (which was the same shade of green as a June beetle – a distant cousin of the scarab), showed I was clearly *not* crazy. Of course, Jung probably would not have approved of me telling my brother Lee that I was the love child of Police guitarist Andy Summers, but no theory is without controversy.

My love of The Police could be divided into two different facets. There was the part of me that was attracted to their fame. I wanted to have millions of adoring fans. I wanted to be fêted. In doing so, I hoped to feed my budding narcissism and recover the sense of belonging that had escaped me since my parents' divorce and the subsequent overgrowth of foliage on our front lawn. Then there was the other side. I wanted to meet Sting. Not to get his autograph, or make out with him. That was for loser groupie types. I was looking for a deeper relationship. Something more along the lines of what Bono and Christy Turlington have. Rock star as father-figure, confessor and mentor all wrapped up in one. I wanted to be understood and I felt that Sting would somehow see the real me. We would bond over a shared love of T.S. Eliot and Jung. We would work together to advance the causes that Sting felt were important (though I'd get him involved in my fight for early literacy). We'd hang out with that South American dude with the plate in his mouth and sing songs about Steven Biko. And years later, following the Bono and Christy Turlington paradigm, Sting would walk me down the aisle when I married Matt Dillon. I saw it all so clearly. It was there, in my consciousness, waiting to be formed into a reality. If only I could figure out a way to reach him. A way to make myself known.

And all at once it came to me. I needed to become a Rock Star. I would start my own band. A power trio named The

Clergy, after my mutual love of saints and parallel disdain for the hypocrisy of the Catholic religion. I would be the front girl and we would model our career after The Police, playing small venues at first, until we built up a following and hit Budokan with a vengeance. In addition to dropping names like Eliot, Biko and Jung during all print interviews, I made a mental note to bring up the fact that like Nabokov, I suffered from a condition known as Synesthesia. Synesthesia is an involuntary physical experience in which the stimulation of one sense modality reliably causes an additional perception in a different sense or senses. For example, I had always been able to describe the color, shape, and flavor of someone's voice, or upon seeing the color red, I could detect the scent and sound of red in addition to its color. Armed with all this fodder, there was no doubt in my mind that somewhere along the way, Sting would read my interviews and be drawn to me.

Of course, my mom was fully supportive. The "Daughter as Rock Star/Member of a Think Tank" concept appealed to her, because deep down my mom was a complete adventurer. This was confirmed when, at the tender age of six, she slid a narrow wooden plank from the roof of her seven-story apartment building to the building next door and then nimbly walked across the span like an expert tightrope walker. And rather than focusing on the positives and commending her daring grace, my mom's family chose to obsess over the fact that she could have plunged to her death. After that, any and all signs of fearless behavior were promptly quashed. The upside for me was that when I announced my burning desire to be a Rock Star, she didn't even blink. This raised the ire of all our extended Irish family, who upon hearing of my impending rock stardom would roll their eyes – not just at my insane dream, but also at my mother's indulgence of it. But their disapproval meant nothing to me. And with my mom's support I felt that anything was possible. I just needed to learn to sing, play guitar, and write hit songs and the plan would be in motion.

Never one to shirk a challenge, I surveyed my landscape for options and found just what I was looking for. My then stepmother, Ming the Merciless, had an aunt named Ruth, who bore a striking resemblance to Martha Stewart. Ruth was married to jazz guitarist Bucky Pizzarelli, which made him my great stepuncle, although I'm not really sure he ever even knew my name. Bucky was a "musician's musician," which is another way of saying a good player with not much pizzazz. He played a 7-string guitar, pioneered by George Van Eps, the so-called Underground Guru of Guitar, so named because no one knew who the hell he was. Bucky had done a lot of studio work. I think the most famous person he ever recorded with was probably Carly Simon, though I couldn't tell you which album. He was an odd bird, not a big talker, and he kind of reminded me of Dean Martin in that he mumbled a lot and never seemed to make much sense. Bucky was born in 1926 in Paterson, New Jersey, where a large community of Italian Americans had settled around the town's textile industries. Bucky's parents ran a grocery store on Union Avenue and he had two uncles, Peter and Bobby Dominick, who were virtuoso banjo players and they taught him to play banjo. When he got older, he switched to guitar, though he always said the banjo playing did him a world of good, although there was no way in hell I was going to be playing a banjo.

At this point, Bucky's big gig was at the Pierre Hotel, where people would sit around with tight smiles listening to his solo-guitar interpretations of Bix Beiderbecke compositions, while secretly wanting to kill themselves from the tedium. I figured he had nothing but time on his hands and teaching me, his plucky step-great niece, would be a fun, rewarding experience for him. I saw myself spending long hours hanging out in his sprawling Saddle River home. Bucky would take me under his wing, teach me everything he knew and then we'd hit the grass for a few rounds of bocce ball before Aunt Ruth would call out wondering if I'd like to stay for dinner. Hell, we had all the makings of a *Tuesday's with Morrie*-type bestseller. But instead, Bucky pawned me off on his son John Jr., who was sort of like the poor man's Harry Connick Jr. and later went on to be the official theme-song crooner for Olive Garden and Connecticut Indian Gaming. It wasn't the perfect scenario but beggars couldn't be choosers. Although, to add insult to injury, John agreed to teach me for thirty bucks an hour, which at the time was a hefty sum. I felt that since I was "family" (albeit step), charging me was "sheer bosh." I complained to my dad about the deal, he made a few phone calls and it was agreed that the thirty-buck clip would stand, but the Pizzarellis would throw an Ampeg tube amp into the deal. I needed an amp, so I agreed. Armed with my new George Benson Ibanez guitar, the plan was in motion.

Of course, no plan is every complete without its fair share of glitches. And the first unforeseen glitch was that Becky moved out of our basement and in with her bandana-wearing, free-loving, flatulent boyfriend, Al. Becky's move came after Al's dad had been arrested for making silencers, which he had then sold to the mob (allegedly). Becky was outraged. After all, Al's dad looked like Willie Nelson and smoked pot, so how could it be that he was doing business with the mob? While we tried to explain to Becky that Northern New Jersey was crawling with mobsters and various hit men and at least once a year there was a rub-out up on Sam's Hill, Becky refused to believe it. She stood firm in her belief that Al's dad was making silencers for hunters. We all rolled our eyes and tried to humor her. "Sure Becky," my mom would say, "everyone knows there's nothing a hunter hates more than the din of gunfire."

Still, Becky wasn't going to let this go without a fight. She reunited with her lawyer father to mount a defense for Al's father. With Becky out and my "I am the love child of Andy

Summers" lunacy blossoming, my mom decided to move me into the basement with Stacie. This abrupt decision, and her refusal to even negotiate with me on it, sent shockwaves through my world. Could she not see that all those perfectly placed posters, album art, and decaled wall mirrors had fused together to form an invisible, trilateral force that was fueling my creative fires, which would in turn lead to the formation of my own power trio, which would then lead me to fame and more importantly, to my father-figure-mentor-personal-guru Sting! I tried to explain it to her, but she had long since learned to tune me out when it came to The Police (though she did think The Clergy was a good name for a band). My mother served me a 24-hour eviction notice and it was done. Like any self-respecting teenager, I did the only thing I could do. I took to my bed and wept. The next morning, I was awoken by Stacie, who must've heard my desperate cries throughout the night. I rolled over and found her perched on the edge of my bed, "It's gonna be okay you know," she began. "We can hang up all your posters and it'll be just like your room down here."

Now before I could even fully process the fact that Stacie was a) Up at the crack of dawn and b) In my room trying to be nice; a long, slender, beam of light came shooting through the space in the curtains. It looked just like the ray that illuminated the location of the Ark of the Covenant in *Indiana Jones*. It was so bright and so piercing that Stacie and I both stared at it in wonder as it moved across the room and hit the center panel of my homemade Police collage, illuminating the holy face of my personal savior, Sting.

"Holy shit!" Stacie cried, as she clutched my arm. "That's amazing, oh my god, Kris. I'm freaking out!"

In that moment, I was saved. It was pretty clear to me that the universe was working with me. I had merely lost faith in the process. I was going to meet Sting. Moving to the basement wasn't going to change that. I was happy to have

Stacie there to witness the moment and I was certain that this would only help to make us closer.

Sadly, the power of the moment quickly faded once I was basement-bound. My bed was in the corner and I had one portion of wall, next to the closet with the broken doors, in which to recreate my shrine. My ratio of posters to wall-space was off, and I found myself chasing the dragon for the better part of a week before giving up. To make things worse, Stacie ran the place with a very messy iron hand. If I even attempted to clear her clutter, she'd rip me a new one. If I turned my amp too loud during practice, she'd yell at me. If I spoke when I wasn't spoken to, I was barked at. Once again, I felt forsaken. The universe was testing me and like a hothouse flower, I began to wilt. Then, one night, something bizarre happened. I was in my bed, tucked behind the far side of the fireplace, in front of the closet that contained the furnace, which would growl and boil all night long. The smell of dank dampness, which is the hallmark of mold, was wafting through the air and I was rolled up in my new Calvin Klein bedding ensemble. The CK bedding had been a secret retaliatory purchase in response to my mother's coldhearted decision to move me into the basement. She had given us a credit card and sent us to Bloomie's to buy a gift for my stepdad. While everyone was looking at wallets, I snuck off and bought the bedding. Sadly, I couldn't wash said bedding because then my mother would have seen the contraband, so they still had that store bought smell and that itchy starched feeling and were giving me a rash. What I did have though was the smug satisfaction of knowing I was sleeping on 100% cotton, which none of the other members of the household could say.

I was roused from my sleep by Stacie's voice.

"Kris ... Kris ... Wake up," she whispered.

I rolled over and asked, "What's wrong?"

"There's someone in the room. He just grabbed my tit

and now he's in the corner. I can hear him breathing," was her response.

I found myself paralyzed with fear, which was surprising because despite my myriad phobias, I always considered myself brave. My first impulse was to ignore the situation and say, "Just go back to sleep. Maybe he'll leave," which clearly was not the answer my stepsister was looking for.

"He's *here*. I can't go back to sleep, we have to do something. Call Mom."

I looked down and saw my phone next to the bed. We had a separate line and I could have easily called upstairs, but I'd seen one too many slasher movies and was suddenly convinced that if I called upstairs, the heavy breathing, tit-grabber's accomplice would pick up the phone and inform me that he'd bludgeoned the entire family. I stuck with my initial impulse. "Go back to sleep," I hissed.

But Stacie was not letting this thing go, which was irritating to me because I really was comfortable pretending this wasn't real. It was like a Jungian inverse; if fantasy could be reality, then why couldn't reality be fantasy?

"I can hear him *breathing*. He's on the steps! *Get over here now*!"

I knew I could no longer ignore the situation. He was on the steps, which meant he could be heading upstairs to bludgeon Jenny, who, apart from being moody, demanding, and a sore loser, didn't deserve that fate. I summoned all my courage, grabbed the phone, which as luck would have it had a ridiculously long cord and hightailed it over to Stacie's bed. I clung to her like a marsupial as she dialed my mom. At this point, I could hear the heavy-breathing perv as he sat crouched on the staircase that led to our room. And in short: I was afraid.

Of course, no sooner did she answer, then I could hear my stepfather's voice bitching from the other end, "Who the hell's calling at this hour?! Someone better be dead!"

But Stacie got right to the point. "There's someone in the house. He grabbed my tit."

At the same time, the heavy breathing pervert made his move out of the house. Stacie and I screamed in unison, "He just went out the back door!"

"Good, then go back to sleep!" yelled my stepdad.

But my mother wouldn't have it and despite his protests, a plan was hatched. The first step: We would meet in the living room.

Stacie and I clung to one another and headed up the steps. There was no sign of the tit-grabber, but we were unable to stop screaming until we finally made it to the recently purchased, vaguely Scandinavian living room sofa. As usual, my mother was running late, but she finally emerged from the bedroom, wielding a wooden coat hanger that would've made Joan Crawford proud. Following behind her was my stepfather, who just seemed to be repeating the phrase, "Go back to bed," as if it were a prerecorded loop.

Our screams had awoken Nak, who joined us in the living room. Lee and Jenny didn't have hearing aids on and remained asleep, completely unaware of how close they had just come to dismemberment. While my mother plotted a response that involved scouring the neighborhood, making phone calls, and getting the police in so we could issue a report, Nak became a Doubting Thomas, questioning the validity of our story. "Who the fuck would want to feel your fucking boobs?" he asked.

My stepfather agreed. "This is crazy, you must've dreamt it!"

To which Stacie started crying, "I didn't dream it. He grabbed my tit. I'm a C cup! Why is that so hard to believe?!"

This went on for a solid fifteen minutes with my stepfather saying things like, "Hon! We're not calling the Feds!" and "Vigilante justice is never the answer!"

To which Nak would add, "That fucking Charles Bronson is fucking excellent. Fucking better than fucking Dirty Harry."

And Stacie would yell, "I heard him breathing!" and I was sort of in the middle, because a) He hadn't grabbed my tit and b) I had wanted her to go back to sleep in the first place.

Ultimately, my mom, being the super-sleuth that she was, made us do a walkabout for clues. She determined that the back door, much like the front door, had not been locked. We never locked doors, so whoever came in clearly knew to turn the doorknob. She then took this to the next level. Our German shepherd Rima (named for a Hindu goddess) barked at strangers but not at people she knew. Since Rima hadn't barked, she must have known the perp. My mother felt that whoever did this was not only a sociopath, but also a person who potentially lived in the neighborhood. My brother Nak backed up her thinking by adding, "Of course, Ma. Who the fuck would drive to our house to feel her tit?"

But my mother wasn't listening. She was too busy staring at the track marks in our front hallway.

"Whoever did this had small feet," she said.

My brother eyeballed the tracks. "Fucking Converse sneakers. The only one who wears those is that fucker Kevin Albee."

Kevin Albee was the nine-year-old boy who lived two houses up and had a strange family.

"A nine-year-old felt you up and you get us out of bed for that?" my stepfather yelled.

"I didn't know he was *nine*!" shouted Stacie.

My mother wanted to call his mother, but my stepfather felt that it was too late for phone calls and we all agreed. Stacie was disappointed that her perp didn't even have chest hair and I was bummed that I had been such a chicken shit because I could have totally taken Albee.

The upshot of all this was that shortly thereafter, Stacie began dating a Marine, which was sort of bizarre since Stacie was a burnout, or at least she had been, and as such didn't gravitate toward people in uniform. I suspect she was so freaked out by her boob-grabbing violation that she just needed a person in a place of authority who could make her feel safe. Needless to say, my parents liked him because he had short hair and said "Yes, sir" a lot. I thought he was fine, mostly because he was really into The Who and we both agreed that *Quadrophenia* was a seminal piece of filmmaking. But the most important thing to come from this in terms of my future as a rock star was that Stacie moved in with her Marine, thus leaving the sprawling confines of our moldy basement in my hands. I no longer had to practice with headphones. I was free to move my bed around. Free to toss out the Victorian hippie-chic lamps adorned with peacock feathers that were her favorite modus of lighting.

Once the room was mine, the CK bedding had been washed, and the furniture had been moved to create a space that I felt Sting would have felt comfortable in, it was time to focus on my impending rock stardom.

If I was to be a rock star, I needed to start partying like one.

I began holding parties every Friday and Saturday night. Invites were easy to come by; you just had to show up. It is a testament to just how loud my stepdad liked his TV that my mother never heard the roar of mopeds pulling into our driveway, or the assortment of kids partying in my basement. Jenny, of course, found the whole situation to be delightfully subversive. For her, the basement had morphed into Rodney Bingenheimer's English Disco and she was the gatekeeper. She stood at her post by the back door, deciding who got in and who was turned away. Substandard footwear was a surefire way to get rejected and kids soon knew that they had to face Jenny and they were afraid.

Inside it was the usual cast of characters, plus whomever Jenny decided to admit.

The regulars included Todd, the guy who got drunk, then took off his clothes and played air-guitar to Rush. Mark, the captain of the football team and resident manslut. Halina, the Penny Lane of the bunch. Jason, the soccer star and all around nice guy, whose endless knowledge of Monty Python made him hilarious. There were the O'Connor twins, known for their wit. Bryan McCann, now the foremost authority on Brazil and Radio, who, at the time, would drink and paint sexually explicit DeKooning-like drawings in permanent marker on the walls of my fireplace. There was Eric, the cutest Jewish kid in the tenth grade and the object of my affection since the fourth, and finally, there was Brown Bob, named for his love of brown corduroy. Brown enjoyed playing sad songs on my guitar and spitting booze into the fire in order to impress Jenny, who was bemused by Bob's idiocy, but clearly not impressed. There were other kids, but this was the core.

We'd get together every weekend, get drunk and talk about whatever was on our mind, until someone threw up or Todd got too drunk and tried to destroy my guitar. They were my posse. And together, we would become a seminal group that would influence fashion, politics, and of course music. Eventually my invites begat other invites and soon the basement was quiet as we took the show on the road. I started drinking *way* too much. Entire nights were erased from my memory. I'd twist my ankle and not remember doing it. Or wake up in the morning with a shrub stuck in my hair. I probably should have cut back, but for some reason I couldn't stop myself. I was having too much fun. I never realized how far I'd fallen, until my parents went out to dinner with Sarah, the former wife of my stepdad's *ex-wife's* new husband. Sarah was visiting from Ohio, where she had been exiled after the divorce. She was passing through and mistakenly thought it might be nice to hook up with my stepdad. The upshot was, they had just come from their fun-filled reunion dinner, when I, operating under my strict "I drink, but never drive" policy, called them for a ride. Why anyone allowed me to do this is a mystery. I had drunk enough Jack Daniels to kill a horse, or at the very least an aged burro, and getting into a packed car with my parents, Sarah, and her two teenage daughters, one of whom was mentally challenged and the other a devout Hasidim in training, was not a good idea. Of course, it seemed like a fine idea to me at the time and I even asked if we could give Halina and Eric a ride home.

There isn't much I really remember about the event, most of it was told to me in bits and pieces by my sister Jenny, who was on hand and delighted by the turn of events. I have a vague recollection of driving home, though I don't remember screaming obscenities out the window or waving wildly to passing cars that I had mistakenly thought were oncoming mopeds. According to Jenny, I was out of control. For some reason, I insisted on calling Sarah "Babs" and told her not to "sweat her fat ass." When the retarded girl commented that Eric's house looked like a church, I apparently screamed, "He's a Jew! They don't live in churches, dumbass!" And I capped that off with a little shame. "Some Jew you are!" I yelled. At this point, the prudish Hasidim-in-training sister began weeping. Then we dropped off Halina, who I believe actually jumped out the window in order to avoid further humiliation. In a wise move, I was dropped off with Jenny, leaving my mom and stepdad alone to drive Sarah and her shell-shocked daughters back to the hotel. My mom said the awkward silence in the car was so thick, she could've cut it with a machete. Of course, I had no clue. I could barely walk. Thankfully, Jenny helped me stagger inside, where I promptly fell asleep in a pool of my own vomit. The next day, I woke up completely clueless. I noticed that no one was talking to me, but I was really too hungover to care. My mother told me she had never been so mortified in her whole life and I just blinked. My stepdad had mercy on me and gave me aspirin. I believe this stemmed from the fact that he got kicked out of Syracuse for drinking and was secretly amused by my Belushi-like antics. But I was sick, seriously sick, for the entire day. My mother would come into my room from time to time to remove my barf bucket and just say, "This is God's way of punishing you."

But in fact, God had nothing on my mom, who forced me to go to dinner with Sarah and her daughters the following Friday at Hunan Pan. I did my best to be nice, charming, and funny, as if the recent drive home had just been a play I was in. My mother enjoyed my discomfort to no end and I vowed to stop drinking for possibly the rest of my life. Lesson learned, it was time to focus on music.

First order of business in my newfound state of sobriety was to stop the lessons with John Pizzarelli. He didn't seem to care about teaching me; in fact, half the time he didn't show up. Instead I found a new teacher, a great guy named John Caridi, who charged me less and taught me more. I started jamming with kids in town, dragging Bucky's old tube amp around with me. I even made the school stage band. We performed a lot of bad Maynerd Furguson arrangements but we also played lots of blues, which was fun. It didn't hurt that I got to sit next to a super cute piano player named Dave. From there I began branching out. Dave actually invited me to join his garage band because they were looking for a front person and he felt that I'd be a good fit. We practiced and got enough music for a set together and then, one day, we played a party. Nothing major, a boring white bread country club set, but it was a party and we were there to perform and I was upfront and center, ready to knock 'em dead with my Patty Smyth Scandal covers. I was comfortable with the notion, even excited by it. Until I got on stage and looked out at all those strange faces staring back at me. My throat went dry and suddenly I could hear my heart beating. Coupled with the giant phallic microphone jutting into my facial region, I suddenly froze. Froze might be putting it mildly. Choked might be a better description. I could not deal with the crowd looking at me, I couldn't even deal with the mike in my face, or the slight delay that it caused my voice. Panic set in, followed immediately by dry mouth, fatigue, and a vague sense that I was going to vomit, which thankfully I did. Dave ended up singing all the tunes and I hightailed it out of there.

The fact was, I had horrible stage fright. And suddenly, the dream of being a Rock Star had to be amended because apparently I wasn't as narcissistic as I thought. Sure I could be in the band, but don't put a mike in front of me and call me front-girl. Let's just say Sting would not have been proud.

I returned home a complete and utter mess. I didn't tell anyone about what had happened because I couldn't take the humiliation. My mom was waiting for me when I got home. She had a nervous look on her face. I wondered if word of my swansong had reached her. But instead she looked at me and said, "The Police have split up," which completely floored me of course. What did this mean? How could this have happened? How was Andy Summers going to earn a living? After all, he made about two cents on those stupid Robert Fripp duets he liked to record on his downtime.

"No, it's not like that," my mom assured me. "Sting is going off on his own. He's got some new thing going with jazz musicians and he's going to have his own band with them."

It was an interesting synchronic development to say the least. And perhaps the dream of my impending friendship with Sting wasn't lost. I mulled it over in my basement salon and after countless hours spent listening to well-produced Michael McDonald and James Ingram records, the dream shifted. I decided I wanted to be a Studio Musician. If I could become a star studio musician, I could be hired by Sting to be in his band. This way I didn't have to start my own band. I could just join Sting's band and the mentor-confessor-father-figure relationship could still unfurl. It was in many ways an easier route.

I enrolled myself in Saturday classes at the Manhattan School of Music. Members of Sting's new band, like Branford Marsalis, had affiliations with the school so it seemed like a good idea to me. So what if I wasn't going to be the rock star? I could still work for one. To pay for the tuition, I used my car accident settlement money that had been sitting around accruing interest since I was four years old, which was when that drunken driver had hit my mom and me. To pay for my bus fare into the city, I cleaned houses on Fridays after school. Clearly, no one could accuse me of not being driven. But I knew that if I were going to be hired by Sting, I would have to become more proficient in jazz. The only trouble was that I fucking hated jazz. Sure, I had a few faves – Miles Davis *Four and More, Porgy and Bess, Kind of Blue* and of course anything by Steps Ahead, but the rest of it really made me want to kill myself. In a testament to hard work and my underlying burning desire to meet Sting, I sucked it up. I became a shut-in, practicing five, six, sometimes seven hours a day. My mom would make me coffee and bring me down plates of dinner. And I got good. So good that I made the McDonald's Tri-State All-star Band, although there were those who said I only got the gig because I was a girl. Still, I met a lot of interesting people. There was Justin DiCioccio, who now runs Manhattan School of Music's jazz program, but at the time was at Music and Art High School. Justin was a teacher in the truest sense of the word. I learned more about music and life from him than from just about anyone else I've ever known. I liked the idea of learning from disparate people whose paths I would have otherwise never crossed. With that in mind, I would just pick people that I wanted to meet, get their number from the Musician's Union Book and call them. This was how I met Miles Davis' über guitarist Mike Stern and David Letterman's first guitarist Steve Kahn. Steve and I became pretty friendly in an after-school-special kind of way. He was perplexed by me, but admired my sheer brass balls. I'd cut school and go to his apartment and we'd talk about his dad (legendary songwriter Sammy), look at his extensive collection of Folon paintings and talk about modal playing. Then there were those who befriended me, like Brooks Kerr, the blind, bipolar piano-player who came up with Michael Brecker (of Steps Ahead fame) and was an expert in all things Duke Ellington. Like most people, Brooks took to my mom. He would call and even without so much as a "Hi, it's Brooks," he'd jump into a long, winding discourse about Fats Waller and Louis Armstrong. My mother said that though Brooks confused her, she didn't mind taking his calls because it kept her off the phone with Schwabie, who had suffered brain damage in a car accident and was now like a lost eleven-year-old. In his somewhat altered state, Schwabie wanted my mother to adopt him and would often call her at all hours of the night to discuss this.

I started meeting other kids from Manhattan School of Music Pre-College and we'd get together and go to clubs like 7th Avenue South, the 55 Bar and the now-defunct Barry Harris Jazz Collective, where Barry Harris himself once screamed, "Get that girl off the stage!"

I was moving in some sort of circular vortex that had me on the periphery of where I wanted to be. I even rode up in an elevator with Branford Marsalis once and out of the blue, he told me that he felt that everyone should learn drums, which of course prompted me to do just that. I was doing everything I could to make this dream true and I should've been happier, or at least more satisfied with all that I had accomplished in such a very short period of time. But instead of feeling fulfilled, I just felt worn out. I remember going to parties and feeling horribly alienated from the rest of my friends. I was barely seventeen but I felt much older. Living inside this dream of mine had made me lonely and isolated. I was inside my head so much that a sense of disconnect began to overwhelm everything else. The only Think Tank that would have me would have been full of depressives. One night, my friend Bryan asked me, "What do you love best about music?" and I began to cry. He put his arm around me and said, "What's wrong?" But I couldn't tell him. The sad truth was that the thing I loved best about music was not playing, or practicing, or even the people I'd met.

The thing I liked best was the quiet bus ride back and forth from my house to the city, staring out the window, searching for signs of home.

3. BUCKY PIZZARELLI IS A BIG dICK

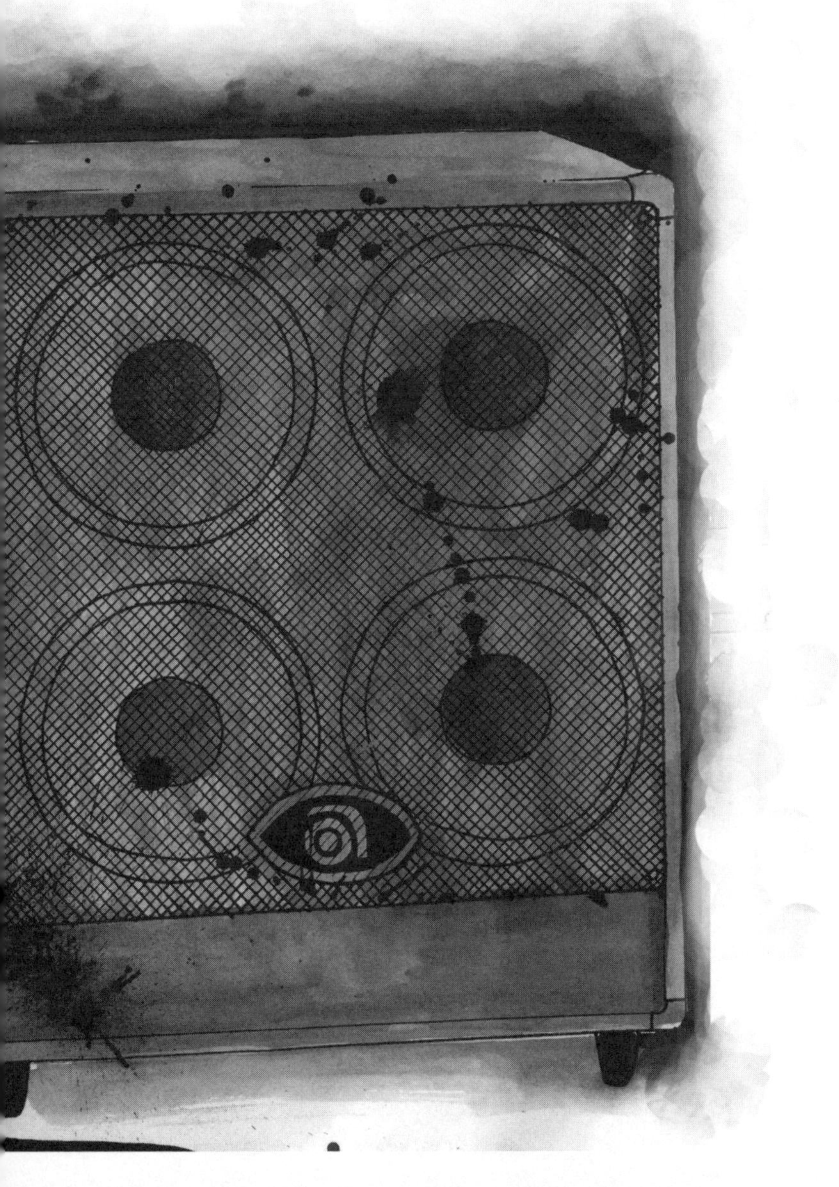

BY DECEMBER OF MY SENIOR YEAR, I had been accepted to Manhattan School of Music. Trouble was, I couldn't help but wonder if I had done the right thing. After all, my motives for becoming a musician in the first place were a little warped and now that I had accomplished at least part of what I had set out to do, I felt strangely unsatisfied.

Upon learning of my admission, my pal Jason called my mom and asked, "Is Kristen excited?" My mom took one look at me sprawled on the sofa, staring blankly at the ceiling, and replied, "You know Kristen, not much excites her."

Which was true. Accomplishments had never meant much to me. I was more of a journey person. As such, reaching the destination always felt anticlimactic. But there was more to my malaise than this. I was beginning to think that maybe I'd made a big mistake. Truth was, I didn't care that much about music. All I really wanted was to meet Sting and be a part of a Think Tank that shaped global policy, but here I was going to Manhattan School of Music. It was a fine mess.

I sleepwalked through winter vacation. The only time I left the house was to go to Jason's to watch Monty Python movies. Meanwhile, I kept getting these annoying phone messages from Bucky Pizzarelli, asking about the crappy old Ampeg tube amp he had lent me years earlier. I had no idea where it was, as I had long since moved on to Mesa Boogie amps and I thought he should probably have done the same.

When school went back into session, I was sullen and disconnected. Since I'd already been accepted to music school, I really didn't see the point of my attendance. It had all the makings of a long winter of discontent. But the gods smiled upon me and sent me Hank the Upright Bass Playing Sub, who appeared one day, as if out of the blue, in one of the many music practice rooms that our gynormous high school offered. Hank was about thirty and not horrible looking, but what impressed me most was that he sounded *exactly* like Eddie Gomez. Gomez was the bassist from Steps Ahead, whose album of the same name was on my daily listening chart.

Hank saw me standing there looking sort of shocked and introduced himself.

"Hey, I'm Hank Sabre. I'm the new permanent sub."

I had a bad history with permanent subs, but this one smelled like a winner.

"You sound exactly like Eddie Gomez," I said.

Hank smiled, "I studied with Eddie."

My Geiger counter was going berserk.

"I love Steps Ahead, they're my favorite," I offered.

"Yeah, I know all those guys."

My head was spinning. A sudden wave of joy washed over me. Perhaps I had been too quick to write off my musical aspirations as the demented dream of a disaffected youth.

"You're working here? Every day?" I asked.

Hank smiled, "Yeah, every day. I'll be here."

"'Cause I play guitar, I'm going to Manhattan School of Music. I know Steve Khan and Mike Stern too..."

I could not get the words out fast enough.

"I study with John Caridi," I told him.

"I know John. How is he?" he responded.

He knew everyone that I knew and he had a close, personal relationship with Eddie Gomez. I played the movie in my mind. I would cut the bulk of my classes so that Hank and I could jam all day and by the time I went to MSM in the fall, I'd be so good that I could drop out, go on the road with a small venue band, say Rickie Lee Jones or someone like that and from there, I'd be right on track to get the gig with Sting!

The trouble was Hank was usually too hung-over to do much playing. But he did love to talk. He talked about the year he lived in his car. He talked about the time he got the clap from a Russian hooker. He talked about the time he had to beg Eddie Gomez for money because he had a loan shark on his back. Hank was barely thirty and it's fair to say, he was completely washed up; and now he was a living, breathing cautionary tale. Yet I hung in because I really needed to do extra work on rhythm changes and he was the only one who could help me. But Hank was more interested in grabbing bites to eat than playing. And sure, I thought it was strange that he insisted on driving to Mexican chain restaurants that were over an hour away just so, "no one would see us and get the wrong idea." But it was going to take a lot more than an oversized tostada to get me to drop trou. Besides, I had higher hopes for Hank. I thought perhaps he could be redeemed. I saw us starting a small band, getting a local gig and maybe becoming the next best thing. Of course, while I was feeling sorry for Hank there were darker forces at play.

As spring neared, Hank suddenly became chipper. He started taking me to jam sessions over at William Paterson College, where Rufus Reid ran the program. It was great. I got to play nearly every day, although Hank never seemed to do any playing. In fact, he'd drop me off and then just disappear for hours at a time. I didn't really care. I needed to get in playing time. Without a juke joint on every corner, it was tough to get good at improvising. You could only sit in your room playing along to Miles Davis records for so long. Everything seemed to be going well. But back at my high school, trouble began to brew in the music department.

The other teachers in the department didn't like Hank. I suppose this was because he showed up late and did virtually nothing, but again, that had nothing to do with me. What *did* have to do with me was this big battle of the school bands competition, which was going to be happening the same weekend that I had a concerto competition at Manhattan School of Music Pre-College, which I was still attending on Saturdays. The music department at my high school got into a war with the music department at the Pre-College, because they wanted me to attend the battle of the bands. However, the Pre-College wanted me to attend the concerto competition because it was the biggest event of the year and the programs had already been printed. I was stuck between a rock and a hard place, but ultimately decided on the concerto competition because I had been practicing the piece for nearly a year, and more importantly, I was going to be attending the school in September and it would have been detrimental from a political standpoint if I had not shown up. I figured that my high school teachers would understand, but instead they turned on me. Next thing I knew, word in the halls was that I was sleeping with Hank! This was preposterous, because *first,* I was hot for a boy at Juilliard and *second,* if I were going to snog anyone at school, it would've been the piece of ass Varsity Soccer Coach, Ollie Pimm, and no one else. I tried to explain this to my teachers, but they didn't want to listen. I was forced to go to Hank with my problem, interrupting the architectural drafting class, where Hank was subbing for the day.

"They think we're seeing each other," I told him quietly.

And he looked around, like a criminal, and said, "Lay low, just lay low with it."

"Lay low with what?" I wanted to know.

"No matter what, don't tell them anything. And don't worry, I won't let them know about those beers you drank after the jam sessions at William Paterson."

I knew a veiled threat when I heard one, but I couldn't understand why Hank was doing this to me. The entire thing was a mystery. I decided that being around Hank was toxic and did my best to avoid him at every turn. But the damn guy wouldn't leave me alone. He was always winking at me in the hallway or brushing up against me in the cafeteria. It was unreal. Finally, one afternoon, I was called down to the office to speak with the dreaded vice principal. The guy was not my biggest fan, mostly because he didn't understand why I was throwing away my "smarts" to play guitar.

"We have a situation," he said.

I was hoping against hope that this wasn't going to be Hank related. I didn't want to be forced to play the "Check my hymen – I'm still a virgin" card, but then I remembered that I had actually broken it horseback riding and that line of defense wasn't going to work.

I was seriously screwed.

"Hank Sabre's car was spotted by your house, three days in a row. We're asking Hank to leave the school and we would appreciate it if you would cease any relations you are having with him until school is over."

I was so grossed out. The vice principal thought I'd given it up to Hank! I wanted to scream out, "*EWWWWW!!*" but then I remembered what Hank had said, about not telling them that I had drunk beer with him after a jam session, and kept my mouth shut.

I nodded my head and agreed to the vice principal's terms because it seemed to be the easiest thing to do. As Joe the Janitor once told me, "The shortest distance between two points is simplicity."

Back at home, I racked my brain, trying to piece the

situation together. I even got Jenny involved because she had read a ton of Encyclopedia Brown books and knew a thing or two about blackmail and deceit. She started scouring the neighborhood looking for signs of Hank. Something was afoot and she was going to get to the bottom of it. Each day, she'd set out, trying to get her man. Sure enough she did it.

It was a Tuesday night, around dinnertime and she came running into the house. "You need to come with me right away," she said.

I looked out the window; it was awfully dark out there. "Do I have to? I hate the dark," I said.

"*Now*," was her response.

Against my better judgment, she and I skulked out of the house and then crawled commando-style into the woods, near the grave of Sheba the snake. While Jenny was very nimble and devious, she always forgot to keep her voice down.

"Don't let them see you!" she yelled.

I whispered, "Who?"

"What?!"

"You're *yelling*," I whispered.

"I can't read your lips 'cause it's dark. Just shut up and follow me," she said.

I pulled her face close to mine so she could read my lips in the moonlight.

"Whoever it is that you don't want to see us, is going to *hear* us if you don't shut up," I explained.

"Oh, right. Sorry."

We got back to crawling through the woods, until we reached the small creek that ran along the outer edge of our property. We took cover behind The Sorrowful Evergreen and then Jenny pointed. I followed her hand and looked across the way into the cul-de-sac.

And sure enough, who was parked there? Hank the Sub in his purple Celica. My mind was in overdrive. Was Hank some crazy pederast? Was he looking through my windows and touching himself? Did Hank think my boobs looked good?

Jenny brought me down to earth by kicking my shin.

"Focus!" she hissed. I snapped out of it as we moved in for a closer look and saw Hank with Bridget Crawford, the slack-jawed chick from up the street, whose front teeth were so large, she could eat corn through a fence. Bridget Crawford? She drooled! She played bassoon. She was in the marching band. She would stand next to me and say things like "You're so pretty" and "I wish I could be cool like you."

Frankly, we all thought Bridget was a budding lesbian. But no, Bridget was a calculating hussy. And Hank was all over her like white on rice.

"Bridget set you up because *she* was in fact screwing Hank the Sub," Jenny explained, feeling no doubt like Encyclopedia Brown's gal pal, Sally Kimball. Talk about calculating! Talk about brilliant! I almost had to respect Bridget and her deceitful tart-like ways.

My sister and I sat in the woods piecing it all together. I wondered when things started between Hank and Bridget.

"Maybe they were seeing each other before he started working at the school. Maybe she got him the job," I mused.

"No, you dumb-ass, she didn't get him the job. Since when do high school seniors make job recommendations? No, they didn't know one another before he got to the school," she explained.

"How can you be sure?" I asked.

"He was a loser, smelled of gin and smoke and then, all at once, he started bathing regularly."

This was true.

"It's amazing how much you hear when you want to," I pointed out.

"Shut up. Listen," Jenny was on a roll. "He came to the school to work because he needed cash badly. Those who can, *do* and those who can't, *teach*, so we know where the music was going with him."

I nodded my head. She was right. Hank had spent so much time trying to sound just like Eddie Gomez, he never found his own sound. And being a great musician was about expressing yourself, not trying to mimic someone else. As such, Hank's musical career was sort of doomed.

"But then something changed," she continued. "Suddenly he's dragging you all over the place. I think he had met Bridget and started up with her, but you became the patsy."

"But how come he didn't want to play with me and then suddenly it was like, 'Let's go to the jam session' central?" I asked.

"Dumb ass, don't you know that Bridget's father works at William Paterson. She was there and Hank dragged you there 'to play' so he could go run off with Bridget."

It was so diabolical.

"He used my love of Steps Ahead."

"Yes, he did. He used you and you fell for it."

"Can you believe that?" I asked.

"Of course I can, you're very naïve," was her response.

"But what does he see in her?" I wondered.

"Her mother is an heiress. She has major cash."

"An heiress?!"

How did my sister know all this?

"Her mother is the granddaughter of the guy who invented the typewriter. I go to school with her younger sister, duh!"

It was amazing, Hank the washed out musician was hustling slack-jawed Bridget to get to her money and I was the fall guy.

I was disappointed in myself for not seeing it all sooner. What's worse, Jenny was insufferable for having figured the whole thing out. At this point, Nak and Lee joined us in the woods. My mom had left for Parents' Night at her school and my brothers, who had been watching us from the dining room window, felt it would be fun to pelt Hank's car with eggs.

I just went inside, tired of the whole sordid affair, and took a shower. I had just finished drying my hair when the doorbell rang. I immediately thought it was Hank coming to scream about the egg job that my brothers had no doubt done. But when I looked out the front window, I saw that it was not Hank. It was a couple. Jehovah's Witnesses maybe. I was in no mood for their crap and figured I'd give them a piece of my mind in an attempt to displace my anger over the Hank situation. But when I opened the door, I found Bucky Pizzarelli and his Martha Stewart look-alike wife Ruth standing on my doorstep.

It was a stunned moment. I couldn't figure out what they were doing here. And then Ruth cut to the chase.

"If you do not return it at once, we are going to take you to the police," Ruth declared.

I just stood there, trying to figure out what the hell they were talking about.

"That's right, missy," said Bucky. "You think you can screw with me?! I want it back!"

The *amp*. They had called asking for it about a month earlier. *This* was what they were after.

"You better stop with the games. We want it back now," said Aunt Ruth, looking like she was going to strangle me. With my mother not home and my siblings off in the woods on some sort of egg smashing odyssey, I found myself at a loss. For whatever reason, I wasn't able to just tell them the truth; I didn't know where the amp was. If I had just done that, they would have been mad, but they certainly wouldn't drag me to the police station. Telling them that would have been the sensible thing to do, but before I could get the sensible person in me to speak, the people pleaser in me blurted out, "It's at my friend Eric's house."

I had left it at a jam session at Eric Goldstein's house about a year earlier. I tried to remember if I'd seen it after that, but couldn't. So I went with that.

"I can get it for you tomorrow," I offered.

"No, we'll go get it now," said Bucky, with a menacing tone reserved for hit men from Paterson. Like a complete fool, I got in the car. We drove across town to Eric's sprawling, churchlike home, where I had indeed left the amp about a year earlier. All the while, Bucky and Ruth took turns berating me from the front seat.

"People like you just take advantage of a situation," said Ruth.

"Someone does something nice for you, you spit in their face," countered Bucky.

I wanted to point out that charging me thirty bucks for a half hour lesson and then not showing up wasn't exactly all that nice. But, "Don't you have other amps?" was all that I could manage.

"That's not the point! It's not yours! It's *mine*!" Bucky was like a rabid dog at this point.

"You will do time for this!" cried Ruth.

Honestly, it was insane. As I was considering jumping out of the moving car, we reached Eric's house. My plan was to escape from Ruth and Bucky, get to the door and explain the situation to Eric. I was hoping he'd pull me in and lock the door and I could hide out at his place until my mom came home. Unfortunately, Ruth and Bucky escorted me to the door. There would be no private face time between Eric and me. In fact, Eric wasn't even home. I was stuck with his mother, who was overworked and tired and didn't really want to deal with a missing amp. She checked her basement, but the amp wasn't there. This was not the answer Ruth and Bucky were looking for. I jumped in and suggested that Eric must have had it with him and that he would bring it back later and all would be well. As I did this, I began to blink a distress signal, using syllables inside my head (that I hoped she would understand telepathically) to send my message, which was:

"Please-help-me-I-am-be-ing-held-hos-tage-by-these-cra-zy-fuck-ers."

I blinked this over and over again, hoping against hope that Mrs. Goldstein would understand my Former Chief Inspector Charles Dreyfus syllabic blinking technique and help me. But she just thought I was insane.

Bucky and Ruth gave her their phone number. They wanted Eric to call once he got in. This pissed off Mrs. Goldstein, who insisted that her son didn't have their amp and that he would most assuredly not be calling them any time soon. Why she couldn't have said the same for me, I don't know.

Bucky and Ruth forced me back into the car. The drive home was brutal. There was more talk about the police, Juvie Hall and how I wasn't raised right. As they continued their rant, I began to wonder if, like Hank the Sub, there wasn't more to the Case of the Missing Amp. Why had Bucky suddenly turned into Bugs Meany? The fact was that the man had a hundred amps stacked up in his basement. Why the obsession with this one? Was there hidden money inside? Stolen jewels? White gold?

Bucky and Ruth dropped me off and issued their final ultimatum, "You've got until tomorrow night to get it back to us, or *else*." Then they screeched out of my driveway in their diesel Mercedes sedan, leaving nothing but a big cloud of black smoke.

I went inside the house. My brothers and sister had long since gone to bed, and my mother had just gotten back from Parents' Night. She was standing in the kitchen eating a hamburger that she'd just fried for herself.

"Where've you been?" she asked.

"Nowhere," was my answer.

I had a bad tendency of not telling things to my mother that were upsetting. Plus, years of living under Ming the Merciless' rule had instilled in me a guilt complex the size of Detroit. Despite the fact that I was innocent, I couldn't help feeling like I'd done something terribly wrong. I went down to my room and began making calls. I literally phoned the entire town of Upper Saddle River in an attempt to find this amp. Switchboards were lighting up like Christmas trees, as I worked to keep my ass out of jail. I was skipping school if I had to. It was all so stressful. I pushed on through the night and it became clear that the trail of the amp was a long and windy one. One person thought it had last been seen at Alyssa Epstein's Bat Mitzvah, another recalled spotting it at a pool party at Dave Reilly's house, while yet another thought it was locked in the custodial closet at the local grammar school. Despite the conflicting stories, I persevered. Following its trail, phoning students who I didn't even know, some as far away as Ho-Ho-Kus, in a quest to find the damn thing. It was like the short-lived TV series *Gun,* which chronicled the life of a gun as it passed from owner to owner. The amp, too, had had quite the adventure. Ping-ponging from one jam session to another, being lent, borrowed, returned, borrowed again, only to find itself in yet another car trunk, en route to a blues festival in Hartford. If the amp could have spoken, oh, the stories it could have told. By two a.m., I had narrowed its location down to a fifty-mile radius and by eight o'clock the next morning I received a call from some kid named Joshua, who informed me that the amp was in the basement of the Lutheran Church on Saddle River Road. I wept with relief.

After school, Brown Bob drove me to the church to get the amp. As we pulled into the driveway, I recognized the Goodwill bin where my mom once dumpster-dived for clothing for us. It was one of those full-circle moments.

Bob went in to get the amp because I was too exhausted to move. Then we drove to Bucky's house for the drop-off. As we neared the house, something inside me grew fearful and I decided to lie in the back of the car, much like O.J.

Bob parked and handed Bucky the amp, but Bucky looked in the car and saw me lying there. All I could think to do was shut my eyes and pretend to be dead. It was a pathetic moment and one that I wish I could live over again. Because if I could live it again, I would've thrown the amp out of the moving car and screamed, "Fuck you motherfucker!!! I always thought you were overrated!"

Instead, I hid.

The guilt complex morphed into a persecution complex. I started wearing pajamas to school. If every teacher was under the impression that I was a substitute-screwing, amp-stealing, drug addict, then I was going to give them what they wanted. The days blended together until finally I couldn't take it anymore. I was in a required history class, one that I had tried to opt out of by taking an AP class, but apparently, moronic history was a requirement. The teacher was a woman in her fifties named Miss Mahoney, who was so overweight that lecturing was like a full aerobic workout. She would wheeze and sweat and often times collapse from the sheer exertion of it all. Mahoney was also tight with the music teachers and thus, hated me. On this particular day, Mahoney was talking about the Triangle Shirtwaist Fire of 1911 and this dope named Monica raised her hand smugly and asked, "Why didn't they just airlift the workers out with a helicopter?"

And instead of ripping her head off and saying, "You moron! They didn't airlift them because there *were* no helicopters!" Mahoney said, "That's a good question, Monica."

I literally slammed my head down on the table. Mahoney started yelling at me, "Get a better attitude, Buckley!"

It was all spiraling downhill.

The next day, I cut history class and went home. My mom was finishing her dissertation and I liked sitting with her in the dining room while she edited on the big table.

"Shouldn't you be in school?" she asked.

"I can't deal with it."

My mom, bless her heart, never questioned me on stuff like this.

"It's a long year," she nodded.

Trouble was, Mahoney knew I cut and was going to make an example out of me. They were going to fail me in the class, which would mean that I would not be able to graduate and I would lose my slot at Manhattan School of Music, which had a waiting list the size of Missouri.

I couldn't take much more and so I went to my mom with everything. Hank the Sub, The Stolen Amp and now the impending GED. And my mom, being the cagey survivor that she was, hatched a plan to get me out of trouble. She wrote an epic note, in which she explained that I had cut class because I was about to be kidnapped by my insane mobster uncle. Had I not left the school, I would have risked not only kidnapping, but perhaps, a rather messy death. The letter went on for a full page. It was a tale of intrigue, shock and, dare I say it, titillation. And it worked like a charm. Mahoney never gave me any crap again.

Meanwhile, my mom, who was fucking pissed about the Amp of it all, contacted my dad looking for answers. He and I hadn't been speaking ever since a run-in involving my perfect score on the PSAT English exam and his completely inappropriate response, which went something like, "That's nice, but why can't you try harder to get along with your stepmother?"

To which I replied, "But Dad, it was a *perfect* score. And I didn't even study for it."

To which he replied, "If you'd try a little harder, maybe things would be better."

Which was the last straw on this camel's back.

The rest of the conversation was a blur, mostly because I lost my mind and started screaming at him until my voice gave out. Then I collapsed in a heap on the floor. My dad countered by not speaking to me for the better part of two months, thus making him the reigning champ of the Curious Silence Game.

Still, my mom wanted answers, so she broke the silence and learned that he was divorcing Ming the Merciless. He went so far as to admit that the abusive amp-retrieval incident and our prior PSAT conversation were all somehow part of that ugly breakup.

My mom was disgusted with my dad for letting me bear the brunt of his screw-ups and in the spirit of reconciliation, she got him to agree to write a note saying I had mono so that I could take the last six weeks of school off.

It was the nicest thing he ever did for me.

I spent most of my days lying in bed listening to Sade. I was, needless to say, really tired. Sometimes I'd burst into tears for no apparent reason and just lay there crying for hours. My mom would stand over my bed and ask, "What's wrong?" but all I could do was shrug and roll over. Words seemed to fail me. I was mired in a deep existential funk, one that had been brewing for a long time. It was bigger than me, even bigger than my mom, and the truth was neither of us was equipped in any way to deal with it.

I tried to sleep it off.

When that didn't work, I got up.

It was the end of an era and I felt that none of us had come away unscathed. Nak was wrestling, and sullen because he was hungry due to the constant need to make weight for his matches. My brother Lee became distant. Jenny's best friend Fat Lip had moved away. Even Midge, with her Dalmatian flags, had stopped smiling at us. My mom finally finished her PhD and we celebrated by going out to dinner at the local Chinese restaurant. As we sat around the table eating, I couldn't help but think that we'd finally made it back to the surface. Yet in surveying the vast ocean around us, there was an overwhelming feeling that we had somehow been blown off course.

14. SAVING GRACES

SINCE MANHATTAN SCHOOL OF MUSIC had no dorms, other living arrangements had to be found. Knowing that it would be tough to find a place toward the end of the summer, I convinced my mother that we should start looking earlier. We spent the last few weeks of my fake-mono illness searching for apartments, until we boiled it down to a choice between a room in an all-girl boarding house on West End Avenue and a studio apartment in a residential hotel on 91st and Broadway called The Greystone. The boarding house had nice crown moldings and high ceilings, but it also had a curfew, which really went against everything I believed in. The Greystone had no curfew, and in addition, I knew a cute boy from Juilliard who lived there. As such it was my first choice.

"Cute boy from Juilliard is not a good enough reason," chided my mom.

But it was more than the cute boy from Juilliard. When I considered the upcoming movie version of my life as a New Yorker, I saw myself attending openings and convening with hip, like-minded people in art galleries and outdoor soirees. I felt that The Greystone, with its pre-war dilapidated charm, bought me a sort of Early Junkie cachet that just wasn't going to happen at the All-Girl Boarding House with Curfew. My mother maintained that the cute boy from Juilliard was my prime motivation, but I assured her that she had raised me correctly. It was the Early Junkie cachet that I was after.

Still, my mom could not be persuaded. Day after day, it was the same litany of complaints: "It smells like urine ... The apartments are small and dreary ... There are always crazy people milling around in the lobby with their coats on ... It's like that hotel in *The Shining*..."

"What are you talking about?" I'd argue. "There's not a single topiary anywhere!"

It was going to be a tough sell, but I had read enough real estate ads at this point to know how to handle this type of situation.

"Quaint, charming. Old World Feel!" I'd yell through the bathroom door.

"Cozy... Emotional!" I'd cry out at the breakfast table.

"Wonderful location, great subway access," I'd blurt out while I hugged my mom goodnight.

This went on for weeks, until one particular afternoon, we were at Grand Union in Allendale doing the weekly shopping. My mom was whizzing down the aisles with the cart while I followed behind shouting, "Antiques galore! Gothic Old World Charm! Literary!"

She was ignoring me, which I hated. I was just about to throw in the towel, when we passed the aisle marked Feminine Hygiene and I decided to go to a dark place.

"Didn't you say you needed another douche, Mom!?" I yelled at the top of my lungs.

This got her attention.

She spun the cart around and yelled back, "Yes, yes, I know... Crown moldings, high ceilings, blablabla! It smells like urine!"

"Urine is not bad for you mom. If you're in a pinch, trapped at the bottom of a well, you can drink it and ..." before I could even finish, she zoomed out of the aisle. But

I would not be stopped. I began shoving cereal boxes out of the way, until I spotted her in the next aisle.

"Don't knock urine!" I cried. "There might come a time when it's your best friend. Your last line of defense!"

My mom was about to respond, when we both spotted a very angry clerk standing at the end of the aisle. We exchanged a glance and decided to table the discussion for home. An hour later we were putting away the groceries.

"Why are there so many old people sitting in the lobby all the time?" she asked.

"Do you have something against the aged, Mom? 'Cause I think they like to be called seniors. And lest you judge, not everyone can do volunteer work or become a docent... Some of them may have rheumatism."

"Is that why they're always wearing coats and hats?" she asked.

I responded to her question as if she were a retarded six-year-old.

"Mom. They wear coats and hats because this was the way people dressed during their era. And frankly, I think that a little more formality wouldn't be such a bad thing these days."

My mother eyeballed my ripped jeans and rolled her eyes, but I was pulling out all the stops. I was so close to making my escape, I just didn't want anything to go wrong. And with graduation approaching, I needed to march down that grassy aisle with the satisfaction of knowing there was a studio apartment waiting for me in the city. "What about that crazy lady who screams?" she asked.

She was referring to the Lobotomy Lady, who often wore nothing but a trench coat and, according to the cute boy from Juilliard, would flash people on the stairwell at night. "She's a method actor. A big name. Can't remember exactly, but she's in tight with Strasberg. She gets so inside the character it's tough for her to get out ... She's playing a crazy lady in a play and once it closes, she's going back to her sprawling, four-plus-two with deco touches on Central Park West."

My mother wasn't buying it. But I was going for the hard sell.

"That's commitment to the craft, Mom," I sneered.

"That's something," she agreed.

Thankfully, the heavens aligned and blind piano great and Duke Ellington aficionado Brooks Kerr phoned. Brooks launched into his usual improvisational conversation, "Just got in from a concert featuring Bebop Daddy Babs Gonzales and Three Bips and A Bob. It was a tribute concert for Willie The Lion Smith. Man that cat had a lyrical bent. You see it especially in his late stuff, like Echoes of Spring."

My mother was in no mood for this and improvised her own response.

"Kristen's arguing about the curfew at the boarding house, but I say The Greystone smells like urine."

Our phones were equipped with volume control for Jenny and Lee so I could hear everything that was being said. I figured Brooks was going to come back at my mom with some obscure fact regarding Cozy Cole or Tal Farlow, but instead he said, "Man, The Greystone used to be a happening joint. Duke Ellington used to hold court there and Lance Heywood, the blind Bermudian piano-player who has a steady gig at The Village Corner, lives on the eighth floor. You probably know Lance for his work with seminal Bahamian Jazz guitarist Ernest Ranglin ... "

My mom looked like she was ready to kill herself but I jumped in immediately.

"Lance Heywood, Ma!" I yelled, even though I'd never heard of the guy.

"He's the most famous blind piano-player to ever come out of Bermuda!"

"You mean Bahamas," my mom corrected, mildly annoyed.

"Yeah, my mistake, I confuse him with Altovese Huxley, the great Bermudian guitarist."

My mother just rolled her eyes.

"Are you familiar with Ranglin?" Brooks' voice bellowed from the receiver.

"No, Brooks, I can't say that I am," she answered.

"Man, the cat loved Charlie Christian; you could hear it in his playing. People say it was Bird in there, but I tell you it was Charlie," he said.

My mother looked at me and mouthed, "Who are these people?"

"He and Charlie Parker invented bebop, although they were in different cities," I explained quickly. "Charlie Parker was from Kansas City and Charlie Christian was from Oklahoma. They were doing the same thing at the same time, like the Egyptians and the Aztecs with their pyramids."

My mom nodded her head, mildly interested despite herself. Meanwhile, Brooks had long since departed our trio and was taking a wild Ornette Coleman-like conversational solo, "When Cozy Cole first came up he used to tell Diz that there was no way a boy like Lance could cut his teeth on the three, six two five progression ... "

Brooks began to laugh hysterically, which forced my mom into a fake laugh as well. My mom eyeballed me and then tried to hand me the phone. I jumped away. "I want to live at the Greystone!" I said.

"Behave yourself and take the phone," she demanded.

"Not until you agree," I countered.

"I will not be blackmailed," she said.

"Then enjoy yourself," I hissed.

My mother threw me a look as she went back to muttering "uh huh" and "hmm," and fake laughing with Brooks, until he said, "You've got to check out this early recording of Lance and Herb 'The Comeback' Chess. I got it off a one-legged cat I know from Amsterdam. Let me go find it."

Brooks had a bad habit of playing music over the phone for my mother. Being blind, it often took him a long time to locate the record he was looking for. And worse than the wait, was the music itself. My mom loathed jazz and the thought of listening to some obscure cutout was the straw that broke the camel's back. "I'd love to hear it Brooks! But I've got to go! Kristen's moving into The Greystone and I have to run because we need to fill out forms. Another time though ... "

My mother hung up and I threw my arms around her in joy.

I moved in the week after school was over. Jenny and my pal Jason helped me move my stuff in. Some clothes, my guitar, an amp, a record player. I was traveling light. After we unloaded everything, Jason and I had a quick goodbye, as I had no interest in some sort of drawn-out, Don Henley *Boys of Summer* moment.

"I'll see you soon," I told him. "And don't disappoint me by joining a stupid fraternity."

Jason smiled and hit the road back to Jersey. Jenny helped me unpack and then around dinnertime my mom popped in to drop off some groceries and to take Jenny home.

Not one for long goodbyes either, my mom gave me a kiss, said, "Don't move in with any boys," and made a hasty exit with my sister.

And there I was inside my very own sixth floor studio apartment. I surveyed my tiny universe. A twin bed, a table, a dresser, a chair, and two lamps. I had wished for an apartment at The Greystone and my wish had been answered. And once the reality of that sank in, all that was left were the overwhelming stench of urine and the stillness of absolute silence. Both of which made me nervous. But rather than spiraling into some vortex of doubt, I stayed positive and focused on the Early Junkie charm, imagining all the interesting characters who once inhabited the halls. Burnt-out writers, pug-nosed pugilists, cheap call-girls. And suddenly things were looking up again. I phoned the cute boy from Juilliard's apartment. But according to his outgoing message he was in Tanglewood for the summer. My hopes of spending madcap summer evenings with him dashed, I decided to go meet my neighbors.

It took me three days to summon up the nerve to go knocking door to door. But the delay served me well as I had at least gotten a working sense of my region of the floor.

Across from me, three doors down, lived The Prell Lady, so named because of her multi-tiered shrine, featuring empty Prell bottles, which was set up just to the right of her door. Prell Lady suffered from short-term memory loss and lived with a "gentleman friend" named Jerry, who bore a striking resemblance to the actor Vincent Schiavelli. Every morning Jerry would go out for coffee and return, knock on the door and say, "It's me, Jerry." And the Prell Lady would say, "Who?!" and he'd say, "Jerry!" and this would continue for the better part of fifteen minutes until Prell Lady's memory of Jerry was jarred and she'd let him in.

To my right, were two twenty-something guys, each in his own studio. One was named Greg, the other Vincent. They were both struggling actors, drawn together by their shared membership in the rogue Buddhist sect known as "Chant for What You Want."

This self-centered Buddhist faction was formed when a Tibetan monk took a Norman Vincent Peale seminar and fused the Power of Positive Thinking with Buddhist chants to create a viable potent force that could allegedly get you what you wanted (the two big celebrities in this bizarro Buddhist offshoot being Tina Turner and jazz great Wayne Shorter).

According to Greg and Vincent, it was simple; you had to spend five to six hours a day repeating the phrase *nam-myoho-renge-kyo* over and over, while envisioning whatever it was that you wanted – new car, record deal, cuter boyfriend, etc. They swore up and down that it really worked. Although when pressed, they admitted that they hadn't gotten anything yet.

"These things take time," said Greg, who was definitely not good looking enough to be an actor.

"And we're willing to give it our all," added Vincent, who was good looking, but sadly suffered from a preternaturally small head, which was a big "no-no" for actors, since a gigantic noggin has always been a prerequisite for stardom.

But Vincent and Greg were not going to be stopped. They chanted all night long, in unison and actually made the walls in my apartment vibrate. Tuvin throat singers had nothing on these guys. Of course I didn't have the heart to complain. I figured the sooner they got what they wanted, the sooner they'd move out.

The corner apartment was occupied by a woman named Rosa, who bore a striking resemblance to Mighty Mouse and for whom frying fish was a way of life. I knocked on her door a few times, but the din from her fryer was just too loud. And so I gave up, though I did make a point to smile and make eye contact when we were on the elevator together.

Across the hall from Vincent and Greg was a two-bedroom apartment that housed a fleet of television transcribers. These were the people who typed up transcripts of shows like *Oprah* and *20/20*. The transcripts could then be purchased by curious viewers for a small fee and a self-addressed stamped envelope. The Greystone was strictly residential and as such, the business was on the down-low. It was run by a heavyset woman named Margaret, who as it turned out, had a tumor on her ovary the size of a cantaloupe. She gave daily tumor updates to anyone who would listen. "Boy, she's swollen up today!" she'd intone. Or, "I'm feeling gassy but it's just the tumor playing mind games!"

I would always just nod my head politely and mutter, "Wow" or, "That must be strange," then hurry off as quickly as possible. But there was something about the way she'd eyeball me in the hallway. With the bevy of scraggly girls in their twenties who worked for her, I was pretty certain Margaret was looking to bring me into the fold. Sure enough, she offered me a job transcribing but thankfully I was able to decline, since I didn't know how to type. But I did need to get a summer job, because the cash I had was already running low. Margaret told me that she knew the manager of Symphony Space, which at the time was a rundown theater up on Broadway and 95th Street where I had gone to see the *Paper Bag Players* as a kid. The manager, Artie, was always looking for ushers. Margaret was nice enough to pass my number along to him and he phoned me the next day to see if I wanted to work a shift the following week.

The idea of working there really appealed to me. It would be a great way to meet new people. It was easy money and I'd get to watch live performances as well as movie revivals. My heart nearly skipped a beat when I saw that they were going to be showing *Quadrophenia*! This was going to be an auspicious beginning for me indeed.

In the meantime, I enjoyed my free time. I was taking a self-imposed sabbatical from playing because I'd gotten a bad flare up of tendonitis. I figured a few weeks off wouldn't kill me and with the free time, I could get acclimated to the city. Since the egoistic Buddhists were still on the p.m. chant cycle, I took to sleeping all day, then roaming the streets at night.

I was a castaway investigating my new island. All those years of being lost at sea and I'd finally washed ashore on the island of Manhattan. And there was so much to discover about the city. The beauty of it was that there was time at night. Time to see the city with all its secrets and hopes and dreams. I loved that you could walk down a street and see a thousand different faces. One that looked like me. One that looked like my sister. One that looked like my grandmother. And I loved to watch the people. Waitresses and busboys. Garbage men and ER doctors. All those tiny microcosms orbiting each other. I loved the cobblestone streets of the West Village and the shiny speckled sidewalks off University. I loved standing outside Automatic Slims on Washington, peering inside the small window at all the stories unfolding inside. I loved the tired greengrocer who peeled perfect slices of papaya for his icy front bin. More than that, I loved the buildings and their lighted windows. I would consider all the people inside and the enormity of their collective experiences. I'd just stand there, ruminating on all the possibilities, until my wide eyes would be drawn upward and out because there was something about the shape of the city at night. It felt so open and porous, as if with the exodus of commuters it was able to spread out and breathe under the blanket of night. There was a different rhythm, a different look, even a different smell. This was the real New York.

A week rolled by quickly and it was time for me to report to Symphony Space for my first night of work. I came a bit early and met Artie, who it turned out, was a struggling comedian. He did improv at the Westbank Café on Saturdays and I promised him I'd come down to see him, though he didn't really seem very excited by my enthusiasm.

"Don't let anybody in until seven, cause that's when the doors open," he said.

I nodded my head dutifully, "Got it. No one in until seven."

"I gotta go to an audition over at Caroline's so I'll be back later. Ben and Vaughn'll be working with you, so just stick with them."

I nodded my head enthusiastically, hoping Ben or Vaughn would make eye contact with me, but they were too busy reading their sport sections to look up.

"You can change in there," Artie pointed to a closet. "I'll see you all later."

Once Artie left, Vaughn and Ben began discussing baseball.

Ben mumbled, "Yanks really need to win this next series, they're three and a half out."

My Geiger counter was going crazy. This was my in! I knew *all* about the Yankees! I had once dreamed of being the first female Yankee manager, though I felt we weren't close enough to discuss that yet. I opted for my go-to Yankee ice breaker, "I grew up in a Yankee town and when they won the '78 Series, they actually had a parade at my school."

I stood there for a moment waiting for a reaction. But Ben and Vaughn didn't even look at me. I thought maybe they didn't hear me. Perhaps this was the problem, because surely, they couldn't be ignoring me. It was a long moment and I began to feel like a moron, which I knew wasn't possible, but still it was unsettling. And instead of just letting it go, I repeated myself. Which was such a mistake because Ben and Vaughn just exchanged a glance and then Ben said, "We heard you the first time."

Which, frankly, was a shitty thing to say and sort of crushing from a social perspective.

Completely mortified, I headed into the closet to change into my polyester tuxedo. Suddenly, there was an abrupt banging on the door and Vaughn yelled, "We're going to get some food!"

"Oh, okay, just a sec ... ," I yelled back, pulling on my cummerbund quickly. Things were looking up. I was getting an invite. But then Vaughn added, "Don't let anyone in before seven." My heart actually sank when I realized they weren't inviting me. Lame and pathetic? Yes. But it's not so easy being eighteen and all alone in a big city, even if it was the greatest city on Earth. I focused on the positive; at least no one would see me emerge from the closet in my ill-fitting uniform.

After they left, I read the newspaper for a while, poked through a few of the desk drawers and wandered around the theater, which was dusty and also smelled like urine.

At around 6:15, I walked past the front entrance and noticed an inordinate number of people lined up at the doors staring at me, with the glassy-eyed look reserved for the living dead. I tried to scurry out of view but it was too late. They spotted me and began banging on the glass.

"I was in the Holocaust!" one of them yelled.

I didn't know how to respond so I went with, "I'm sorry to hear that."

"Let me in!" screamed another one.

I turned and looked at the marquis board and saw that tonight's screening was a documentary about the Holocaust, which explained the throng of agitated Jews at the doors.

"We are survivors!" one cried.

"Let us in!" demanded another.

And then a voice from the crowd screamed, "I was in Auschwitz!"

And they all began banging and screaming in unison. And despite the fact that it was barely twenty after six, I did the only thing a person could do in this situation: I opened the doors and let the survivors in. I thought they'd calm down but in an effort to get orchestra seats they turned on one another. It was a stampede into the theater. I was knocked down in the melee and when I finally managed to get to my feet, I ran into the auditorium and saw that they were all arguing with one another.

It was a cacophony of voices.

"I was in Dachau!"

"I was in *Auschwitz*!"

"I have to have an aisle seat!"

"The aisle is mine!"

"I suffered enough!!"

"I will not take a center seat!"

"You don't know from suffering!"

"They starved us!"

"We went two months without food!"

"This row is taken!"

"Two months!?"

"That's a rainy day in Disneyland my friend!"

"I'm saving these seven seats for my cousins!"

"How dare you take all those seats?!"

"How dare *you*?!"

Then the fighting really began. They ripped out seat cushions and arm rests, and then they ripped out each other's hair and various articles of clothing. Using their purses as weapons, old women took turns bashing each other over the head. Desperate to try and control the situation, I started singing my sister's *If You're Jewish* song, but no one heard me.

Ben and Vaughn walked in at five of seven, saw the disaster and were forced to call Artie who had to leave his audition. Ben and Vaughn spent the better part of an hour breaking things up, while I sat in the office explaining things to an understandably irate Artie.

"They said they were in the Holocaust," I explained.

"So? That's not some free pass. My grandmother was in the Holocaust, I still wouldn't let her in before seven."

"Really?" I asked. "You wouldn't let her sit in the office or something? 'Cause you wouldn't want to be rude to your own grandmother, would you?"

"That's not my point!" he yelled. "Jews have the monopoly on rudeness, you have to be able to stand firm in the face of it, 'cause if you don't ... ," he pointed to the fistfight just outside the door involving three octogenarians, "this is what happens."

I stared in shock as Artie continued, "There's nothing more brutal than Jew on Jew violence," he said shaking his head. "I need to know that you can handle this type of thing, 'cause we have a huge portion of subscribers from the JCC."

I swallowed hard. "I've got a step-grandmother in Fort Lauderdale."

From his face this was not enough for Artie who sighed and said, “I'll call you if I need you.”

Dejected and depressed from what was probably the first true dismal failure of my life, I walked the city for hours. When I returned home, it must've been around 5 a.m. My apartment was oppressively hot so I opened the windows, which faced the courtyard that housed the dumpsters belonging to a Chinese restaurant. The morning stench was just beginning to rise, but I was too desperate to cool off to care. I pulled the bed over to the window, yanked off all my clothes and fell asleep dreaming of the Arctic. I woke up around 4:30 in the afternoon, feeling clammy and exhausted. My head hurt and my eyes were blurry. I looked over at the windowsill and saw that it was covered in feathers. Mounds of them were everywhere, as if there had been some sort of violent altercation. I looked around and saw *more* feathers strewn all over the floor beside my bed. Completely freaked out, due to an irrational fear of birds that I had inherited from my mother, I jumped up and pulled on some clothes. Then I proceeded to clean up all the feathers, which I decided unwisely to flush down the toilet. This of course clogged the toilet. And instead of just leaving the toilet alone to digest the offending quills, I continued to flush it, over and over, until water began to shoot out from under the toilet itself, creating a rather horrid mess. Though it pained me to do so, I called the front desk to see if the janitor could come up, only to be informed that he was away having his teeth cleaned. I asked if they had a toilet plunger but was told to just “make do.” I was nearly broke and plungers were out of my price range. And the man at the hardware store refused to lend me one. I went back to my apartment and assessed the situation. I could pee in the tub if necessary, but going full potty was going to be an issue.

I needed a damn toilet plunger.

After much debate, I knocked on the door of my Mighty Mouse look-alike neighbor, Rosa.

"Hi, I'm your neighbor, remember?" I said, pointing to my door.

"You're the noisy one. Everyone's talking about you."

Which was a big shock because I hadn't touched my guitar since I'd moved in.

"Everyone's talking about me?" I asked.

"Yeah, you're on thin ice," she said.

Clearly she had me mistaken for someone else. "I don't understand. I'm so quiet and most of the time I'm not home."

She narrowed her gaze, "We all hear you and your racket."

"Are you sure you're not confusing me with the chanting Buddhists?" I tried.

"The *who*?" she asked.

This was clearly going nowhere and I had an explosion of bird feathers and fecal water in my bathroom that needed to be cleaned up.

"I just need a favor, if you don't mind," I started.

Rosa opened the door and let me inside. The apartment was a shrine to velvet art and judging from the Jarco Electric Twin Pot Fryer, the art of frying food.

"They don't know I've got these," she said proudly of her fryers. "It's against code, 'cause these babies can cause fires like that," she snapped her fingers to illustrate. "I blew one up down at the Chelsea. That's how I ended up here."

"Your secret's safe with me," I joked as I eyeballed the fryer, which was located on the opposite side of the wall where I slept. I made a mental note to move my bed to the other side of the room, so as to avoid being blown to smithereens when the fryers went.

"So, what's your story?" she asked.

"Um, I just need to borrow a … "

"No, not why are you *here*, what's your story?" she said.

"I don't really have one," I said.

"Everyone has a story," she insisted.

"I'm just here because I'm going to music school and the rents were reasonable," I explained, leaving out the part about the Early Junkie charm.

"Let me tell you something sweetie, everyone in this place either comes in with a story, or goes out with a story. You haven't found yours yet, but trust me, before it's all over, you're gonna have a story to tell."

I wasn't sure what to say to this; there was an ominous quality to her voice.

"Well, hopefully it'll be a good one." I said.

"Don't know about that," she said, dumping another vat of fish into the fryer. "But it'll be yours."

"I suppose."

"So, what brings you to my abode?" she finally asked.

"I really need to borrow a toilet plunger."

She looked at me like I was insane.

"A toilet plunger is a very personal object."

"I know but I put feathers down the toilet and it backed up all over the floor."

"Honey, I'll give you the shirt off my back, but I won't give you my plunger. It has my doo on it and I can't have *your* doo, getting on *my* doo."

"But there's no doo involved," I reasoned. "It's just bird feathers."

"Even worse. They're filthy creatures you know. Sorry, no can do. Try sticking a broom down it."

I left feeling dejected and depressed and spent the better part of a day cleaning up the bathroom. Later, I found out from the night guard that the janitor had never had his teeth cleaned in his life and was going to be away for a week. He was nice enough to look for a plunger, but it turned out they didn't have one.

With no running toilet water and pooping in the tub like a cat not an option, I took to the streets in search of bathrooms. Had this been Ancient Rome or Ancient Crete it would've been no problem, but this was New York where the lack of public bathrooms had been well documented throughout history. Even Henry Miller once complained, "I know that I am in distress when I walk the streets of New York. Wondering constantly where the next stop will be and if I can hold out that long."

I tried the public toilets in Central Park, but they were filled with flashers, perverts, rapists, and more often than not rats. Then I tried the subway toilets. There were something like seventy-eight of them, but every one I found was locked. Police stations were clean, but the assortment of unsavory criminal-element types put them way down on the list. Public libraries had big bathrooms, though they were surprisingly dirty, thus debunking any connection between literacy and hygiene.

The bigger issue in my public toilet odyssey had to do with frequency. Not in urination but in appearances. If you used a public bathroom too often and were spotted by a city official, you risked getting pegged as a vagrant. As a result I had to mix it up. One day I'd start my morning at the 20th Precinct, then hit The Lincoln Center Listening Library before lunch, with a quick slash at Avery Fisher after. Hotels were good for the night shift, although the key to success was to blend in with the tourists. This usually involved carrying a large bag of sorts and nodding to the concierge. The Waldorf-Astoria had very gaudy décor but was a great choice if you were near 50th Street. The Plaza was tricky because their doorman was very officious, but the bathrooms were *very* nice. My personal fave was The Royalton, although the doors were always locked and you'd have to loiter until someone with a key came along and slip in behind them. However, once inside, the modern works of art made it well worth the trouble.

Since I was running out of money fast, I took to eating Knorr vegetable soup for every meal, as it was cheap. On the downside, I was starving, but on the plus side, I lost a lot of weight. And thanks to all the walking and a lack of sunscreen, I got quite the tan.

Back at The Greystone, things were pretty grim. After the feather incident, I refused to open my windows. Without air-conditioning, the apartment was oppressively hot. In addition, if I made the slightest sound, Rosa would bang on my wall with a broomstick. I was forced to tiptoe around in socks, listen to music with headphones and whisper on the phone. All I *could* do was sweat profusely and try to ignore the steady trickle of water seeping from under the bathroom door onto my carpet.

"Why am I having so much trouble hearing you?" my mother asked one night as we chatted on the phone.

I was lying face down on my bed, with a pillow over my head so as not to disturb Rosa's bionic hearing.

"I signed up for summer choir at school and I'm saving my voice for rehearsal."

A complete and total lie, but I figured my mom would be steamed if she thought I was misbehaving and making too much noise, which I wasn't. "Your sister has joined the choir, we'll have to go in and hear her," I heard her say to Jenny.

"Mom, she's deaf, she can't hear music," I responded.

"Helen Keller said that she often enjoyed the vibrations."

Whatever. I wasn't going to get stressed about my mother thinking I was in choir and her subsequent plans to attend a nonexistent performance.

"How's the job going?" she asked.

"It's good, they're all nice." I hadn't gotten around to telling my mother about my colossal failure.

"Oh, tell me more," she pleaded.

"Not much more to say, we just let them in and they watch the show. Then we all go home."

I hated lying to my mom on so many fronts but I had

bigger issues to think about. Aside from a toilet that didn't work because the janitor was still "at the dentist" and the fact that I was broke, there was yet an even larger problem looming.

My friend Flo was late.

I had never been late before, so I was sort of shocked when my date rolled around and she didn't show up. I didn't want to be one of those girls who was all irregular and had to go on the pill. Were my ovaries suddenly shutting down? Was this somehow related to the use of public toilets? Did a seed from Margaret's cantaloupe tumor escape and pollinate on my ovary? What was going on? I envisioned horrible health problems and frequent visits to the gynecologist. As is the wont of every girl in my predicament, I amped up my public bathroom use. After about four days of this I staggered home from yet another long day's journey into public toilets and bumped into Rosa.

"You're glowing!" she cried.

"What?"

"Glowing ... Look at you ... Wow, when's it due?"

"When's what due?!" I said.

"Your baby," she patted my half-starved, concave stomach.

"I'm not pregnant!" I blurted out.

Rosa rolled her eyes at me and muttered, "Suit yourself," as she went into her apartment.

But of course this left me in a tizzy. I went inside and stared at myself in the mirror. I was indeed glowing, though I was too exhausted to realize that my glow was the residual effect of sweat, sunburn and starvation. With that dreaded word "pregnant" ping-ponging through my brain, my eyes came to rest on a lone white feather sitting under my dresser, which had apparently escaped my frenzied cleanup a week earlier. And I thought of the feathers. The massive array of them everywhere. The sheer violence of it all. And then I recalled with horror that I had been completely naked! Being naked was not normal for me because I grew up in a repressed Catholic household. Nakedness was really bad, as it led to sex, which was *super* bad, because sex led to things like unwanted pregnancies, hairy palms, and blindness. It also occurred to me that I had missed the unit on sex-ed during my fake-mono illness and as a result, I wasn't completely clear on the ins and outs of interspecies reproduction, which I assumed would have been covered.

But despite my ignorance, the evidence in favor of pregnancy was mounting. Something had happened while I was sleeping. There had been an invasion of birds, or perhaps it was just one bird, a giant pigeon maybe, and it had come into the room, coupled with me, and now I was pregnant with a mutant half-breed child! I considered this for a while and then realized I was being ridiculous. After all, the child wouldn't be half-bird, because obviously the bird had really been a god (disguised as a bird) and so the child would not be born with strange wing-like arms or a beak for a nose. Rather, it would be an illustrious, godlike offspring, much like Hercules or Helen of Troy. But was *this* to be my story? Young girl leaves the mean streets of New Jersey only to get pregnant when a Greek God (disguised as a pigeon) takes advantage of her overheated naked body? The child would be born with superhuman traits that would inevitably cause all sorts of strife. My heart was pounding from the stress of it all. Until things took a turn for the worse and I realized that this was not the work of a Greek God, because as everyone knew, they had been defeated by a more powerful singular god. No, my virginal pregnancy could have only been the work of one spirit and one spirit alone ...

The Holy Ghost.

Everyone knew that he often appeared in the form of a white dove. And damn if those feathers weren't super white.

I took to the streets, trying to figure out what to do. I didn't want to be carrying the next Messiah. The stress was unbearable. How would I explain this away? Obviously I couldn't get rid of it, because that would surely peg me for eternal damnation. I'd known Hell in sixth grade and wasn't going back. No, I was going to have to have this baby and I was pretty sure I was going to be persecuted and ridiculed. And my dreams of becoming a musician (and meeting Sting) were going to be put on hold. I didn't know what I was going to do. I prayed to Saint Gregory, patron saint of musicians, to help me out. And I began to feel so bad for Mary (mother of God) because I never realized how hard it was be to the recipient of an immaculate conception. But still, that was back in the day when women didn't have dreams like meeting rock stars and forming think tanks to influence culture. For Mary it was probably more of a shock than an inconvenience, but for me, the timing was *awful*. I needed an immaculate conception like I needed a hole in the head. Worse yet, if this was the *True Messiah*, then this meant I'd be leading the Jews who were the only group still waiting for their savior to arrive. And if my one night working as an usher at Symphony Space was any indication, I'd be steam-rolled by my own people and they'd steal my baby and it would all end badly.

Days spent crisscrossing the Upper West Side in search of bathrooms had taken its toll on my Plantar warts, which had never fully healed. I sensed an outbreak, which was really the last straw. There was only one person who could help me in this time of need and that was my sister Jenny. I phoned my mother and told her that I needed my sister to come in. She could stay the weekend with me and I'd sort this all out with her. She'd know how to handle this, because unlike me (who was prone to hysteria) she had an ability to detach from the situation and approach it clearly and rationally. All I had to do was convince her that I wasn't crazy and then we'd figure the whole thing out. I phoned my mother and arrangements were made for Jenny to be dropped off that night.

Just as I was rehearsing my opening salvo, there was a knock on my door. Thinking it was Jenny I jumped up, opened the door and blurted out, "I'm a virgin, but I'm pregnant!"

Trouble was, it was the janitor, newly returned from his weeklong teeth cleaning with a plunger in hand and quite the sparkling set of chompers. He purged the feathers of the Holy Ghost and just like that, plumbing was mine. I could go to the bathroom! What joy! It really was the little things that made a difference. In my happiness, I began jumping up and down. My Messiah baby and I were going to be fine. I thanked the dentally restored janitor profusely. As he left, I noticed that he bowed his head to me, which was sort of strange, but I was too happy to really consider it. With all my jumping up and down and rejoicing over the return of indoor plumbing, I felt a sudden quickening. I ran to the bathroom and lo and behold ... Flo had arrived!

My joy was boundless. I thanked Saint Gregory for letting me off the hook. Obviously he had seen that I wasn't cut out to be the mother of a Messiah. Maybe an apostle or a high-ranking church official, but Messiah, not so much. By the time my sister arrived I was so deliriously happy I still couldn't stop jumping up and down. My sister was happy to see me too, and even though jumping up and down wasn't her style she partook in a slight hop. Even better, my mother had slipped my sister a twenty, which might as well have been a million dollars. It was time to go have a feast, to give thanks for all that we had.

As we headed out of the building I heard whispers spreading among the hat-wearing seniors in the lobby, who had been clued in by the gleam-toothed janitor.

"Look at her, so full of herself, thinks she's a big shot cause she's carrying the Messiah," mumbled a woman named Estelle.

"Please, Estelle, you'd be celebrating too if you were carrying the Messiah," argued her husband.

"What you don't know, Saul, is a lot," snapped Estelle.

The conversations regarding my imaginary immaculate conception spread like wildfire, but I was too happy to care.

Outside, it was a perfect New York summer's eve. It was still light out and the setting sun was glinting off the buildings all orange and yellow. The sky looked so beautiful, it made you happy to be alive. From our vantage point we could even make out the gleaming Hudson River and just beyond it, New Jersey, which was where our story had begun. We headed south and then crossed over to Amsterdam to get a bite to eat. We settled on an Italian place near 76th because Jenny liked the fact that it had glass doors that opened onto the street.

"It looks classy," she insisted.

We sat down and after perusing the pricey menu, settled on a simple pizza, which no doubt annoyed our waiter. Then we got caught up. Jenny told me everything that had been going on in recent weeks. Nak had shagged a flight attendant on his way home from wrestling camp. Stacie had attended a Jackson Browne concert and was back on her world peace bandwagon. Lee was working part-time at the Chinese restaurant up the street and one of the waiters, a guy named Fong, had decided that my mom was his new best friend and kept showing up on Sundays (unannounced) to discuss his life choices with her. And finally, Midge from across the street decided that flags were passé and had begun wearing giant Dalmatian pins on her lapels instead. In short, nothing had really changed.

After a few drinks, I told my sister all about my false pregnancy and she laughed so hard soda came out of her nose. It was a great night and there was a lot to be happy about. Namely, we had each other. Then of course there was the fact that I had a working toilet and, the best one yet, I was not pregnant with the Messiah.

Pretty soon, the waiter brought the biggest pizza we had ever seen and we dug in with the relish that can only come after eating instant soup for a month in humid weather.

As we ate, my sister's eyes grew wide. "Now there's something you don't see everyday," she laughed.

I turned and saw a disheveled homeless man peeing against the window by our table.

While everyone around us politely ignored the rogue slasher, I began to laugh hysterically. The sheer brazen quality of it, coupled with my understanding that public bathrooms were indeed hard to come by, made me feel simpatico with our urinary offender. And all I could think to say was, "Isn't this the greatest place ever?"

Jenny nodded, "You are *so* lucky!"

And I was lucky, because no matter what happened, if I didn't become a famous musician, if I didn't meet Sting, if I was never part of a Think Tank (that influenced culture and politics), I had this moment. After all, how many people could say that they had sat in a clean, well-lit restaurant and enjoyed a delicious piece of pizza while a homeless man peed all over the window?

Only in New York could such disparate elements fuse together so seamlessly and wonderfully. I became a citizen of New York in that moment. The city revealed itself to me and I saw my place within it. I didn't know about my future. I guessed that all that would sort itself out. Like Rosa said, everyone left with a story. One way or another.

What I did know was that there was a place for me. And that for the first time, in a long time, I knew I was exactly where I belonged.

In my mind's eye I remembered that fateful day, so many years ago, when my dad had left. I remembered clinging to my mother for dear life. I remembered how she had said to me, "Everything is going to be fine."

For a long time after that I resented the statement

because everything wasn't fine. Had she said, "Everything will be different," or, "Everything will be difficult," or maybe, "Nothing will ever be the same," I would have at least had the luxury of being able to believe her.

But so much time had passed and so many tears had washed my eyes clean that on this night, I was able to see that moment again through clear eyes. And it occurred to me that she hadn't said, "Everything is going to be fine."

What she had said was, "You are going to be fine."

You being the operative word. It was a statement of intent. My mother's own complicated history may have been a mangled disaster, but there was hope for me. I would have the freedom to think and dream; the freedom to define my own life on my own terms. I would not be forced to be less than the sum of my parts. And with my mom at the helm of our wounded ship, I'd made it to the other side, and washed ashore on the wondrous island of Manhattan. My feet planted firmly on dry ground. My future spread out above me; all my hopes encased in vertical lines of concrete and steel.

Just beyond the island, I could hear storm clouds raging, yet I knew everything would be okay. I knew this because I could see my mom in the distance. She was out there lying in wait on the rough seas. An unwavering beacon to any lost soul who needed a little help finding their way back to dry land.

INDEX

1. FIVE AND A HALF STAGES OF GRIEF

ASBURY PARK

Once a thriving boardwalk and beach along the great Atlantic Ocean, Asbury Park fell on hard times during the 1970s, when race riots started what was to be a 30-year decline in the city, which now resembles bomb damage assessment photos from Iraq.

BRUCE SPRINGSTEEN

Author Jim Cullen sums Springsteen up best when he writes, "Springsteen's music clarifies, revises and reinterprets the myths and symbols of American culture."

To this end, nothing sums up life in New Jersey better than these lyrics.

Baby this town rips the balls off your back
It's a death trap, it's a suicide rap
We gotta get out while we're young
'cause tramps like us, baby we were born to run

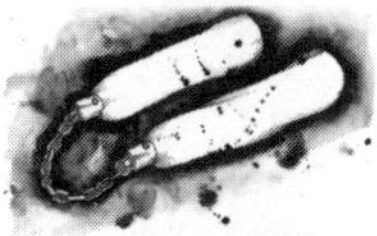

On the Web

www.brucespringsteen.net/news/index.html
www.greasylake.org/

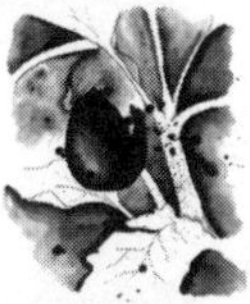

MAUD GONNE

The "Joan of Arc" of Ireland. She was a fiery orator, a patriot, a noteworthy actress, a good writer, an adventuress (who ran off to France with radical journalist Lucien Millevoye), and a mother.

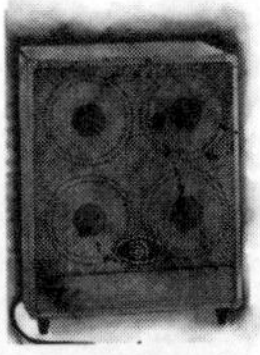

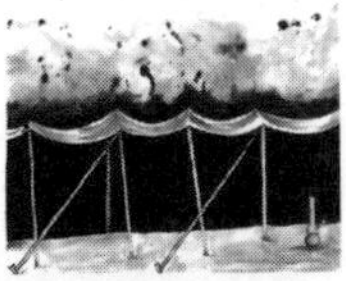

A shortlist of her accomplishments:

- She founded the Daughters of Ireland in 1900, which opened the door of 20th century politics to Irish women.
- She fought for the Irish who were the Treason-Felony prisoners on the Isle of Wight.
- She single-handedly averted famine by helping the Irish to hoard their food supply.
- She was 5' 10".
- She helped establish the Abbey Theatre in Dublin.
- She was the muse of William Butler Yeats, who wrote about her often in his poetry. Among his most memorable lines:

How many loved your moments of glad grace,
And loved your beauty with love false or true;
But one man loved the pilgrim soul in you,
And loved the sorrows of your changing face.

From "When You Are Old," William Butler Yeats

Her daughter Iseult Gonne had a torrid affair with the writer Ezra Pound.

Her son Sean MacBride was the co-founder of Amnesty International.

Essential reading

The Autobiography of Maud Gonne: A Servant of the Queen.

The Gonne–Yeats Letters 1893–1938 by Anna MacBride White (Maud's niece).

ROMANTICISM

A secular and intellectual movement in the history of ideas that originated in late 18th century Western Europe. It stressed strong emotion, legitimized the individual imagination as a critical authority, and overturned some previous social conventions. There was a strong recourse to historical and natural inevitability in the representation of its ideas.

Romanticism is also noted for its elevation of the achievements of what it perceived as misunderstood heroic individuals and artists who altered society.

ROMANTIC POETS

John Keats summed up the Romantics best when he coined the phrase "Negative Capability," which meant being able to exist within the mists of uncertainty, mystery, and doubt without concern for fact and reason.

The poetry of the romantics helps us step outside of ourselves to realize a more fully understood existence. They stress the importance of imagination, courage, and truth. Reading them (Blake, Wordsworth, Coleridge, Byron, Shelley, Keats) with an open heart can change your life.

Great websites

www.poets.org/
www.poemhunter.com/

SEPTIC TANKS

Apparently the French were the first to use an underground septic tank system, back in the 1870s.

ST. RITA

Patron Saint of Desperate Cases

St. Rita was born in Spoleto, Italy in 1381. Like most saints, she had the calling at an early age, though her parents refused to listen to her and forced her to marry a horrible guy. After his death, Rita found herself alone in the world and finally able to fulfill her childhood dream of becoming a holy nun. Shunned by the nuns on account of the fact that she wasn't a virgin, St. Rita did her best to outholy everyone, putting all her efforts into piety, self-denial, and obedience. Her work was rewarded when by some miracle a thorn (presumably from His crown) flew into her forehead. There it festered until the other nuns were obliged to give a wide berth to Rita and the stench surrounding her. She continued in this life of holy mortifications for fifteen years and upon her death, the stench from her festering wound became that of a rose. There are those who maintain that the sweet fragrance permeates the atmosphere of the convent, where her incorrupt body is on display under glass.

WHITE TRASH

According to the Oxford English Dictionary, "white trash" first came into common use in the 1830s as a derogatory term used by the slaves of upper-class Southerners against poor whites, who worked in the fields and were below even the status of yeomen. At the time, "white trash" was synonymous with the slurs "sand hiller" and "clay eater" because they were assumed to farm ineptly on poor land and therefore had to resort to eating clay in order to survive.

For Great Moments In White Trash please go to: http://snltranscripts.jt.org/

Key Words: *White Trash; Appalachian Emergency Room*

2. FORT APACHE

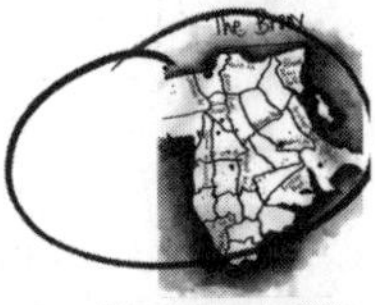

THE BRONX

The Bronx is the only section of New York City that belongs to the North American mainland. The borough got its name from the Swedish immigrant Jonas Bronk who acquired a massive piece of land that later became known among locals as "the Bronks land".

Quintessential reading

In the South Bronx of America by Mel Rosenthal, Martha Rosler, Barry Phillips

South Bronx Rising: The Rise, Fall, and Resurrection of an American City by Jill Jonnes

Ladies and Gentlemen, The Bronx Is Burning: 1977, Baseball, Politics, and the Battle for the Soul of a City by Jonathan Mahler

Quintessential viewing

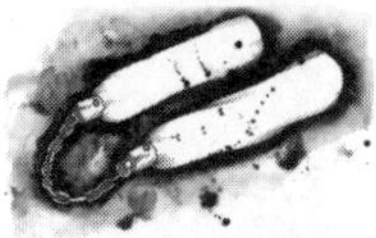

A Bronx Tale
Fort Apache, The Bronx
The Warriors
Marty
Mac
Finding Forrester

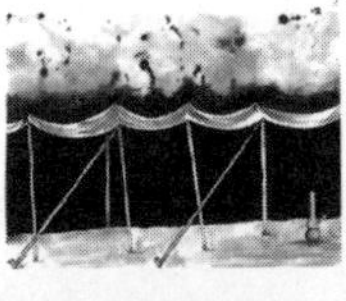

DOMINICAN VOODOO

If you are geographically challenged then you might not know that the Dominican Republic and Haiti are the same island. It was first called Hispaniola, then the French came and took over and it became Haiti, but locals fought French repression in favor of Spanish oppression.

JACKSON WHITES

Folk belief was that the Jackson Whites were descendants of runaway and freed slaves ("Jacks" in slang) and whites (including Dutch settlers and Hessian soldiers) who had supported the English during the American Revolution and were forced to flee to the mountains after the end of the war. In his book *The Ramapo Mountain People*, historian David Cohen found that the old stories about these people were legends, not history.

On the Web

www.ramapoughlenapenation.org

KEN WAHL

Actor Ken Wahl was tall, handsome, athletically gifted, and best of all, he oozed on-screen appeal to both sexes. Unfortunately, taking his cue from Jan Michael Vincent, he smashed up his face in a car accident. Though he managed to survive, he spent many years battling several addictions in an attempt to ease the chronic pain.

Must-see Ken Wahl movies:

The Wanderers
Fort Apache, The Bronx
The Soldier
Purple Hearts

MELUNGEONS OF TENNESSEE

The Melungeons were "discovered" in the Appalachian Mountains in 1654 by English explorers and were described as being "dark-skinned with fine European features," (meaning they were not black) and as being "a hairy people, who lived in log cabins with peculiar arched windows," (meaning they were not Indians). They practiced the Christian religion and told the explorers in broken Elizabethan English that they were "Portyghee," but were described as being "not white," that is, not of Northern European stock, even though some of them had red hair and others had VERY striking blue or blue/green eyes. Recent research suggests that they may be a combination of Turks, Spaniards, Portuguese, Moor, Berber, Jew, and Arab.

PARENTS WITHOUT PARTNERS

If you are a parent without a partner, then this is the group for you. Unless you are like my stepsister, who attended once and ran screaming from the building. Clearly it is a hit-or-miss proposition.

www.parentswithoutpartners.org/

QUINN CUMMINGS

d.o.b. August 13, 1967

The Meryl Streep of child actresses. At 10 she starred with Marsha Mason in *The Goodbye Girl* (1977) for which she received an Academy Award nomination. She eventually left the film business and went on to invent the Hiphugger baby sling.

http://shop.store.yahoo.com/thehiphuggeronline/faqs.html

RECIPE FOR MANGU

Before starting to cook: Peel the plantains and cut into 8 pieces.

Ingredients

4 unripe plantains
4 tablespoons of butter
2 tablespoons of oil
2 large onions
1 tablespoon of vinegar
1 cup of cold water
Salt

Preparation

Boil the plantains adding 2 teaspoons of salt to the water. When the plantains are very tender, turn off the heat.

While the plantains are boiling, heat a tablespoon of oil in a shallow pan. Saute the onions, add the salt and the vinegar. Reserve.

Take the plantains out of the water and mash them with a fork. Add the butter and the cold water and keep mashing until it is very smooth. Garnish with the onions and serve with scrambled eggs or deep-fried slices of salami.

Serves 4.

ROANOAKE COLONY

In 1587 over 100 men, women, and children journeyed from Britain to Roanoke Island on North Carolina's coast and established the first English settlement in America. Within three years, they had vanished with scarcely a trace. Creepy stuff indeed.

www.thelostcolony.org/

VOODOO V. CATHOLICISM

Similiarities

- Both venerate a supreme being.
- Both believe in the existence of invisible evil spirits or demons.

- Both believe in an afterlife.
- Both focus their ceremonies around a centerpiece, i.e. an altar in Catholicism, a pole or tree in voodoo.
- Both the services include symbolic or actual rituals of sacrifice and consumption of flesh and blood.
- Both have "saint" equivalents, though in voodoo they're called Loa.
- For example, Legba, an old man, is said to open the gates between Earth and the world of the Loa, much like St. Peter traditionally throws wide the gates to heaven.

Differences

- Westerners tend to believe in free will and personal choice. Not so in voodoo. The Loa are believed to determine our lives to an astonishing degree and are always present in great numbers: There might be two people in a room, but there are also twenty Loa.

. TAKING THE BATH

ANTI-FRIZZ

Life with curly hair has made me an expert in the art of controlling unruly tresses.

Here is my foolproof routine for perfect curly hair:

- Start with a good cut. (Bad cuts will cause you to "triangulate" giving you the look of an Egyptian pyramid.)
- Find a hairdresser who is Italian, as they seem to be the best with curly hair. (If you find yourself in Beverly Hills go see Alex LaPiana at Umberto Salon.)
- Never brush your hair. Ever.
- Purchase the proper products, and don't skimp! For best results use the brilliantly innovative product line *Me to You* formulated by the aforementioned mad hair genius Alex La Piana.
- Shampoo once every two weeks.
- Condition daily.
- Apply a large amount of Styling Cream to wet hair working it through each tress evenly. Then allow to dry.
- Scrunch dried hair with fingers to eliminate any of that dreaded DeBarge "wet look" and enjoy your day of perfect hair.

CARVEL CAKES

You can't live your life without eating Fudgie the Whale and/or Cookie Puss at least once.

www.carvel.com/

JAPANESE NOVELS

Long before *Memoirs of a Geisha*, Japanese writers have been thrilling readers with their depictions of upper class Japanese life.

The Heian Period (794–1185) in Japan is associated with aristocratic and courtly elegance, art and poetry, literature, and religious learning. Out of this period emerged two classics.

The Tale of Genji, written by Lady Murasaki, is the world's first novel and contains 54 chapters, which chronicle the life of the aristocracy.

For more information check out: www.taleofgenji.org/

The Pillow Book by Sei Shonagun is another literary masterpiece of the period, which reveals the observations and musings of an attendant in the Empress' court.

MARX BROTHERS ESSENTIAL VIEWING

Horse Feathers (1932)
Duck Soup (1933)
A Night At The Opera (1935)

www.marx-brothers.org/

RELIGION

Judaism

Defining Theme:	Chosen People
Favorite Son:	David
Culinary Tradition:	Matzo Ball
Big Moment:	Moses parts the Red Sea
Essential Reading:	*I and Thou* by Martin Buber

Catholicism

Defining Theme:	Meek shall inherit the earth
Favorite Son:	Jesus
Culinary Tradition:	Spaghetti and meatballs
Big Moment:	Jesus resurrects

Essential Reading:	*The Golden Legend* by Jacobus de Voragine

Protestant

Defining Theme:	Screw tradition
Favorite Son:	Gutenberg
Culinary Tradition:	Tuna noodle casserole
Big Moment:	King Henry wants a divorce
Essential Reading:	*The Mischief of Sin* by Thomas Watson

. IN PURSUIt OF LEISURE

BULLSHARKS

Bullsharks have special features that enable them to live in freshwater. A gland near the tail helps them retain salt, and the kidneys are designed to recycle the salt already in the body.

In July 1916, three swimmers were killed by a shark dubbed "The Matawan Manhunter" that swam into the Matawan Creek River. Scientists now think it was a bullshark because they are the only shark breed with the propensity toward venturing into fresh water.

"The Matawan Manhunter" was the inspiration for Peter Benchley's book *Jaws*.

www.nationalgeographic.com (key words bull shark)

THE (NOT SO) FLYING WALLENDAS

Arguably the most famous tightrope act of the 20th century. Led by their loopy patriarch Karl Wallenda, there was pretty much nothing they wouldn't do: Seven man pyramids, trotting across skyscrapers, balancing on chairs... The only thing was that Karl didn't believe in nets, and as a result, about five Wallendas plunged to their deaths and about five others were paralyzed in falls.

Their story was immortalized by the late, great Lloyd Bridges in the 1978 TV movie, *The Great Wallendas*.

Visit www.wallenda.com for performance information.

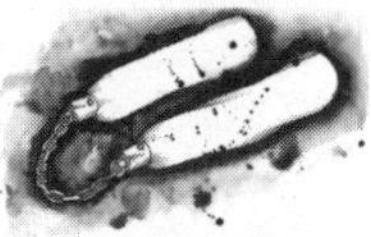
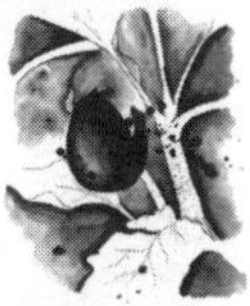

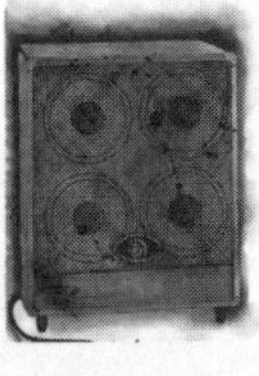

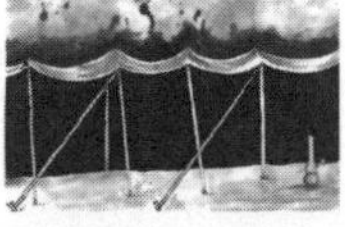

MINOANS

The Minoans were a pre-Hellenic Bronze Age civilization in Crete in the Aegean Sea, flourishing from approximately 2600 to 1450 B.C. when their culture was superseded by the Mycenaean culture (i.e. the first Greeks), which drew upon the Minoans.

The three characteristics that make the Minoans unique in the ancient world are their focus on female versus male deity; the strong possibility that their rulers were not men but women; and, arguably, their avoidance of warfare.

Essential reading

Minotaur: Sir Arthur Evans and the Archaeology of the Minoan Myth by J. A. Macgillivray

On the Web

www.uk.digiserve.com/mentor/minoan/
www.theplumber.com/crete.html
www.explorecrete.com/

SIX MILLION DOLLAR MAN

aka *The Bionic Man*

Lee Majors played Colonel Steve Austin, a NASA test pilot who survived a near fatal crash and was reconstructed and refurbished by Dr. Rudy Wells at a cost of $6,000,000. Steve was fitted with atomic-powered legs, arms, and a left eye (complete with built-in grid screen). Steve then went to work for The Office of Strategic Investigations where he battled foreigners, spies, and villains. He also occasionally fought aliens and extraterrestrials. There was eventually a Bionic woman, a Bionic kid, and a Bionic dog. His marriage to Farrah Fawcett was for many of us a first foray into celebrity marriage.

5. tRUtH OR CONSEQUENCE

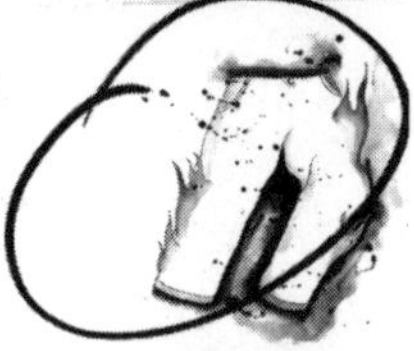

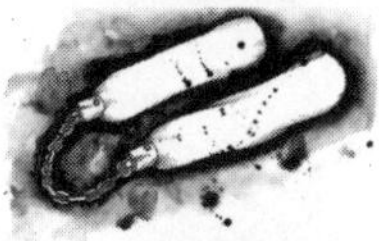
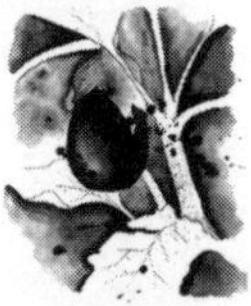

CAMILLE CLAUDEL

French sculptor and graphic artist. Born in 1864, Claudel displayed a fascination for sculpting from the time she was a child. Eventually she became an assistant to Rodin, and then his muse and lover. Beautiful, talented, and fiercely independent, Claudel struggled to find her own place out of the shadow of Rodin. Unrivaled in her ability to convey narrative through her sculptures, Claudel became a brilliant sculptor in her own right. But like many women, yearning for freedom and struggling against a male-dominated system, Claudel became paranoid and depressed. People labeled her as crazy and she was eventually shipped off to a mental asylum where she lived the rest of her life in complete solitude without so much as a visit from a single family member. She died in 1941.

Essential reading

Camille Claudel & Rodin: Fateful Encounter by Auguste Rodin, Camille Claudel, Antoinette Lenormand-Romain

Essential viewing

Camille Claudel (1998) starring Isabelle Adjani and Gerard Depardieu. The ending will haunt you forever.

www.camilleclaudel.asso.fr/ (great web site – all in French)

CHER

In a career that has spanned five history-making decades, Cher has managed to do it all. From her early days as

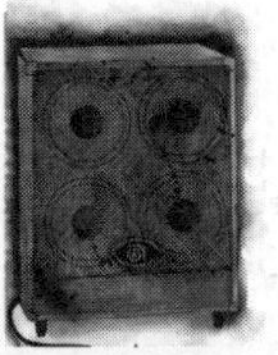

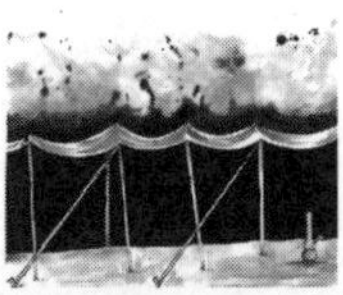

an angry "half-breed" to her later work selling skin cream, everything Cher touches seems to turn to gold, which is why she has earned a place in the Diva Trinity which includes the other single named stars, Blondie and Madonna.

Her longevity is the inspiration for the famous quote "After a nuclear holocaust, all that will be left are cockroaches and Cher."

Essential viewing

Mask
Moonstruck
Silkwood
Witches of Eastwick
Mermaids

www.officialcherfanclub.com

LYING

It is assumed that man invented lying millions of years ago, out of necessity. Life in a state of nature was most certainly "nasty, brutish, and short," and to paraphrase the immortal Babs Streisand, people need people, and because of this, early man learned to lie so as to ensure reciprocal altruism on the part of his cave neighbor.

As man developed, lying became a taboo experience. Early human history held lying as a sacred act of transgression that was not just interpersonal, but against the gods, the fates, or the cosmos. This is what led to things like Confession and Purification rites.

However, recent sociological research has found that the lie is losing much of its taboo power. In fact, many people (celebrities, politicians, you name it) are adopting a fast and loose attitude with the truth in order to fulfill or protect their self-image, thus leading to the recently coined Stephen Colbert word "Truthiness".

Essential reading

Why We Lie : The Evolutionary Roots of Deception and the Unconscious Mind by David Livingstone Smith

If you are a big fat liar in need of a little instant absolution check out:

www.notproud.com
www.dailyconfessions.com

Particularly skilled liars who find themselves in England can participate in The World's Greatest Liars Competition, which is hosted in Nottingham, or The Festival of Liars which is held in Cumbria.

THE MERCHANTS OF VENICE

Much like Ancient Crete, Venice was a nation founded on trade. But if the Minoans were the first accountants, then the Venetians were surely the first investment bankers. The Venetian merchant aristocracy was a close-knit group. This created a spirit of mutual trust that in other cities seldom extended outside the family circle. Because of this, the Venetians were unique in their capacity for quick, efficient business administration.

Interestingly enough, the practice of using surnames originated in around 1000 A.D., when merchants in Venice needed to know who owed them money.

TAE KWON DO

Modern-day Tae Kwon Do is influenced by many other martial arts, the most dominant being Japanese karate. This is because Japan dominated Korea during 1910 until the end of World War II. During World War II, Korean soldiers were trained in Japan, and also during this occupation of Korea, the Japanese tried to erase all traces of the Korean culture, including the martial arts.

On the Web

www.baistaekwondo.com/
www.sjkim-taekwondo.com/

5. RIDICULE

BEN JONSON

Jonson was a pal of William Shakespeare, but was often attacked for being a lesser poet. Jonson countered by saying that Shakespeare was a sellout. Jonson was a funny guy, with a killer wit and an argumentative personality. After English theaters were reopened during the Restoration of Charles II, Jonson became the dominant influence in shaping English theater. He died in 1637 and was buried standing up in a two-by-two section in the nave at Westminster Abbey.

Essential plays

Volpone
The Alchemist

DANTE

For everything you ever wanted to know about Durante "Dante" Alighieri, check out Columbia University's Digital Dante Project:

http://dante.ilt.columbia.edu/new/

HAMMURABI'S CODE

The very first written code of laws in human history. Hammurabi's laws focused on theft, agriculture (or shepherding), property damage, women's rights, marriage rights, children's rights, slave rights, murder, death, and injury. My two personal faves:

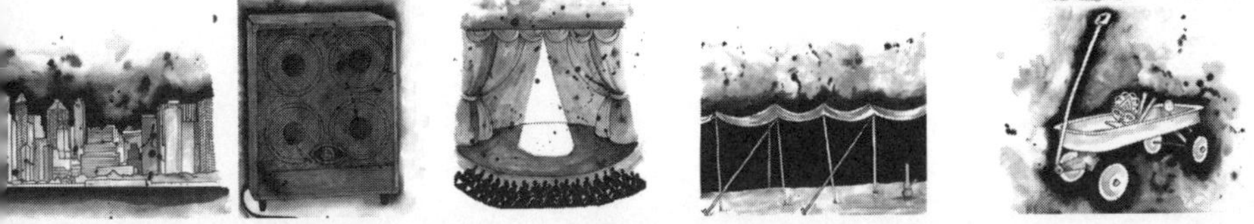

142. If a woman quarrel with her husband, and say: "You are not congenial to me," the reasons for her prejudice must be presented. If she is guiltless, and there is no fault on her part, but he leaves and neglects her, then no guilt attaches to this woman, she shall take her dowry and go back to her father's house.

53. If any one be too lazy to keep his dam in proper condition, and does not so keep it; if then the dam break and all the fields be flooded, then shall he in whose dam the break occurred be sold for money, and the money shall replace the corn which he has caused to be ruined.

RELIGION

Zoroastrianism (Persian)

Defining Theme:	Good thoughts, good words, good deeds
Favorite Son:	Zarathustra
Culinary Tradition:	The kebob
Big Moment:	Seven-year-old Z survives poisoning attempt
Essential Reading:	*The Avesta*

Hindu

Defining Theme:	Karma
Favorite Son:	Krishna
Culinary Tradition:	Chicken tikka masala
Big Moment:	Lord Vishnu opened his eyes
Essential Reading:	*The Upanishads*

Lutheranism

Defining Theme:	Scripture alone
Favorite Son:	Martin Luther
Culinary Tradition:	Cheese whiz and olives on rye
Big Moment:	Charles V issues Edict of Worms
Essential Reading:	*Book of Concord*

7. dOJANG BLUES

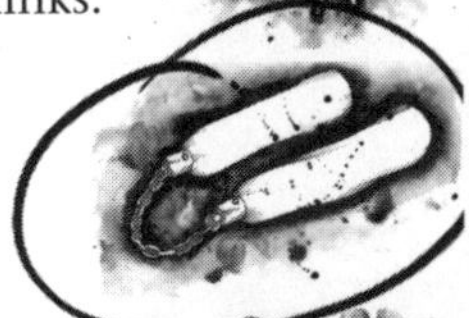

GENERAL TSO

An intelligent and able scholar-administrator, Tso was particularly gifted as a logistical planner; his long-distance campaigns in northwest China and Sinkiang compare favorably with contemporary operations of European armies. Equally remarkable was his unusual stamina, for most of these operations were carried out while he suffered from recurring bouts of malaria and dysentery. He was a founding member of the Self-Strengthening Movement and no doubt, a great lover of chicken.

KUNG FU MOVIES

On the Web

www.kungfucinema.com/ – Contains reviews, history and links.

www.kungfumovies.net/ – An amazing selection, listed by category. Everything from classic Kung Fu, to Shaolin, to Wu Tang, and even Zatoichi the Blind.

www.rarekungfumovies.com/ – Great selection of obscure Kung Fu movies.

SHAOLIN TEMPLE

Chinese Buddhist monastery known for its long association with Zen Buddhism and martial arts. According to legend, Kung Fu was invented at the temple, in part to help the disciples cope with the rigors of Zen Buddhism and also to

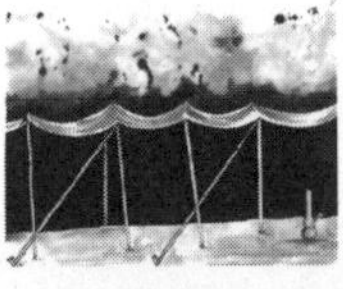

help the monks defend against the attacks of invading hordes that frequently marauded in the area.

SUN TZU

Author of the definitive grand strategy known as *Art of War,* which was required reading for every corporate raider back in the 1980s.

Related: The *36 Tactics* which sums up every war maneuver including the oft maligned "If All Else Fails Retreat" tactic, which was the origin for the pseudo-sexual term, "When in Doubt, Pull Out."

7.5. I AM THE EGGPLANT

AMERICAN DREAM – EVOLUTION TIMELINE

1600s

- The Original American Dream starts with the Puritans and was religious in nature. Basically, God would provide if people formed a community to honor him.

Mid 1700s

- As people realized that they could only count on themselves, Dream becomes less about salvation through community and more about salvation through personal redemption. Lots of fire and brimstone.

End of 1700s

- Jefferson says, "Life, Liberty and Pursuit of Happiness" (unless you are poor, female, or black) – which instills a vision of unmitigated possibility.

Mid 1800s

- Transcendentalists led by Thoreau (who, it should be noted, often left his Indian servant outside during winter nights to guard his canoe – so much for his egalitarianism) start yammering about "Living The Life You Imagine," a precursor to Joe Campbell's "Follow your Bliss."

- Manifest Destiny redefines American Dream as imperial conquest.

Late 1800s

- After Civil War, country a mess, the Dream becomes all about economics. A hope that your kids will do better than you.

1900s

- Sans taxes, tons of people pull themselves up by their bootstraps and get super rich a la Andrew Carnegie (who then donates to charity on an epic level). American Dream becomes about getting rich so you can help others.

Mid 1900s

- Post-World War II – Boom economy. Television. Media. People doing well. American Dream becomes primarily about fame and wealth.

1970s

- Elvis Presley dies on the toilet. American Dream becomes tempered with the reality that it can quickly turn into a nightmare.

Essential reading

Main Currents in American Thought Volumes I and II by Vernon Louis Parrington

ESSENTIAL GANGSTER MOVIES

Chinese Triads – *Year of the Dragon* starring Mickey Rourke

Irish Mob (aka Westies) – *State of Grace* starring Sean Penn

Jewish Mafia – *Once Upon a Time in America* starring Robert DeNiro

FIVE FAMILIES

After years of turf wars, these five families ended up dominating New York, and by default, New Jersey.

Bonanno
Colombo
Gambino
Genovese
Lucchese

Essential reading

Five Families; The Rise, Decline and Resurgance of America's Most Powerful Mafia Empires by Selwyn Raab

For more information, check out Court TV's Crime Library: www.crimelibrary.com

MANZANAR

Manzanar is the best known of the ten camps in which Japanese Americans, both citizens (including natural-born Americans) and resident aliens, were detained as a "precautionary measure" during World War II.

On the Web

Check out Ansel Adams' Manzanar photographs at the Library of Congress website: www.loc.gov/index.html

Key words: *American Memory*.

Reading: *Snow Falling on Cedars* by David Guterson

Film: *Infinite Shades of Grey* by Toyo Miyatake

MAFIA PLEDGE

"I (NAME GIVEN) want to enter into this secret organization to protect my family and to protect my brothers. 'Morte alla Francia Italia anelia!' With my blood (a knife is used to place a cut on the right index finger or hand) and the blood of all the saints, and the souls of my children (the sign of the cross is made) I swear not to divulge this secret and to obey with love and omerta. I enter alive into this organization and leave it only in death."

1 A code of silence – Never "rat out" any mafia member. Never divulge any mafia secrets, even if threatened with torture or death.
2 Complete obedience to the boss – Obey the boss' orders, no matter what.
3 Assistance – Provide any necessary assistance to any other respected or befriended mafia faction.
4 Vengeance – Any attacks on family members must be avenged. "An attack on one is an attack on all."
5 Avoid contact with the authorities.

PETER CALABRO

Peter Calabro, a corrupt New York City cop, was shot to death in Upper Saddle River on March 14, 1980 after a tour of duty with the Queens Auto Crimes Division.

While in jail, Richard "The Iceman" Kuklinski claimed that he was hired by Sammy "The Bull" Gravano to carry out the execution. But there are others who believe the hit was financed by the family of his first wife, Carmela, who drowned under suspicious circumstances.

PINKY AND THE BRAIN

Arguably the greatest duo in the history of world domination. For the most comprehensive collection of AYPWIP (Are You Pondering What I'm Pondering) files check out Tom and Matthew's Pinky and the Brain page: www.duryea.org/pinky/.

ST. ROSALIE OF PALERMO

1130–1166 – Born to a wealthy family, St. Rosalie decided to keep it real and go live in a cave instead. There she dedicated her life to solitary prayer and penance.

The devotion to St. Rosalie stems from the fact that centuries later, when plague was decimating the city of Palermo, she appeared in a vision to a humble soap maker and revealed her final resting place to him. She then instructed him to exhume her earthly remains and parade them around the city. Legend tells that wherever her bones passed, the sick became well and in a matter of days the city was freed from plague.

8. PET PEEVES

BOA CONSTRICTOR

The world's oldest recorded snake was a boa constrictor called Popeye who lived at the Philadelphia Zoo and died in 1977 at the age of 40 years.

CRONOS

Cronos was the youngest and most wretched child of Gaia (Earth) and the chronically abusive Uranus (Sky). Cronos ended up castrating his father and then became the ruler of the universe (interestingly enough, he tossed the castrated penis into the water, and from this sprung Aphrodite). Soon Cronos was prophetically informed by his parents that he would be dethroned by his own son. Ever the optimist (and clearly having never read Oedipus), Cronos figured that if he swallowed his offspring at birth, he could avoid such a fate. Cronos ate all his kids, until bloat got the better of him. Then he vomited them all up, and, together with Zeus, they fought and defeated him.

ELIZABETH ENRIGHT

Essential reading: *The Melendy Quartet,* which follows siblings Mona, Rush, Miranda, and Oliver. First published in 1941, *The Saturdays* starts the series and centers on the foursome's Independent Saturday Afternoon Adventure Club (I.S.A.A.C.), an allowance-endowed venture formed so one fortunate Melendy can enjoy a solo outing each week. In *The Four-Story Mistake* (1942), the family moves

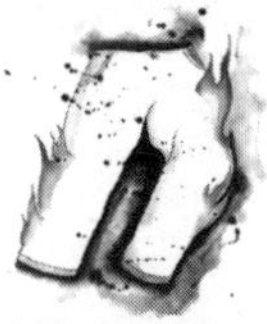

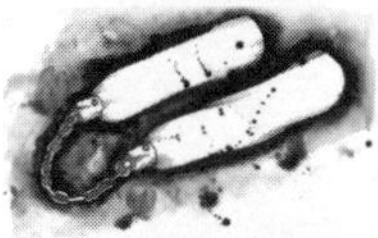
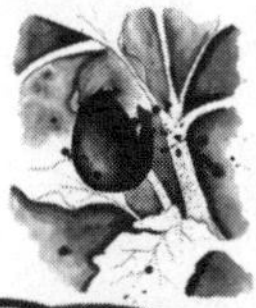

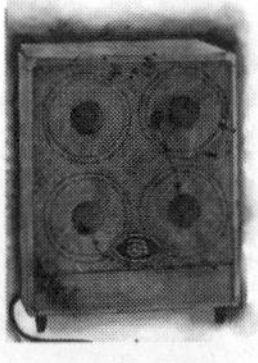
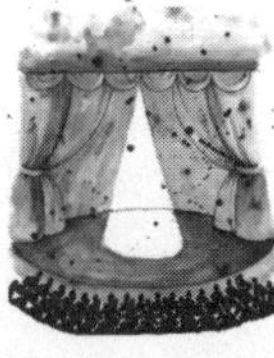
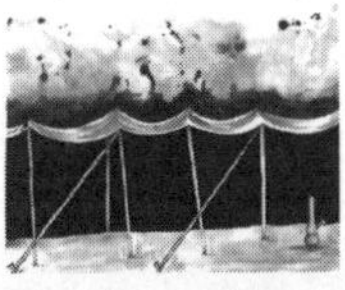

from their city brownstone to the country; *Then There Were Five* (1944) describes what happens when the siblings befriend an orphan; and finally there's *Spiderweb forTwo: A Melendy Maze* (1951), in which Randy and Oliver are left to solve a mystery.

LOST TRIBE

Ever since the Assyrians exiled the Lost Tribes of Israel in the eighth century B.C., the mystery of what happened to the Ten Tribes has deepened inexorably with time. Where did they go?

Recent tests suggest two finalists: The Lembain people in Africa and the B'nei Menashe in India. But my money is on the Mormons.

WOMRATH'S

My favorite bookstore ever. Currently located in Tenafly, New Jersey. Check them out on the web at womraths.com and support independent booksellers!

9. THE EXTERMINATOR

DIRTY SANCHEZ

After having anal sex the giver pulls out his member and rubs it on the upper lip of the receiver's face.

KOREAN NAME THING

For a comprehensive look at Korean names, check out Arthur's Korean Page: www.unsu.com/names.html.

MARXISM (AND RELIGION)

Liberation theology is an important, sometimes controversial school of theological thought. At its inception, it was predominantly found in the Roman Catholic Church after the Second Vatican Council. It is often cited as a form of Christian socialism and has had particularly widespread influence in Latin America and among the Jesuits, although its influence has diminished within Catholicism in the past decade.

Related

OSCAR ROMERO: BISHOP OF THE POOR

Oscar Romero gave his last homily on March 24. Moments before a sharpshooter murdered him he said, "One must not love oneself so much as to avoid getting involved in the risks of life that history demands of us, and those that fend off danger will lose their lives."

Essential viewing

Romero (1989)
Salvador (1986)

Essential reading

Bread and Wine by Ignazio Silone

RATS

Known for their intelligence, playfulness, and sociality, the rat makes a fine pet. Like many other domesticated animals, rats can be taught entertaining tricks, and they are extremely clean. If only my family had known that.

Essential reading

Rats: Observations on the History and Habitat of the City's Most Unwanted Inhabitants by Robert Sullivan

Mrs. Frisby and the Rats of Nimh by Robert C. O'Brien

.0. JENNY WREN

ALICE ROOSEVELT

February 12, 1884 – February 20, 1980

Daughter of President Teddy Roosevelt. Alice was the original wild child. Independent, irreverent, and beautiful, she was often called the other Washington Monument. President Roosevelt often commented that he could control the affairs of state, or control Alice, but he could not possibly do both.

Essential reading

Princess Alice: The Life and Times of Alice Roosevelt Longworth by Carol Felsenthal

HAROLD BLOOM

The Mac Daddy of Critical Theory. The defender of Romanticism. The man who makes thinking look sexy.

Essential reading

Deconstruction and Criticism (1980)
The Book of J (1990)
The Western Cannon (1994)
Shakespeare: The Invention of the Human (1998)
How To Read and Why (2001)
The Best Poems of the English Language (2004)
The Meaning of the 21st Century (2006)

THE GLASS FAMILY

Created by J.D. Salinger, the seven Glass siblings were all geniuses who earned a fortune on a fictional radio quiz show called *It's a Wise Child*.

Seymour	(Eldest and most revered brother who committed suicide)
Buddy	(Salinger's alter ego)
Beatrice	(The most well-adjusted of the Glass children)
Walt	(Died in Japan after World War II)
Waker	(Walt's twin. A Catholic priest)
Zachary	(The best looking, yet most bitter, of all the Glass children)
Franny	(Actress. Prone to nervous breakdowns)

Essential Glass Family reading

Nine Stories (published in the U.K. as *For Esmé – with Love and Squalor*)

Raise High the Roof Beam, Carpenters

Franny and Zooey

SON OF SAM

During the late 1970s, serial killer David Berkowitz killed six women with a .44 caliber handgun. The press had a field day with his crimes, dubbing him the ".44 Caliber Killer." The name incensed Berkowitz, who wrote a long letter to the head of Operation Omega, (the task force created to find him) in which Berkowitz named himself "Son of Sam."

For more information, check out: Court TV's Crime Library

11. GYPSIES, tRAMPS AND tHIEVES

MR. JIGGS

2. BEST LAID PLANS

BRAZIL

To understand the role of popular music in the making of modern Brazil check out:

Hello, Hello Brazil by Bryan McCann

JAZZ ALBUMS

My personal Top 10 list in no particular order.

- Johnny Hartman and John Coltrane – *Lush Life*
- Miles Davis – *Four and More*
- Miles Davis/Gil Evans – *Porgy and Bess*
- Jimmy Smith – *The Sermon*
- Sonny Rollins – *Live at the Village Vanguard*
- Bill Evans – *Waltz for Debby*
- Wayne Shorter – *Speak No Evil*
- Steps Ahead – *Steps Ahead*
- Pat Metheny – *Rejoicing*
- Dave Holland – *Seeds of Time*

RODNEY BINGENHEIMER

Bingenheimer was the ultimate LA scene-maker and consummate DJ who was responsible for introducing "Glam Rock" to the States.

Essential viewing: *The Mayor of Sunset Strip*, a film by George Hickenlooper.

On the Web: www.rodney-b.com

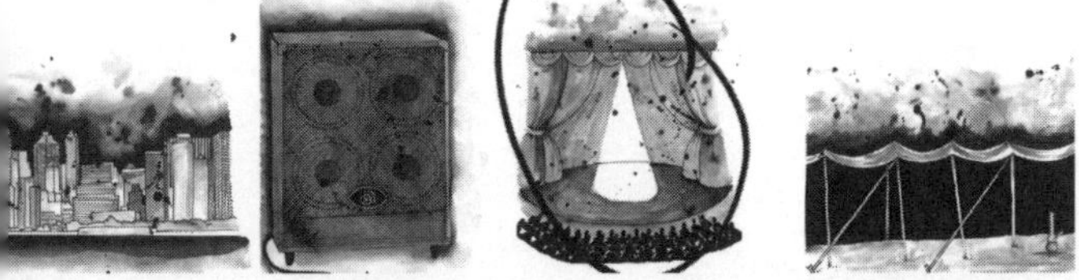

STEVE KAHN

For an amazing collection of handwritten solo transcriptions of classic jazz solos go to www.stevekhan.com.

Check out his album *Eyewitness* and listen to the sound of drummer Steve Jordan's snare drum. It's like nothing else.

STEVEN BIKO

Steven Biko was one of the founders of the Black People's Convention, which worked on social projects around Durban, South Africa. Arrested under anti-terror apartheid legislation, Biko died as a result of injuries sustained during a scuffle with security police.

The brutal circumstances of his death made him an instant martyr and a symbol of black resistance to the oppressive apartheid regime. As a result, the South African government banned a number of individuals (including Donald Woods) and organizations, especially those black consciousness groups closely associated with Biko. However, Biko's death caused a world outcry, and The United Nations Security Council responded by finally imposing an arms embargo against South Africa.

Essential listening

Biko by Peter Gabriel

THINK TANKS

Check out the Institute For the Future, which is the hippest think tank going.

www.iftf.org/

3. BUCKY PIZZARELLI IS A BIG dICK

ENYCLOPEDIA BROWN

Encyclopedia lives in Idaville, Florida, which is often referred to as a typical American town. He's aided in his investigations by his best friend, Sally Kimball, who plays Watson to his Holmes. The perennial villain in many of the stories is Bugs Meany.

GARMENT INDUSTRY

At the turn of the last century, many immigrant women and children, among them my own grandmother, found work in New York's thriving garment industry. They worked 15-hour workdays in cramped, dangerous, filthy factories for no benefits and little pay.

Essential reading

We Were There by Barbara Mayer Wertheimer (Pantheon Books)

On the Web

www.ilr.cornell.edu/trianglefire/
www.historyplace.com/unitedstates/childlabor/

This site features photographs of child laborers taken by Lewis W. Hines.

THE PINK PANTHER

To understand my usage of the Chief Inspector Charles Dreyfus' syllabic blinking technique check out:

The Return of The Pink Panther (1975)
The Pink Panther Strikes Again (1976)

4. SAVING GRACES

AUTOMATIC SLIMS

Washington and Bank Street. My favorite NYC bar ever.

ST. GREGORY

In addition to having a giant bald head, St. Gregory was a major prude, who felt that sex was always evil. He was named Pope in 590 A.D. and promptly tried to win converts by promising to slash the rents by one-third of any Jew who would become a Christian. A lifelong sufferer of indigestion, Gregory turned to music to sooth his bloated belly. He was a huge promoter of “plainsong,” which later became known to all as Gregorian chant.

NEW YORK CITY

Essential reading

Here is New York by E.B. White
The Colossus of New York by Colson Whitehead
Celluloid Skyline by James Sanders

On the Web

Gothamist	www.gothamist.com
Joe’s NYC	www.joesnyc.streetnine.com/
Overheard in New York	www.overheardinnewyork.com/